EMERGING MARKETS

OTHER ECONOMIST BOOKS

Guide to Analysing Companies
Guide to Business Modelling
Guide to Business Planning
Guide to Economic Indicators
Guide to the European Union
Guide to Financial Markets
Guide to Investment Strategy
Guide to Management Ideas
Guide to Organisation Design
Guide to Project Management
Numbers Guide
Style Guide

Brands and Branding
Business Consulting
Business Ethics
Business Miscellany
Business Strategy
China's Stockmarket
Dealing with Financial Risk
Economics
The Future of Technology
Globalisation
Headhunters and How to Use Them
Mapping the Markets
The City
Wall Street

Essential Director
Essential Economics
Essential Investment
Essential Negotiation

Pocket World in Figures

EMERGING MARKETS

Lessons for business success and the outlook for different markets

Nenad Pacek

and

Daniel Thorniley

THE ECONOMIST IN ASSOCIATION WITH
PROFILE BOOKS LTD

Published by Profile Books Ltd
3A Exmouth House, Pine Street, London EC1R OJH
www.profilebooks.com

Typeset in EcoType by MacGuru Ltd
info@macguru.org.uk

Printed in Great Britain by
Clays, Bungay, Suffolk

A CIP catalogue record for this book is available
from the British Library

ISBN 978 1 86197 843 1

The paper this book is printed on is certified by the © 1996 Forest Stewardship
Council A.C. (FSC). It is ancient-forest friendly. The printer holds FSC chain of custody
SGS-COC-2061

FSC
Mixed Sources
Product group from well-managed
forests and other controlled sources

Cert no. SGS-COC-2061
www.fsc.org
© 1996 Forest Stewardship Council

To our two wonderful daughters Natasha (DT) and Nina (NP)
who make it all worthwhile

Contents

Preface

Welcome to the second edition of *Emerging Markets*. We would like to thank all those who read the first edition for their comments and feedback. We are delighted that so many people found the book useful.

Since the first edition appeared there have been five developments that make a new edition all the more necessary. First, corporate strategies designed to conquer emerging markets have been evolving rapidly and will continue to do so. Second, emerging markets are becoming increasingly competitive, calling for a new set of ideas on how to preserve and build business. Third, emerging markets' contribution to the global economy has grown faster than most observers ever expected. Fourth, with a build-up of global economic imbalances and vast speculative flows from cash-rich developed markets into emerging markets' securities, cash and commodities, economic risks and the forces that shape them that could derail good corporate plans in emerging markets are worth explaining in even more depth, as is what executives should do to protect their companies and their careers. Fifth, the outlook for the global economy and the regional and selected country outlooks covered in Part 2 have changed.

The underlying theme of the book (particularly Part 1) remains the same: why are some companies more successful than others when doing business in emerging markets? What kinds of strategies will make companies successful in the foreseeable future? Why do so many companies fail to reach their targets? What are the mistakes made by so many companies in the past 20 years?

The contribution of emerging markets business to the bottom line of international companies has been rising as more and more companies have recognised the opportunities for growth that less developed markets offer.

This book covers everything that businesses need to think about, understand and act on in order to be successful in emerging markets. Real corporate experiences are used wherever possible to illustrate the points made and we are grateful and indebted to the many people who over the years have shared with us their lessons of business success and failure in emerging markets. There are many references to conversations with and remarks made by them, but as a professional courtesy and because it makes no difference to the points we illustrate, we have chosen not to give names even when conversations were on the record. Where names do appear, the remarks and quotations were not made to the authors personally and are in the public domain.

We are grateful to our colleague Delia Meth-Cohn, who continues to inspire us with her sharp intellect and warm friendship; to colleagues in The Economist Intelligence Unit, Corporate Network, Asia, for insights into business in South-East Asia; and to Stephen Brough and Penny Williams for the parts they have played in the book's creation.

We are keen to hear from anyone who would like to give us feedback and to share their experiences of emerging markets or would like to know more about The Economist Intelligence Unit's advisory service Corporate Network. You can email us on nenadpacek@economist.com and danielthorniley@economist.com.

Nenad Pacek and Daniel Thorniley
May 2007

PART 1
LESSONS FOR BUSINESS SUCCESS

For many companies and for a long time, emerging markets were a strategic sideshow, largely tackled in an opportunistic way. This partly explains why so many companies ended up disappointed with their sales and profit growth. However, there have been notable exceptions and this book examines the lessons that can be learned from those who have been taking emerging markets seriously for years.

More and more companies are thinking of emerging markets in a strategic, systematic way and are recognising that emerging markets must be an integral part of their long-term global strategy. Indeed, for some companies emerging markets are now central to their strategy.

The reasons for this increased strategic focus on emerging markets are as follows:

- Achieving growth in the developed world has become harder so companies have been forced to look for growth outside the big markets of the United States, the European Union and Japan.
- More and more companies now realise that even their most opportunistic endeavours in emerging markets are yielding better sales growth than can be found in the developed world. Companies that have been taking emerging markets seriously for years say that sales and profits in absolute terms are also becoming large and interesting for the total global business. This has prompted many companies already involved in them to start talking about "step-up" efforts – how to go faster and what is needed to do that. "If we could get some good returns without doing much, think of the returns we could get if we do it more systematically," the thinking goes.
- Emerging markets are quickly becoming commercially mature despite a still much lower average standard of living than in the developed world. This is driven by booming competition as both international and domestic companies expand at unprecedented speed.
- Economic growth in emerging markets outpaced growth in the

developed world by 4.5 percentage points between 2000 and 2005, and it is generally believed this trend will continue.

◪ Despite rising commercial maturity in emerging markets, it is still easier to capture market share more quickly in them than in the developed world. This is because competition is still not as fierce and because brand loyalties are not as entrenched as in the developed world. Buyers are still easier to influence than in, say, Germany or the United States, even though there is much more loyalty to brands in emerging markets than there was a decade ago. This means that it will not be long before it becomes as difficult and costly to acquire market share as in the developed world. For any company wishing to strengthen its market presence, the window of opportunity for *systematic stepping up* is closing fast.

Defining emerging markets

The term emerging markets was first used by Antoine W. van Agtmael of the International Finance Corporation back in the early 1980s. These days it is used loosely. Some observers include only extremely low-income economies under the emerging-market umbrella; some include only countries that are expected to experience high economic growth; and others include all countries that are not considered developed. This book looks at what are generally called developing countries and includes Central America, Latin America, the Middle East, Africa, central and eastern Europe, and the whole of Asia apart from Hong Kong, Japan and Singapore, and Australia and New Zealand. It may not appear to make sense to include countries such as South Korea and the United Arab Emirates within emerging markets, but they are included because companies still tend to have them as part of their emerging Asia division or Middle East/North Africa division. Companies manage these more developed markets as part of wider regions and often face similar strategic and operational issues as in other emerging markets.

According to estimates by *The Economist*, emerging markets reached an important milestone in 2005: their combined economic output was just over 50% of total global output. This was calculated on a purchasing power parity basis instead of market exchange rates – a good measure for business since prices (particularly of services) are lower in emerging markets. The purchasing power per dollar in India is higher than it is in the United States. At market exchange rates the emerging world is still smaller than the developed world, accounting for just under 30% of total world GDP or about $11 trillion–12 trillion. Add to that 30–40% grey/black economic activity, and emerging markets at market exchange rates are probably producing output worth at least $15 trillion–17 trillion – one and a half times that of each of the United States and the European Union and about three times that of Japan. With continuous fast economic growth (official and unofficial), emerging markets are adding an estimated $1 trillion–1.2 trillion of output every year, more than double the output of the developed world.

Companies that like to consider the long-term implications of their strategies should be aware that emerging markets are behaving not so differently from the way they did some 200 years ago. According to Angus Maddison, an economic historian, emerging markets accounted for 80% of world output in the first half of the 19th century, and before the impact of the Industrial Revolution, China and India produced about half the world's total output.

The strategic importance of emerging markets is evident through other statistics too:

- In 2005 they accounted for more than 80% of the world population.
- Every month, the population of emerging markets grows by more than 6m people. At the same time, the developed world adds only 300,000.
- Emerging markets' share of world exports is now just under 45% of total global export activity compared with around 18% in the late 1960s.
- In 2005, emerging markets consumed 48% of the world's oil.
- 70% of all foreign exchange reserves are now held by central banks in emerging markets, demonstrating their new economic strength and an unprecedented cushion against unwelcome economic crises and sudden currency depreciations (on the latter see Chapter 14).
- More than 50% of developed world exports are now sold in emerging markets, an all-time high.
- If emerging markets continue to grow three times faster than the developed world in the next three decades – which is a plausible scenario – their share of global output at purchasing power parity will rise to over 65% in 20–25 years.

Chief executives are taking notice of all this. The 2006 edition of *CEO Briefing*, an annual Economist Intelligence Unit survey of chief executives, revealed an unprecedented finding. Leading chief executives believe the single most important force shaping global business today is demand originating from emerging markets. The economic changes taking place and the new corporate obsession with emerging markets will change the business environment in those emerging markets hugely – and much sooner than many anticipate. This presents challenges that some companies will rise to and others will not. This book sets out to help those who are determined to be one of the success stories.

1 Why companies fail

If I want sustainable profits, I am going to invest in the longer term, even if it has a negative impact on the short term. For some of the members of the financial community, whose timeframe is between half a year and a year, it is very difficult to explain what it means to build up a business in Korea or China or Russia, where you have to invest for five to ten years before you get into profitability.

> Peter Brabeck, CEO of Nestlé, who refuses to give short-term financial targets to analysts.

It does not matter how much it costs. What matters is how much money it can make.

> Roberto Goizueta, former CEO of Coca-Cola. (Coca-Cola is the fourth most valuable brand in the world. Since December 2002 it has refused to give quarterly and annual sales expectations to analysts.)

Market leaders in their sector in the developed world often set out to repeat their success in emerging markets, and seemingly put a lot of resources into achieving their aim. This chapter looks at the reasons so many fail – and what can be done to make sure they do not.

Growth is a corporate obsession. After the cost-cutting that followed the bursting of the stockmarket bubble in 2002, companies have rediscovered the advantages of more offensive strategies: Where do we find growth? Where should we allocate resources? In response to these two questions companies are increasingly moving into emerging markets. But they also insist that to achieve growth you have to be innovative (see later and Chapter 7).

But time and time again companies that are market leaders in the developed world fail to replicate that success in emerging markets. Why? And what can companies do about it?

The problem often starts at the top of the corporate hierarchy. A typical scenario goes like this. A CEO sends a manager that he knows and trusts to start "conquering" a group of countries in the developing world. This manager ends up operating from a regional hub. He visits the countries he is interested in, establishes contacts and collects relevant information. He spends months evaluating potential distributors and partners. He decides who he wants to work with and signs the contracts. Sales begin. He hires a few people in the hub to co-ordinate the effort. Sales pick up. He is excited. Business is going well. "We're in. The sky's the limit", or so he thinks.

A year later he is holding a report on market shares. "How can this small player be ahead? Why am I still so far behind?" His CEO calls and says: "I'm looking at the report. It is not bad. But I would like to see us becoming much more dominant next year."

Another year on, the position is much the same. Business is slightly up but not relative to the competition. This time the CEO is less relaxed: "You said you were going to increase our market share. What's wrong?" This is when the regional manager usually says: "I think I'll need more resources to build the business. People don't seem to know our brands here."

The CEO's response is: "Prove to me there is more business there and you'll get more resources." To which the inevitable riposte is: "How can I increase sales if you don't allow me to invest more?"

Getting out of this vicious circle is never easy. The following guidelines show how a firm can avoid getting into it and improve its chances of being successful in an emerging market.

Emerging markets must be a central or at least an integral part of global strategy

The only way to be successful in an emerging market is to appreciate the opportunities it offers and then take it seriously. This means putting emerging markets at the centre of the corporate agenda or at least having them sitting side by side with the developed world in terms of strategic importance. Business success for larger firms in the next ten years and beyond will depend on remaining competitive in large-volume, low-growth developed markets while establishing and increasing presence in faster-growth emerging markets. Getting the balance right for this two-strand strategy will require two distinct approaches and sets of criteria for judging progress and success. This is not easy, especially in publicly listed companies that are under short-term pressure from shareholders (see Chapter 2). Most companies that the authors work with (50% US owned, 40% European owned and 10% Japanese owned) have failed to do so until now. This chapter offers guidelines on how to drive growth in emerging markets.

Ensure there is genuine commitment from the top

Senior management must be absolutely committed to an emerging-market business. It must commit sufficient resources to getting it established and then to sustaining and growing it. Building business in emerging markets is never a short-term affair; the CEO and the board must be prepared to lose money for at least a few years. In companies that prove successful in emerging markets, it is common that once a strategic commitment has been made, the CEO appoints a trusted senior manager who is powerful enough to override internal obstacles and to make investment decisions according to market needs. He champions and drives the emerging-market business. CEOs of companies that are successful in emerging markets have often made a point of convincing analysts and shareholders about the benefits of the long-term growth that emerging markets can help provide. The big change in recent years is that this internal focus on emerging markets at the very top is becoming more intense. Companies that focus on short-term profit maximisation are typically less successful in emerging markets, even if their products dominate the developed world.

A global head of emerging markets is essential

Many international companies have a head of international markets, but they often lump together markets such as Germany and Ukraine. The problem with this is that Germany and similar developed markets require different strategic and operational approaches from underdeveloped markets such as Ukraine. Emerging markets are all about going faster and making massive market share and sales leaps. For this companies need flexibility, focus, investment and attention. As one emerging-market manager put it: "It boils down to bureaucracy versus flexibility."

Make sure heads of regions and business units, not heads of functions, drive business

"Region is the king, then business unit and then function." These words of wisdom come from the man who created more shareholder value for Procter & Gamble than any other manager in its history: Herbert Schmitz, former president of Central Eastern Europe, Middle East and Africa. Companies with many business units often drive expansion solely through those business units. It is common to find that in the same company a unit, say involved with special plastics, is well established in certain emerging markets, while another unit, say involved with speciality paints, is not, simply because the global head of the speciality paints unit is not enthusiastic about emerging markets.

A good formula is to have regional and country managers driving expansion, spotting opportunities on the ground and, in conjunction with heads of business units, driving growth forward.

An arrogant approach is doomed to failure

"We have been producing this product for 26 years and our customers in the United States have always been happy with the packaging, the flavour and the price, and we are not going to change it – certainly not for Russia or China or Paraguay. If it is good enough for the United States, it's good for anywhere else." This is how one executive paraphrased the response of his CEO when he tried to argue for some product development changes. Just using tried and tested techniques, products and services from the developed world in emerging markets is unlikely to yield anything more exciting than a few short-term sales gains. Although these tried and tested techniques do not always fail when transferred from developed to emerging markets, they often do. Success in emerging markets depends on well-researched market entry and market expansion preparation (see Chapter 3), development of in-depth customer relationships built on trust, rethinking former business models and structures, rethinking brand building and marketing processes, and engaging in innovative R&D to respond to the needs of the local markets in various segments.

Avoid resource mismatch

More and more companies are recognising the business opportunity in emerging markets and although senior management may be notionally committed to exploiting the opportunity, they often fail to commit enough resources, with the result that such a half-hearted effort is destined to fail (see more on this in Chapter 7). Companies frequently try to get away with doing things on a shoestring. This may maintain profit margins in the short term, but it is unlikely to build long-term success.

Companies with international boards have an advantage in emerging markets

The 2006 Economist Intelligence Unit *CEO Briefing* identified the biggest challenge facing global companies today: how to understand local customers. One way to address the issue is by increasing local presence (particularly any customer/consumer facing functions). Another way is to build more diverse boards. Recent surveys indicate that boards are remarkably homogeneous. In Japan, Germany and the United States, only 7–11% of board members are foreign nationals. This compares with over

30% in Switzerland and the Netherlands. The advantages of more diverse boards are greater appreciation of the emerging-market opportunity, championing geographic expansion at board level, engaging in top-level government lobbying if and when needed and acting as role models for a growing army of employees around the world. Local employees then see that there is no limit to their career advancement and this drives them to high performance in local markets.

Never take market leadership for granted

Just because a company is a market leader in the developed world, it does not mean that it will become a market leader in an emerging market. Consumers in emerging markets are often unaware of a newly available product or of its brand recognition in the developed world. Companies that are early into the market and put resources into skilful brand building and local presence usually end up dominating the market, even if they are small, local players. Multinationals that underestimate the potential competition from smaller international and domestic competitors do so at their peril.

Toe-dipping often backfires

Either go for it or stay out. Half-baked entry and market testing is dangerous. John Menzer, who took over Wal-Mart's international operations in 1999, told the *Financial Times* in early 2003:

> No more flag-planting and opening a few stores to test out the
> market. Now when we decide to go into a new market, we
> are going to go in with enough mass that we can use our core
> competences.

Wal-Mart learned some bitter lessons in several markets in Latin America where it was beaten by smaller European competitors. While the US giant was testing the market, Europeans were developing it at full speed and now enjoy the benefits of that approach. The company is now changing its tactics.

Don't let economic crises interfere with strategy: adjust performance criteria

A Dow Chemical regional executive for Europe, Middle East and Africa says:

> *Our company accepts that there are regular setbacks and crises*
> *in emerging markets. We know that most of these crises are*
> *largely crises of progress and we do not really adjust our overall*
> *strategic approach. We adjust our tactics but we are never really*
> *concerned about crises. They come and go and we are here to*
> *stay.*

Economic and political uncertainties can easily disrupt quarterly and even annual plans. This goes with the territory and many companies do not even adjust their cost structure in times of downturn, knowing that this can damage the business once the crisis is over. The wisdom of this approach was demonstrated after the 1998 rouble crisis in Russia. In a *Wall Street Journal* interview in 2002, Peter Brabeck, CEO of Nestlé, said:

> *If I had only thought about short-term profit margins, I would*
> *have withdrawn from Russia, like everybody else, during the*
> *Russian crisis. We did not. It very clearly had an impact on*
> *my profit margins, but in 18 months we doubled our market*
> *share. This is the difference between short-term profit margin*
> *maximisation and long-term, sustainable profitable growth.*

It is immensely frustrating for regional managers to be criticised for missing quarterly budgets during crises. Performance criteria should be focused on sustainable, medium- to long-term results, not the next month or quarter. Likewise, management incentive schemes should be related to longer-term results.

Switch off the cost-cutting button

A large international company with multiple business units and a relatively modest presence in emerging markets has recently designed a comprehensive market entry/expansion strategy involving more than 50 countries on three continents. The global CEO was supporting the plan, and after two years of better than expected results, the company created a new "go even faster" strategy, which required substantial investment in resources. But just as it started hiring people to exploit identified market opportunities, it was reported that quarterly results from new regions were falling behind the stretch budget by several percentage points. The global chief operating officer asked what was wrong and demanded a temporary halt on new hires to preserve short-term margins. He also temporarily froze funding for a large project that was supposed to yield results in 12–18 months.

This is a common management reaction, but it is mistaken. If a company really wants to be a player in emerging markets, it should have faith in its strategy and not get alarmed by short-term slippages against budgets – especially stretch budgets. Brabeck says:

Many of our competitors chose streamlining over growth.
They did improve their margins but then they had no growth.
Excessive cost cutting by rivals has left them without resources
needed to invest in new sources of sales growth.

A senior executive of one major packaging company said:

Any company can cut costs anytime and do so quickly. But to
recapture the market share which can be lost due to those cost
cuts can take years or never happen.

Set realistic targets and determine possible sustainable growth in the next few years

Many corporate careers have been destroyed when executives promised or were forced to promise too much and then missed the promised targets. It is easy to get senior management excited about emerging markets these days, but this excitement often leads to unrealistic budgets. Managers should work hard to:

- set the most realistic annual target and then budget less than that;
- have contingency plans in place if volatile demand in emerging markets derails certain projects and plans;
- warn senior management about external risks;
- determine the likely sustainable growth over the next 3–5 years and then budget less than that.

This will leave them with some manoeuvring space and a buffer against external surprises and internally inflated expectations.

Be early to market and go for it

As emerging markets mature, it becomes harder to persuade consumers to switch brands and take market share from established products, as it is in the developed world where firms celebrate if they manage to increase their market shares by 0.5% in a year. What surprises many companies is how quickly a competitive business environment can develop in emerging markets, despite their relative lack of economic sophistication and occasional crises. Companies that allow other players to dominate the market for too long (through a half-hearted approach or by late entry or both) always find it difficult to turn things around. While mighty Wrigley dithered about expanding into Russia, for example, Dandy/Stimorol, a small privately held Danish company, captured almost the entire local market. It took Wrigley years and millions of dollars to catch up.

Step up the effort

Companies engaged in emerging markets are now asking themselves the following questions: If our current approach is giving us sales of 1x, how can we reach 3x or 5x in three years? What resources should be deployed to achieve this? What is the best way to deploy these resources? Companies will always set a stretch target several years into the future, but they should not become obsessed with the target *per se*. If a company plans to reach 3x in three years it may well do so, but it may also fail to capture market share, fail to build local presence and local relationships, and resort to regular quarterly cost cutting (which will diminish future earning power). This is not a recipe for success. It may be better to reach 2.5x after three years through systematically building up local presence and local relationships, stronger brand loyalty and higher market share, and committed business development resources for the future.

Friendship often precedes business

As any emerging market "old-hand" will testify, you have to demonstrate to locals that you are there for the long-term. Building relationships and at least semi-friendships is a time-consuming exercise that can be achieved only with dedicated local presence. A senior executive from a US chemical company operating in the Middle East says: "Every day I thank all my competitors who do it from a distance or with agents." Another executive from a US engineering firm says: "Hand-holding of customers has won us more business than almost any other local tactic."

Local presence is essential but not for back office functions

If there is one ingredient of success that makes a lasting difference, it is a local presence. If a company is well entrenched locally, this will shield it (at least temporarily) from all sorts of external influences. It will also shield it from any headquarters change of heart about emerging markets. Even if a new senior management team is less enthusiastic about emerging markets, an effective local presence will keep bringing in good business, and in any internal corporate debates that is hard to argue against. Even in the smallest of markets, time and time again companies that invest in at least a "one man and a dog" office do better than those who rely solely on distributors. (See also Chapter 7.)

Localise decision-making and empower regional and country managers
A regional manager at Adidas, a German sports equipment company, said in 2005:

> *The bigger the distance from headquarters and higher the flexibility of the local office, the better the business.*

More and more companies realise that more decentralisation is the way to go and that micromanaging from a distance does not work (see Chapter 7). One of IBM's regional bosses for Central Eastern Europe, Middle East and Africa (CEEMEA) says he constantly has difficulties moving corporate decision-making forward. Senior management is slow to allow local managers to step up business development. He comments:

> *We should just let our country managers run the show as they see fit based on local circumstances. We as a centre can provide guidance, all kinds of support and teach them lessons of success and failure from other markets.*

It is clear that companies that give more decision-making power to their local managers – particularly in marketing, sales, pay and bonuses – usually do better than the centralisers. However, companies that leave all the decision-making to their local partners are often just saving on costs. It is local underinvestment that explains what distinguishes losers from winners.

Underinvestment is often a result of focusing on short-term rather than longer-term results, especially in listed companies. Roberto Goizueta, former CEO of Coca-Cola, who championed investments in emerging markets, was famous for taking issue with analysts when they criticised the company for its quarterly earnings and "reckless investments". He also made his regional managers accountable for three-year results (not one quarter or one year). When Goizueta took over as CEO, he was stunned to discover how little say the company had about how its product was marketed around the world because of its reliance on partners to look after such things. Economist Intelligence Unit corporate surveys carried out in 2006 reveal that more than half of all international companies plan to decentralise their decision-making in the next few years.

Pay attention to organisational structure – and to processes

Many companies discuss at length what kind of organisational structure they should employ in emerging markets. They focus on location of offices, reporting lines and where certain business functions should be located. These are all relevant considerations – and for more on corporate structures see Chapter 7.

But what many companies (even those who understand the importance of having an excellent local presence) ignore are the organisational processes. Local managers should be made accountable for results but given considerable freedom of action. Goizueta had the following message for Coca-Cola's regional and local managers:

> I want you to tell me what you need to do to expand your business, what kind of capital you need to do so, and what kind of net return you're going to get.

Adapt to the market

Customers are often more price-sensitive in emerging markets, but many companies stick to their product portfolio and pricing structures instead of adapting their products and marketing to take local sensitivities into account. As a result, their market share remains small compared with lower-priced competitors offering products that local consumers or businesses prefer to buy. One company against which others benchmark market adaptation is Philip Morris, a tobacco company producing many of the world's best-selling cigarette brands. Managers at Philip Morris have developed a detailed and sophisticated approach to market segmentation. Many of their national markets are divided into seven, ten or twelve segments, and the company develops products for each of them. This often means reducing functionality and quality for lower segments and then having to source and manufacture in local or subregional markets (see more on manufacturing strategies in Chapter 9). IT companies such as Microsoft and Oracle are increasingly trying to develop strategies aimed at serving small and medium sized businesses as opposed to giant corporations and large government contracts.

"Value-added" and "strip-down" innovation are both crucial for success

Every company sees value-added innovation as a success factor anywhere in the world. But "strip-down" innovation, or "innovation downwards" as it is referred to in some firms, is becoming an integral part of strategy for any company that wants to be successful in emerging markets. Companies are going back to the product drawing board, assessing whether the current product portfolio is right for various emerging markets. Inevitably, the conclusion for most international companies is that middle and lower segments of the market are often underrepresented in terms of product offering. To address this large market segment, the best practice is to develop products in new R&D centres based in emerging markets and to produce there too using local sourcing. Ideally, these newly developed products should be marketable in as many emerging countries as possible. One factor driving "strip-down" innovation is the rise of domestic competition in a number of market segments, which highlights another way to address lower market segments: to acquire domestic companies already serving the third or fourth tier of the market (for more on acquisitions see Chapter 10). In the words of an executive running a large European brewery, "the business in emerging markets in the next years will be about having a winning portfolio of brands".

Don't underestimate local competition

Local competitors are becoming formidable in a number of markets. They are also increasingly selling across international borders, often in immediate neighbourhoods but increasingly globally. While many of them still hesitate to take on the developed world and focus their activities on developing countries, it is just a question of time before they seriously start threatening big brands in places such as the United States or France. In other words, it is highly likely that the next decade or two will see the rise of new Samsungs and Hyundais. Both of these companies were massively underestimated by big global firms. The strength of such companies is still largely in the lower market segments, but they are increasingly showing their teeth in the upper segments, traditionally dominated by foreign companies. And they are not easy to compete against as they often understand business in emerging markets better than most multinationals. Sometimes they have unclear sources of financing and they may enjoy political protectionism, use dubious business practices, copy the manufacturing and marketing processes and steal the intellectual property of multinational companies, and be willing to sacrifice margin for market share.

This is the reality that large European, American or Japanese multinationals must cope with. Responding to pressures from local competitors often leads back to the drawing board when it comes to product development. As local competition is increasing in the upper segments of the market in the developing world and starting to attack the developed world, smart multinationals are responding. Toyota, for example, is to develop a cheap $5,000 car, and other multinationals are not slow to buy local competitors that may seriously threaten their existence. Multinationals that do not buy their local competitors soon and/or launch products for lower segments of the market and/or develop smarter products for the upper segments of the market are likely to fall behind their global competitors.

Be flexible

Unwillingness to change long-standing practices is probably one of the largest obstacles to success in emerging markets. Different markets require a temporary or even lasting departure from the ways in which a company is used to operating. Rather than saying "We don't do this anywhere in the world", several carmakers gave up their long struggle to find local partners and extended their operations to include sales and distribution of their products. This flexibility was driven by the realisation that they would not succeed without fully committed partners. By taking control, they were able to establish lasting and sustainable market leadership quickly. Such flexibility does not have to be costly; it just has to be creative. When Ford could not find a distributor in Bulgaria it asked its German distributor to do the job. Two years later (while competing carmakers were still searching for good local partners) Ford had a dominant market lead.

Recognise that a worldly business requires worldly people

The senior managers who are making the overall decisions about emerging-market investments must feel comfortable in these places. They need to have a sufficiently international perspective, to have travelled and had experience of operating internationally. The closer to the market a manager is operating, the more important it is that he has a good understanding of the local market, culture and language. It is still fairly common for a company's emerging-markets business to be run by people who had never been outside the developed world before their appointment to run an emerging-market business. Such people start with a handicap that is not easy to overcome.

Never lose sight of economic and political risks that can derail your plan

Economic and political risks should be monitored continuously in emerging markets. Smart monitoring can anticipate sudden currency crises for example (see Chapters 6 and 14 for more details on understanding economic indicators and predicting economic crises). And, if only for the good of their own careers, executives should warn their senior management of any external risks that might be building up. These warnings should be footnotes (written in large letters) to any annual business plan. The last thing anyone running a business in emerging markets wants is to be blamed for weaker sales as a result of sudden currency depreciations. The footnote basically tells top management: "I told you it was bound to happen. The currency was about to fall. Don't blame me and my team."

Don't judge emerging markets on the basis of media reports

Media reports on their own should not be the basis for judging what is going on in different markets. The reporting is often superficial, focusing on the negative and the short term. The problem is that CEOs are often influenced by the headlines – see Chapter 17 on how a majority of companies misjudged the lucrative Russian market largely based on negative and alarming news reports.

Never stop monitoring which markets offer most potential

Few companies have the resources to develop all markets at the same time. So as well as initial market prioritisation, a company needs continuous up-to-date knowledge of external conditions to decide and plan the geographical order in which it should expand its operations. One criterion for deciding which countries will be winners is to look at the sustainability of economic policies and political decision-making. Sustainability of policies goes hand in hand with predictability. For example, with so many east European countries now in the EU it is much easier to say what these markets will look like in ten years, but for many Latin American countries the future remains uncertain.

Accept that you will never have all the information you would like to make a decision

In less-developed markets, there is rarely the range or quality of data you would normally gather in order to make a business investment decision in a developed country. But this should not be an obstacle for expanding operations in a systematic way. Instinct or gut feeling plays an important part in decisions to expand into developing countries. Companies can become more comfortable with such decision-making by, for example, building relationships and networks with people already operating in the markets in question. It is also good to hire senior people who have long experience in emerging markets, and who have the instinct and gut feeling that is needed to make decisions about where to go and how. This is of great help in testing assumptions and in discovering the realities of a market.

Don't ignore smaller markets – they can offer rich opportunities

There seems to be too much obsession with BRIC (Brazil, Russia, India and China) markets at the expense of other countries. A regional boss at Oracle says:

> A $10m contract from the government of Albania is the same as a $10m contract from the government of China. We don't want to let our competitors get that kind of money. At Oracle we say that no market is too small because our competition is there.

China deserves great attention, but not at the expense of other, often equally lucrative and interesting markets. The relative lack of competition in many small and even very poor markets means that early entrants and companies focusing on building a strong local presence often earn fantastic returns on investment. In the poorest countries of Sub-Saharan Africa, for example, one mobile telecoms company has made a return on investment that is six times the level it achieved in richer South Africa.

Accept that demand is hard to predict and volatile

A lack of reliable market information together with all kinds of uncertainties makes it much more difficult to predict demand than in the developed world. But this should not be an obstacle for investing in systematic business development. Demand will go up in most emerging markets but in a more volatile way. The important thing is to ignore quarterly and monthly volatility and focus on what really matters: capturing market share, and building brands and relationships.

Know or anticipate what others are getting into

When companies prioritise the markets they are considering entering, they often do so on the basis of a few key economic indicators. This produces hotspots, with many players pouring into some markets and few into others. For example, as a regional star, Hungary attracted all the major players in the mid-1990s, creating one of the tightest, most competitive markets in Europe where many companies struggled to make any money. However, companies which anticipated how crowded the Hungarian market was going to become and opted to invest more in Russia found themselves in a market that offered less competition, higher margins, quicker profits and more scope to build market share and brand loyalties.

Set high standards and benchmark against the best

Successful companies frequently ask themselves what ideal they are aiming at in emerging markets. They set criteria and then see what they can learn from the companies that are best for each criterion.

Understand that business in emerging markets is more time-consuming

Everything takes longer than in the developed world. Dealing with local authorities, customs clearing or getting a simple licence can take days or weeks. Since time is money, companies should understand the pace at which it is possible to run the business and budget money and time accordingly.

Use your emerging-markets business to benchmark your developed-world business

When some companies reach a certain level of success and comfort in emerging markets, they like to see how their organisational structure and results per employee compare with their developed-world business. Many are surprised that their developed-world business now seems flabby and over-managed compared with their nimble and tightly run emerging-markets business. So companies have realised that a successfully executed emerging-market strategy can have an impact on the company as a whole, and the way it is set up and run, and are using internal benchmarking as a way to increase adaptability and fleetness of foot, and to improve efficiency. Emerging-markets executives often run a more efficient operation for two reasons:

◪ They rarely get the resources they need but still get large growth targets. This has forced many of them to become extremely innovative and to work longer hours than their colleagues in the developed world.

19

◪ Unusually nimble domestic competition and increasing international competition are providing an incentive to run an efficient and creative organisation.

Don't forget that profit margins are often better than in the developed world

Many companies that the authors work with report results like this: "Developing markets account for 30% of our sales but 44% of our profits." This is not surprising since virtually all international companies face massive competitive pressures and price wars in the developed world. There are also emerging markets that have matured commercially far faster than their GDP per head numbers would suggest. However, the scale and intensity of competition are still below what is found in the developed world. Many companies demonstrate that it is possible to be exceptionally brave with pricing strategies. For example, Castrol, a motor oil and lubricants provider, charges 2-3 times more for its engine oils than its competitors in some of the poorest countries in the world. Yet it still manages to gain a commanding market share through its powerful marketing message, which clearly positions its products way above anything else in terms of quality and reliability.

Be aware than manufacturing shift is not only accelerating but also evolving

As foreign direct investment flows to emerging markets hit one high after another, fewer and fewer companies can continue to manufacture in expensive locations and stay competitive (see Chapters 9 and 10). For many years, labour-intensive manufacturing has been shifting to cheaper locations, but in recent years, more and more companies are also shifting to cheaper locations capital-intensive manufacturing, R&D, logistics and services. The advantages of offshoring are clear, but the disadvantages have not always been thought through in terms of both the short and long term. The lesson from this is to weigh carefully costs and benefits, while keeping a careful eye on what competitors are up to.

Don't impose time-wasting exercises on executives running emerging markets

Many companies devote huge amounts of time to budgeting and five-year plans at the behest of the senior management team. Budgets are, of course, essential, but there are disturbing examples of the budgeting process not taking into account the realities of emerging markets - for example, the volatility and unpredictability managers have to deal with and the travel and workload they have to undertake compared with country managers. One manager in charge of Russia and the CIS markets was instructed by his corporate headquarters to redo all his budgets to two decimal places. "Instead of 45% growth, for example, they forced me to waste days and insert two decimal points such as 45.27% growth into a number of our business unit plans." This is just one example of how global business practices often adapt poorly to emerging markets.

Appreciate that staff retention is more complicated

The demand for qualified staff continues to outstrip supply in most emerging economies. The turnover is higher, poaching is rampant and salaries/pay packages are often overheated (see Chapter 12). Retaining talented staff often means that their pay packages are sometimes more generous than those of comparable positions in the developed world. Companies should constantly benchmark with local market conditions and stay competitive, rather than stick regardless to global pay scales. It is also important to understand what makes locals tick and what things matter in addition to pay. The Centre for Creative Leadership has recently conducted a study analysing the differences in needs of local managers in emerging markets and their equivalents in the developed world. These differences – for example, seeking faster promotion, being eager to learn and develop, expecting companies to invest in their education – are notable and have direct implications for retention strategies. Companies should take note.

2 Managing corporate expectations

I never attempt to make money on the stockmarket. I buy on the assumption
that they could close the market the next day and not reopen it for five years.

Warren Buffett

The fish rots from the head.

Old Chinese saying

Business in emerging markets rarely succeeds if it is subjected to the
short-term criteria that companies in the less volatile developed
world are often judged by. But many chief executives of listed companies
are unwilling to adopt longer-term targets. Managing the expectations of
senior management is one of the top three critical issues for developing a
healthy business in emerging markets. This chapter explores strategies to
overcome in-built short-term perspectives and to manage the expectations
of not only board members but also investment analysts and the media,
whose perceptions of a company are crucial in determining its reputation
and share price.

If you look at how companies have gone about building and sustaining
their business in emerging markets, two facts invariably emerge. A short-
termist approach succeeds only in the short term. Private companies, or
those not dependent on equity markets, almost always build stronger and
more sustainable businesses than listed companies. This is because they
are not tied to quarterly results and are able to make longer-term plans.

A short-term approach to building business in emerging markets is the
most frequent cause of longer-term failure. When companies fall behind
their more systematic competition, regional and country managers often
criticise their CEOs for not releasing enough resources to build the business
properly. Many privately accuse their CEOs of caring only about the next
set of quarterly results.

That CEOs take a short-term approach is not surprising for two reasons.
First, reward systems in publicly listed companies have increasingly
favoured those who maximise short-term profits. Second, the complexity
and pressure of running large corporations have steadily decreased the
shelf-life of the average CEO. Consultants at Booz Allen Hamilton reckon
that the average tenure of CEOs for the world's 2,500 most valuable

companies had fallen to 4.6 years in 2006, compared with 9.5 years in 1995. Between 2000 and 2006, half of all *Fortune* 1000 companies had replaced their CEO. Markets give an average CEO less than 19 months to increase the share price, according to Burson-Marsteller, a public relations company.

To the detriment of the long-term well-being of their corporations, a number of CEOs have come to see their job as maximising short-term profits while in charge. This growing short-termism in the past two decades is one of the reasons that only 40% of *Fortune* 500 companies in 1980 are still on the list today. The stockmarket madness of the late 1990s, with the temptation to inflate profits via creative accounting practices, became just an extreme symptom of the same disease.

In the past two decades compensation systems for CEOs have to a large extent been based on stock options and bonuses based on short-term profit maximisation. Rewards go to those who move the stock price up in the short term. Many CEOs will not want to forgo a large annual bonus or a big gain on exercising their stock options by investing in something that will bring returns only when they may well no longer be with the firm. In such companies, emerging-market business suffers the most. Success in emerging markets requires a passion for systematically building business and investments that will not bring in profits in the short term. Unfortunately, investing for the medium to longer term has increasingly been viewed as a cost that squeezes the all-important short-term profits.

Short-termism reached a peak during the stockmarket bubble of the late 1990s. Starting in the early part of that decade in the United States, companies increasingly gave the investment community guidance on what their likely earnings would be as shareholders demanded greater short-term transparency and legal changes allowed companies to quote their quarterly earnings expectations. Many CEOs of listed companies, particularly in the United States and the UK, were under pressure to provide high short-term returns to their increasingly impatient shareholders. Managers operating in emerging markets found themselves (and many still do) impossibly pressured by the contradictions in overall policy. On the one hand they were being told to increase growth (and short-term returns); on the other hand they were being refused the resources to systematically build up business.

Many well-run companies' stock prices were (and continue to be) punished for missing expected quarterly earnings by an unforgiving Wall Street, as if such results really mattered for the overall soundness and future prospects of the business. Good decisions aimed at building a sustainable business are rarely rewarded by markets, and rewarding fund managers and analysts on how well they do in one quarter and how well they predict quarterly earnings encourages herd behaviour. "I buy because others do. I sell when I see that others sell," is how one young fund manager described how he worked.

A study by doctoral candidates at New York University's Stern School of Business, reported in the *Harvard Business Review* in June 2001, found that more than 90% of analysts' questions to CEOs during conference calls were about expectations for the next quarter's earnings. Investments were treated as factors that might jeopardise this "holy" quarterly number. Analysts' behaviour is unlikely to change. They cover many companies, and according to one analyst: "There is really no time to properly research, analyse and think."

No wonder managers who are in charge of real business decisions are immensely irritated by analysts. A senior executive from one of the 100 largest corporations in the world (which has been highly successful in emerging markets) said in a private conversation:

> These 26-year-olds, who have never run any business, come to
> us and interrogate us like the Gestapo. They are not interested
> in how we build business or what we are trying to do. And the
> day after they reveal our plans on CNBC, another damaging
> influence by the way. Because we told them about our
> investments our share price went down 15% in a few hours. We
> should do what XYZ does – give them a vague idea what the
> plans are and tell them to go to hell.

The impact of this on business is clear. Many companies have postponed investments that will help ensure their future survival and prosperity, and for some it may make the difference between surviving or not. One regional executive says:

> We make an enormous number of business decisions that I
> would never do if I were a sole owner of this business. But our
> top management is more obsessed with the steady growth of
> quarterly earnings than investing for the future. We will soon
> run into severe problems.

An exclusively short-term approach is bad for business in general; for emerging markets it is likely to be disastrous. But there are encouraging signs that companies are realising how they need to shift their focus from the short term. In 2003, three-quarters of all publicly listed companies in the United States told the market what their quarterly expectations were. By 2006, this proportion had dropped to just over one-half – a trend that is likely to continue as companies become more focused on not damaging long-term revenue and profit growth. If all that matters to the outside world is the quarterly figures, chief executives with what is likely to be a limited tenure may well be tempted to stop investing in long-term strategic projects and instead focus on cranking up short-term results by whatever means. Those in the investment business seem to have realised that too regular reporting of earnings estimates is harmful – 75% of investment professionals surveyed in 2006 by the CFA Institute say they would welcome the move away from quarterly guidance. This gives companies more scope to become more long-term in their approach and should encourage investment in emerging markets. As companies become more certain that their future must increasingly involve emerging markets, being able to take a longer-term view will allow them more freedom to embark on medium- to long-term investments in those markets. But they probably need to get a move on as the window of opportunity to acquire a sufficient market share will get smaller by the day.

Many companies invest too little in preparing for market entry (relative to the best competition) or have inadequate resources to execute effective market entry and market expansion plans (see later chapters).

So how do emerging-market managers go about managing the expectations of senior management? First they should go through the checklist in Chapter 3 and fight to get the resources to prepare each aspect of market entry properly. Without thorough preparation, any manager will have a hard time growing an emerging-market business, and the task of managing the CEO's expectations will become monumental.

Emerging markets are often more volatile than developed markets. There are years that are spectacularly good but they are often followed by not-as-good or even bad years. How can emerging-market managers predict the sustainable annual growth of business over, say, the next five years? How do they explain the inevitable ups and downs, and how do they get senior management to accept that next year may not be as good as the previous one?

A CEO may assume that because an emerging-market business grew by 30% in the previous year, it can grow by the same percentage or even a higher one in the current year. Therefore emerging-market managers need to communicate constantly what is shaping their business, taking care to point out why a certain level of performance may not be sustainable and the factors and risks which might set things back. Equally, senior management needs to be made aware that there are years when sales fall to unexpectedly low levels, usually because of some kind of emerging-market crisis (see Chapter 14). As with good years, the circumstances that made a year a bad one usually do not last. Markets bounce back sooner or later. Many short-termist companies react to such crises by radically downsizing operations. Although this provides short-term protection, it may have negative implications in the longer term (see Chapter 14).

Many CEOs push regional managers to work to stretched budgets, which simply increases the stress of working in a difficult-to-predict volatile market. Or it is counterproductive because managers simply ignore the budget as it does not take into account the realities of the market. The message from the top is often: "You claim there is a lot of potential in emerging markets, let's see it." And that is regardless of the fact that the risk and uncertainty as well as the potential have been pointed out.

One problem is that many companies push managers to deliver big returns before enough has been invested in establishing local market presence and securing brand recognition. But even in companies that do invest in what they need to, budget games are rampant. Those who meet and beat budgetary targets (regardless of how low they were set) are usually regarded as better managers than those who grow a business faster year on year but keep missing their unrealistic budgetary targets.

Many potentially productive hours of work are wasted on tactics for meeting budgetary expectations. As the regional manager of a large American company says: "I spend too much time managing the bottom line instead of managing the business." Studies by Wharton business school show that setting what managers perceive as overly ambitious goals distorts their behaviour and ultimately damages their companies. Managers start playing games. If they see they can exceed the stretch budget, for example, they try to delay end-of-year sales so they are booked in the next year. They fear that fantastic growth will earn them an even worse budgetary target next year, and they also want to have a good start to the year. Some managers even give up hard work "to prove that the target was crazy" and to play down expectations for the next year. As one manager who lost his job after proving that the target was crazy said: "I lost my job but at least I'll stay sane." The volatility of emerging markets makes the requirement to meet demanding budgets particularly stressful for local and regional managers, with the result that they are even more likely to behave in ways that are not in the best long-term interests of their firms.

Budget games are a fact of corporate life, but for emerging markets the following approach is a good one to adopt.

Determine the sustainable level of business growth in a given market

This assessment should be based on at least three factors: past results (if any); a thorough understanding of the external environment and the risks it carries; and a clear view of the internal capabilities and resources (see Chapter 3).

Decide whether you can communicate this analysis openly

Depending on the company culture and the CEO, some managers are able truthfully to communicate this sustainability analysis to their senior management. But in many companies it is not possible for at least two reasons. One is that pay and bonuses are linked to exceeding targets and, furthermore, missing a target can lose you your job or damage your career.

As a result, many companies have developed a corporate culture of deceit and caution. If a manager thinks his business in an emerging market can grow 30% next year, he will tell his senior management that a sustainable rate of growth is 15% plus, while pointing out a whole set of things that can potentially destroy even this 15% growth rate.

Point out all risks to the main scenario

Clearly outlining risk factors, as a footnote to the budget and business plan, is a smart thing to do in emerging markets regardless of whether a company encourages and rewards truthful communication or is infested with a culture of deceit. In both cases, senior management needs to be aware of the things that can go wrong. There is no shortage of risks in emerging markets. Many companies active in them say that the single biggest risk affecting their emerging-market plans in the 1990s was the unpredictability of currency devaluations. Managers at Sony say that they fear unpredictable recessions and unpredictable consumer behaviour. In many countries, managers worry about political risks and the way they affect sales. In years of uncertain elections, for example, consumers' appetite for spending often shrinks. Perhaps the most worrying thing for many companies is that the list of largely unpredictable market threats is long, even in reasonably well-managed emerging markets. The Mexico crisis in 1994 moved the country from a star to a short-term basket case in a matter of weeks, for no good fundamental reason (see Chapter 14).

Make sure senior management understands and accepts volatility

One of the most important things for senior management to accept is that emerging markets are volatile. Regardless of how much money is invested and regardless of the quality of the people running the operation on the ground, there will be bad years and there will be good years, even spectacular ones. Also keep in mind that not all global emerging markets are down at the same time. The encouraging news is that there are, in virtually all emerging markets, more good years than bad ones. In other words, there is steady long-term growth of revenues and profits. But both good and bad years often come unexpectedly, despite the efforts of forecasters to predict the future.

Establish different performance criteria for emerging markets

Managers operating in emerging markets need to be judged according to different criteria from those operating in developed markets. Performance criteria should focus on sustainable medium- to long-term results. Pay and rewards should be linked to these and not to short-term results. This will encourage more truthful and meaningful exchanges of information and analysis between country, regional and senior managers. It will also create a corporate culture in which emerging-market setbacks are seen as a normal part of business (and often economic progress) and not as disasters.

Educate senior management about risks and opportunities

One of the most important priorities for those in charge of emerging markets is to make senior management clearly aware of the risks and opportunities in their territory. Senior management's perceptions are inevitably shaped by news headlines, which do not tell the whole story, or even the true one. The best type of education is to bring the CEO and senior management to the market. But with such visits it is crucial to convey the realities of a market. For example, in most emerging markets there is a huge difference in development and purchasing power between capital cities and the rest of the country. A CEO who gets only a picture of a booming capital and a five-star hotel might start making unreasonable demands later on. In other words, sell the market to the CEO but do not oversell it.

To provide more objectivity to the visit, bring in outside speakers. These not only provide an expert view of the market, they also bridge any gap in trust between senior management and those on the ground. If an outside expert talks about the opportunities and risks of business in the market, it adds credibility to the local management's arguments.

In a globalised world there is a growing tendency in business to believe emerging markets are less foreign, less different, than they are. Senior managers have to be made aware of these foreign differences and the differences they make to business performance. At the same time, they must not become scared of them; that will lead only to a lack of commitment to a market in terms of resources.

3 Market entry preparation

A traveller without knowledge is a bird without wings.

Sa'di Gulistan, 13th century

Many companies mess up their entry into an emerging market by not adequately preparing the ground. This chapter provides a comprehensive run-down of the issues that must be understood and acted on before market entry is attempted.

Virtually all multinational companies do most of their business and make most of their profits in the developed world, and because their emerging-market business is smaller in absolute terms (and perhaps they understand it less), senior managers often pay less attention to it. Nevertheless, many CEOs put a lot of emphasis on being a powerful global player and being strong in emerging markets. The reality is less glorious. Time and time again, companies enter new markets with little understanding of what they are getting into, and then wonder why their often smaller competitors are beating them hands down.

Thorough preparation is essential for success. Leadership and support in the form of finance and other resources must come from the top of the corporate hierarchy from the very beginning. Any half-hearted effort is eventually bound to fail in the face of international and domestic competition. Making the necessary investment in preparation is usually more expensive than is generally thought, although, strangely, many companies will spend millions after they decide on a market entry or expansion plan but will not spend much trying to understand what they are getting into in the first place. Worse still, many leading firms underinvest in both preparation and execution, and later wonder what went wrong.

Business plans for emerging-market operations must be based on sound assumptions. Understanding the external environment should be a continuous effort, not just a one-off or occasional exercise. It should include extensive and continuous research. But none of this is much use if the company does not have or is not prepared to use internal resources to address the challenges of the external environment.

The external audit

The first priority is to rank markets according to the political and economic environment and the business environment. Many of the things listed below are not easy to find out in emerging markets, and in order to come up with the best possible assumption many will require creative research methods.

1 Understanding the market

Companies should be careful not to be misled by statements such as: "There are 1 billion consumers in India. Every one of them is a potential buyer of our TV sets." In reality, most of the 1 billion will be poor and living outside the cash economy at subsistence level. Does this mean there must at least be a few hundred million who can afford to buy what we sell? Not necessarily. There could be a large domestic player dominating the market in such a low pricing range that no foreign company can match it without radically changing its manufacturing cost structure and being prepared to accept lower margins than usual.

It is also important to bear in mind, especially in business-to-business transactions, that demand can be sudden. This is hard to predict. Hence the importance of local presence and the building up of relationships so that you have your ears close to the ground and hear about likely developments in the market. Questions to ask about the market are as follows.

Market potential
- How large and wealthy is this market? Calculate local production plus imports minus exports.
- What is the history of local consumption of the product/service?
- What percentage of local production is actually sold? How much is lying around unsold?
- Is there unsatisfied demand for the product/service?
- Are there any re-export dynamics that should be considered?
- How important are parallel or grey imports (smuggled or counterfeit)?
- What has traditionally driven local consumption of the product/service?
- What are the current and likely future drivers of local consumption?
- How is local consumption likely to evolve in the next 5–10 years?

Understanding local consumers/customers
- Who are the consumers/customers? What are their characteristics?
- What do consumers/customers want? Interview buyers and dealers/distributors for preferences.

- Where are they in the country in question? Where are the clusters or pockets of purchasing power?
- How do consumers/customers make their decisions?
- What are their spending patterns?
- How much money do they have to spend?
- How do other companies in the sector see the customer/consumer base and how much are they able to sell to them in reality?

Reaching the consumer/customer
- How difficult/easy is it to reach potential consumers/customers?
- Who are the potential local selling partners that need to be engaged?
- How do competitors and non-competitors reach their customers?
- Who can help with contacting potential partners?
- What are the most effective ways to promote the product?
- What kind of advertising/promotion works best?

Competition
- Which competitors are already operating in the market (both international and local)?
- If local competitors are important players, how sustainable is their existence and what is it based on? Is there a danger of smaller local competitors playing a stronger role in the future?
- How strong are competitors that are already there?
- How many people do they employ and what is their organisational structure?
- Are other competitors entering or planning to enter the market?
- What do customers/consumers think about competitors and their products/services?
- What have been competitors' experiences and results, both negative and positive, in the local market?
- If competitors failed, why?
- If competitors succeeded, why?

Understanding lessons learned by non-competitors
- What do non-competitors say about the business environment in the country?
- What have been the largest obstacles to successful operations?
- How can such obstacles be overcome, if at all?
- What is the discrepancy between official statistics and actual

achievable sales? In other words, is there more purchasing power/ money in the country than the official statistics suggest?

- What level of local resources is necessary to avoid the risk of underpenetrating the market or underexploiting its potential? (See Chapter 7.)

Local culture

- What specific aspects of local culture are relevant to running a successful local business?
- What makes this market different from others in the region? Always remember that markets are different and should be examined separately.

2 Understanding the political and economic environment

Questions to ask about the political and economic environment are as follows. (See Chapter 6 for how to interpret economic indicators and Chapter 5 for more on political risk.)

Economic outlook

- How sustainable is economic growth?
- What is driving economic growth?
- How accurate are the relevant economic indicators?
- Even if reasonably accurate, are economic growth indicators misleading when it comes to local consumption, and why?
- If real economic growth is likely, will this mean that GDP per head will also increase?
- What will happen to the exchange rate and inflation rate?
- What is the likelihood of devaluation or depreciation and how large could it be?
- What are the stories and assumptions behind other economic indicators that may have an impact on operations?
- How independent is the local central bank? Are its policies shaped by politics rather than sound principles of monetary management?

Political outlook

- What is the level of political risk and how will or might it affect the business?
- What is the risk and what kind of companies will be most affected by it? For example, is it only those with a large asset investment on the ground that are at risk?

- What subtler forms of political risk (see below) could affect operations?

Government policies and their impact on business
- Does the government allow a level playing field? Is there discrimination against international companies? If yes, potentially how disadvantageous or dangerous could this discrimination be for the business?
- Is the government in the hands of local lobbies and to what extent do local special-interest groups have a detrimental influence on business?
- Does the government protect intellectual property?
- Does the government encourage free trade? Does it allow and even encourage non-tariff barriers?
- Is the government trustworthy when dealing with foreign companies?
- Does the government protect private property and how high is the risk of expropriation?
- To what extent does the government interfere with pricing?
- What is the government record in implementing antitrust policies?
- What is the quality of public administration and government bureaucracy?
- Is it an effective and efficient government to deal with or is it ineffective and inefficient?
- How quick is policy formulation and execution?
- Who are the key government players at the federal, regional and city levels that can make or break plans for a business?
- How open is the government to foreign involvement in the economy? Does it encourage and even provide incentives for foreign investment?
- What kind of local organisation is allowed?

3 Understanding the business environment
Questions to ask about the business environment are as follows.

Finance
- Is it possible to finance operations locally or will it be necessary to rely on in-company finance or sources from abroad?
- What access do customers/consumers have to finance?
- What are the loan conditions for different types of firms and private consumers?

◪ Can finance be raised through local capital markets (corporate bonds or equity)?

◪ How stable is the banking system? How high is the risk of collapse and how good/bad is banking supervision?

◪ How efficient is the banking system?

◪ Are banks willing to lend money to local private individuals, small and medium-sized enterprises and large domestic companies?

◪ Is it possible to repatriate profits freely and is the currency convertible? How difficult is it to move funds in and out of the country?

◪ Is it easy or difficult to transfer money within the country?

◪ What other potential sources of funding (development banks, government agencies, and so on) can be tapped into for the project?

◪ Are there any potential local partners who might co-finance the project?

Labour market

◪ What are the wage/salary rates for the employees who will be needed?

◪ How high are social security contributions and what is the outlook for them?

◪ How aggressive is the labour market (is there a lot of poaching) or not? What is the outlook?

◪ How educated is the labour force?

◪ How unionised is the local labour force? What is the incidence of strikes?

◪ What are the main weaknesses of the labour force? Which areas will require most training?

◪ What are the most effective ways of recruiting local employees?

◪ How flexible or inflexible is labour law and what is the outlook for it?

Taxation

◪ What are the current levels of taxation?

◪ What are the planned or likely changes to the tax system?

◪ What kind of "less obvious/hidden taxes" exist in the market?

◪ What kind of tax holidays and incentives exist at national, regional and city levels?

◪ What is the outlook for tax incentives?

◪ How frequent are tax inspections and are they carried out fairly?

◪ What kind of organisational structure/legal entity is the most advantageous in terms of taxation and local cost structure?

Legal environment

◪ How effective and efficient is the local judiciary?

◪ Can foreign companies rely on local commercial courts?

◪ Is arbitration the best option in disputes and where should it take place?

◪ What is the discrepancy between laws on paper and actual implementation?

◪ Is there a discrepancy between interpretation of the same laws from province to province or from city to city?

◪ Is there any hope that the local legal system will improve? If yes, how long will the process last?

Bureaucratic obstacles to business

◪ What are the most common bureaucratic obstacles for business (permits, licences, and so on)?

◪ How easy or difficult it is to move goods through customs?

◪ How easy or difficult it is to set up business in the country? How long does it take and what is required?

Crime and corruption

◪ Is crime a problem for business?

◪ Is organised crime a problem for business?

◪ Does crime or organised crime affect only local companies or does it also affect foreign players?

◪ What kind of crime is problematic for business?

◪ What should a security policy cover?

◪ How are other companies fighting a crime problem? Is the problem manageable?

◪ What is the level of corruption? How does it affect business? Is it getting better or worse?

◪ Who is corrupt? Which individuals and which government institutions?

Infrastructure

◪ What is the quality of local transport infrastructure?

◪ What is the quality of local telecommunications infrastructure?

Foreign trade environment
- Is the country a member of the World Trade Organisation (WTO)? If it is, how closely does it follow WTO rules?
- Does it belong to any trading blocs or regional free-trade areas?
- Which bilateral free-trade agreements does it have?
- What is the outlook for any future free-trade agreements?
- Do these signed free-trade agreements work in practice? If they do not, what are the problems?
- Are non-tariff barriers significant and what is the outlook in that regard?
- Are there customs bottlenecks and how much would they add to operational costs?
- Is there a problem of illegal/parallel imports (or even counterfeit products)?

Current and future cost of building a business and brand

Estimating the cost of expanding in or entering an emerging market is difficult and frequently underestimated by multinational companies. The most common mistake is to underestimate the time needed to accomplish an action plan. Even the simplest task (for example, getting a stamp on a permit) that would take a few hours in most developed countries can take days or weeks in an emerging market. Companies need to take time during this preparatory stage to understand how long it will realistically take. After all, time is money.

- How expensive is the operational environment and what is the outlook?
- How expensive is it to build a brand and what is the outlook for advertising prices?
- How much time will it take to do what is necessary to get the business off the ground?

The internal audit

Detailed and continuous understanding of the external environment is just one part of the challenge when setting up and running an emerging-market operation. The other is assessing the internal capabilities needed to match market requirements.

The internal audit prepares managers for the internal battle for corporate resources by assessing in detail what is needed to develop business opportunities effectively and to minimise the risks identified during the external research. If an internal audit results in the allocation of adequate resources, the likelihood of business success will jump dramatically.

Most of the emerging markets with obvious potential have now passed the point where strong and profitable market positions can be established without significant investment of resources.

The key questions to ask in an internal audit are as follows:

- What is needed? If this market opportunity is developed systematically, how much time and money will be required?
- Are the CEO and senior management committed to supporting a systematic business development and providing the necessary resources? Note that the commitment of the CEO is sometimes not enough; other senior managers also have to support the project.
- Is the product portfolio right for the market?
- Which existing products have the strongest chance of success?
- Can the business opportunity identified be addressed by existing products and services? Or does the product/service portfolio need broadening to match the needs of local consumers/customers?
- If market research suggests that the product portfolio is wrong for the market, will investment be available for developing new products?
- Would a modest modification of the current portfolio of products/ services do the trick or is something entirely new needed?
- If substantial changes to the product/service portfolio are needed, would this deviate too much from the core strategy? How long would it take to make the changes and how much would it cost?
- What human resources are needed? Is there enough internal human resource expertise to develop the business in these complex markets or will it have to be acquired? What is the view of the human resources department about all HR issues?
- Are processes and structures flexible enough and adequate for what is planned? Will existing internal processes and operational practices help or hinder what is planned? (Many companies give more flexibility to their emerging-market business teams because they have found that structures that work well in mature markets are often too slow and inflexible to respond to day-to-day challenges in emerging markets. The internal audit should identify what operational aspects need to be addressed before going ahead.)
- What existing capacities can be drawn on?

- What existing internal strengths can usefully be built on? For example, before entering the Russian market, one firm realised that it could ship products duty-free from its plant in Kenya to Russia because of an old free-trade agreement. This circumvented enormously high import duties and made a crucial contribution to the success of the business over the years. Many multinationals have used Austrian employees to expand operations into eastern Europe, believing that they are culturally better positioned to establish successful operations than people who grew up in, say, Ohio.
- Is there pressure/encouragement from customers to expand?
- Can the risks that have been identified be managed? Are the internal structure, processes and people up to managing financial and other risks the business will face? (Identifying potential risks is not the same as having the capability to manage them.)
- How would entry be financed? Are the funds available, and if not, how would they be raised? Are there development bank funds or incentive schemes that can be tapped into? Should the cost of expansion be shared with local partners?

After examining their internal capabilities, most companies realise that there is a resource gap which needs to be addressed. Some companies invest time and money to close it and some do not. The latter generally fail.

The next step is a business proposal, based on the external and internal analyses, to senior management. It includes what to do, how to do it and by when, as well as a detailed outline of resource requirements.

4 Market research and business intelligence

Few things foul us up quicker than bad information.

Mort Crim, veteran American broadcaster

Collecting business intelligence in emerging markets is trickier, more demanding and more time-consuming than in developed markets. This chapter explains how to conduct complex research, how to save money doing it, and which methods and sources to use.

Market research takes more time in emerging markets than in developed markets and the outcome of intelligence gathering is often disappointing. In the majority of emerging markets, data are often unreliable, vague and hard to find. Needless to say, this makes senior management and everyone else involved nervous. How can a company make a sound and potentially costly business decision on partially accurate and incomplete information?

There are two ways for emerging market managers to minimise the risks. First, they should rely more on primary research than on secondary research wherever possible. Primary research means going straight to the source, in many cases through interviews with potential customers and other companies. Carrying out primary research in emerging markets is time-consuming and is not cheap. One multinational conducted more than 50,000 interviews with potential customers to improve its market intelligence before entering a cluster of new markets. Benchmarking against companies which devote substantial resources to research is critical. There are many companies willing to spend tens of millions of dollars during implementation which hesitate to spend a fraction of that for the detailed business intelligence research that is essential if they are to understand and succeed in the market they are entering.

A manager who relies solely on desk research is like a ship's captain who sees only the tip of an iceberg; it is the large chunk below the surface that makes or breaks the business. It is this invisible part that business intelligence should focus on most. Desk research may provide some useful background information and basic data, and even local intelligence, but companies should be wary of local media reports, which are often more biased than foreign sources.

Government information sources can also be misleading. For example, a new commercial law may sound good on paper, but what is the chance that it will be implemented and enforced? A reality check with law firms and other players in a market is more important than simply knowing the letter of the law.

Consultants can help, but since data are scarce and unreliable, market research firms often recycle and repackage old information. In some countries one or two sources are recycled over and over again, often repeating information that is wrong and misleading for decision-making. Primary research is the only way to find out the realities of the market.

It is also important to realise that leading consulting firms frequently charge top-dollar rates for conducting primary and secondary research, which they then subcontract to local firms. Substantial savings can be made by going direct to consulting firms which focus on specific sectors or regions.

Qualitative inputs – or gut feelings

The risks of poor market research can also be greatly reduced by devoting resources to qualitative inputs. Many business decisions in emerging markets will to a large extent be based on instinct and gut feeling, and there are two ways to ensure that such instincts and feelings are more than guesswork.

One way is to have a small team of people in charge of co-ordinating business information gathering and analysis. An efficient and quick-witted internal business intelligence team keeps a company sharp and ready to act and react appropriately. This is crucial to staying ahead of the competition, as it means managers are kept up to date with analysis of the business environment and are better able to anticipate any emerging risks and opportunities. These teams can help gather and share information on a regional basis; they can also pass on information and intelligence from one emerging market that could be relevant in another. People hired to run such co-ordination centres have to be good analysts. They should be able to say: "Based on this information, this is the implication for our business and this is why."

The other way to develop reliable instincts is through networking. Building up a good network of contacts and maintaining them is the most powerful business intelligence tool in emerging markets. It is as important for companies entering the market for the first time as it is for those already established, since personal relationships matter much more than in developed markets. Networks provide business intelligence that is unavailable through conventional research. They can help with all aspects of external market analysis as well as with benchmarking how internal assessments were made and how internal resource gaps were closed. They add more comfort to decision-making and decrease the chance of failure.

A business network is a base for continuous benchmarking. Are we underinvesting relative to the competition and by how much? Are we on the right track? Is everyone else facing this complicated issue (meaning that it is not our fault, but a feature of a difficult market)? Are we taking the right steps to try to resolve a problem or is our approach different from other players in the market? All these questions are difficult to answer in any other way.

Personal contact is crucial in all aspects of networking. Business in most emerging markets is intensely personal. Many managers are ignored by government officials and potential partners, suppliers or customers because of a lack of personal bonding. Many companies make the mistake of replacing their expatriate managers every few years, thus damaging their local business. The same goes for retaining key local staff, since when they leave they take their personal relationships with them.

Different kinds of networks are important in emerging markets. The most important are described below.

Peer groups
The best stories about emerging markets are never published; they are told over dinner and during coffee breaks at meetings of regional and country managers. Joining regional and local peer groups and associations provides easy access to useful knowledge. In emerging markets, managers from competing companies often socialise and discuss how to handle generic business issues. The challenges these managers face are so overwhelming that both sides benefit from sharing information and insights.

Government networks
Government policies can be difficult to follow and understand even in advanced emerging markets. At worst, new laws may be applied before the new legislation has been announced.

Most successful companies in emerging markets have an external affairs team comprising managers who are mainly in charge of developing and maintaining links to authorities. Their job is to understand how government policy is shaped and to anticipate any legislative changes that might affect the business. They must also know who is influencing important commercial laws and regulations at all levels of government. This requires relationships with ministers and their deputies and advisers, as well as the lower-level bureaucrats with whom companies have regular dealings.

Other important personal business intelligence contacts
These include the following:

- Existing customers, suppliers and business partners, as well as potential ones.
- Leading analysts and opinion leaders who regularly follow the market and generally know more than they publish. Extracting their intimate knowledge of the market and its challenges is invaluable.
- Influential local businessmen, especially where they have a major influence on government policy and the business environment. Such contacts can help bring substantial additional business. But it can all backfire if the regime changes and your contact is not in favour with the new one. Achieving a balance that allows a company to get the most benefit from its contacts while not exposing it too much should the climate change is a challenge that has to be weighed on a case-by-case basis.
- Business conferences featuring good debates between government officials and business. Networking at events is also important.

Developing a personal knowledge network is neither cheap nor easy, but it is invaluable and goes hand in hand with having strong local presence. It takes patience, time and corporate dedication, but it is as least as important as spending time and money on more conventional research methods. Emerging-market companies need to budget sufficiently for this purpose on a continuous basis.

5 Assessing political risks

You miss 100% of the shots you never take.

Wayne Gretzky, the greatest ice hockey player

There is more business in supposedly dangerous places than many companies imagine. Companies that understand how to interpret the real political risk greatly improve their chances of being among the first to operate profitably in emerging markets. This chapter shows how companies should go about interpreting and assessing political risk. "Only bullets and bombs can prevent our trucks from reaching the consumer," says one Coke bottler. Coca-Cola and some other companies (but not too many) sell their products in some of the most dangerous and politically risky countries in the world. Most political risks are irrelevant if a consumer wants to buy and can pay, and physical delivery is possible. But political risks, even minor ones, can and do disrupt business planning. It is from this perspective that companies need to understand and monitor them.

The first step is to make a distinction between political risks that affect sales and those that affect investments in physical assets on the ground. Many multinational companies have ignored good sales opportunities because their political risk analysis dominated their overall market assessment. The perception of high political risk hijacked their thinking and limited their sales activities.

International media often heighten the sense of political risk. Companies that are interested only in selling to a market need to look carefully at what is behind the headlines and decide whether the bad news is really bad for sales. Following the invasion of Iraq and the toppling of Saddam Hussein, Iran became "high risk" in the media, and yet international companies were lining up to sell to this large market. Even US trading sanctions did not deter American firms, which often licensed their products to local partners to sell. Nevertheless, keen as companies may be to sell to the Iranian market, few will invest directly in it.

Interestingly, there are examples of companies investing in physical assets even in very dangerous places. They take a calculated and strategic risk. Most companies do not have the stomach or leadership vision to do this. But it can be done and risks can be minimised. When Coca-Cola built a bottling plant in Angola, for example, rebel forces were still regularly attacking government forces. Shooting occurred not far from the bottling plant. Coca-Cola shared the risk of investment with other partners; it invested in security, keeping the investment low enough for it not to be a catastrophic loss if the facility was destroyed. In such ventures, the downside is a loss of several million dollars and the upside is reasonable sales in the short term and market leadership.

In some ways, the decision on whether to enter a high-risk market is simple because the reality is stark and the expectations are more likely to be realistic. For those who have the stomach and corporate tolerance for calculated risk (for the sake of establishing strategic market leadership), investing in physical assets and establishing operations in a high-risk emerging market may result in a firm becoming the market leader. Equally, it may result in every dollar spent on the project being lost with little warning.

Subtle, less visible political risks – common to most emerging markets – are in many ways more dangerous, and companies need to invest time and money in understanding them. Those that ignore them generally end up facing unpleasant and costly surprises.

Unlevel playing fields

Government discrimination in favour of local players – sometimes blatant and sometimes subtle – is one problem for foreign companies in emerging markets. Such protectionism may be in the form of subsidies that support inefficient local firms, or it may be simply a matter of connections and "old boy" networks.

Sometimes a government is influenced by local business groups, which shape the business environment in their own interests. One firm, for example, set up an office in a market with the aim of establishing a network of filling stations. Its strategy was to import high-quality gasoline because the gasoline produced by local refineries was low-quality and, over the long term, detrimental to car engines. After the company had committed substantial resources to the project, the government, responding to pressure from the local oil monopoly, introduced quality controls on imported oil. The cost of securing quality approval was set at such a level that the foreign company could not compete and, after lobbying the government for months, it pulled out.

This example illustrates how local firms can team up with governments and damage the business of foreign companies. But it also shows that the foreign company was neither properly prepared to enter the market nor really committed to it. If it had been, it would not have pulled out so quickly after facing its first large obstacle. Eight months later, under pressure from two other foreign companies, the government was forced to abandon its quality control scheme. The company that pulled out is a large player in the United States and Europe but tiny in most emerging markets; this is not surprising given its weak market entry approach.

The interplay between special interest groups and government can take many shapes and forms, but it is a risk that can be anticipated with proper research and, hopefully, it can be dealt with. Companies with or planning operations in emerging markets should have a permanent external affairs team.

Disrespect for intellectual property

Slack intellectual property laws or enforcement amount to another form of government protectionism for local firms. The counterfeiting industry thrives; we live in a world of fake or pirated goods such as software, music and computer games, as well as watches and designer clothing. In recent years there has been a massive proliferation of factories producing anything from fake baby food and pharmaceuticals to fake spare parts for aircraft and cars. The International Chamber of Commerce (ICC) anti-counterfeit division and the OECD estimate that counterfeit products could already account for up to 10% of total world trade. Like any grey-market activity this is hard to estimate, but it is clear that the problem is growing. Master Foods, a US consumer goods giant, has even found counterfeit cat food in certain markets around the world.

What really worries companies is that the rogue products are not coming from small businesses operating from garages and basements. They are real, extensive and sophisticated manufacturing operations financed by organised crime networks and often with the blessing of local or national government officials who have been paid off. They use the latest technology and have even developed the sales and distribution techniques of large international companies. They are fleet of foot and difficult to catch, but it is their links to officials in certain countries that makes it hard to combat them. Pirated music and films are now on sale before the official launch date. Counterfeit versions of curtains designed in France were on sale before the genuine French article.

According to the ICC, China leads the world counterfeit rankings, followed by Russia, India and Brazil – the same quartet that arouses so much international business excitement. Emerging-market intellectual property laws are often good in theory but poor when it comes to the practicalities of enforcement.

Tracing counterfeiters is hugely time-consuming and, as the copiers no doubt exploit, the cost of chasing them is often too much for the size of the local market in question.

So how are companies supposed to fight back? An increasingly common approach is to develop technologies that will identify – and therefore help protect – the genuine article. For example, Du Pont, a chemicals and healthcare company, has developed three-dimensional optically variable devices embedded in polymer film which carry authentication information. 3M, a US industrial conglomerate, produces hidden tags that can be seen only with special lasers and lights. Car manufacturers already use radio-frequency identification to track auto parts. Another strategy is to accelerate innovation for existing products, though some products are never going to be particularly difficult to counterfeit. Other ways of tackling counterfeiting include investing in dedicated in-house resources, often as part of external/government affairs divisions, to work closely with ministries and government agencies. For the managers involved this can be a dangerous game and they keep a low profile for fear of reprisal by organised crime groups. At the same time, companies also invest in educating the public and changing attitudes.

Dealing with autocratic regimes

This is a tricky area for business which is often full of hypocrisy and double standards. American companies thought little of breaking trade sanctions against countries such as Libya and Iran by using third parties, third countries and non-US citizens. Every company in the world happily does business with the communist government of China, while many are reluctant to do business with communist-led regimes in Belarus and Cuba. The size of the market and its strategic importance play a role. Many companies are afraid to be associated with "evil" regimes and feel that negative western public perception of their involvement outweighs the benefits of doing business there. Others argue that their involvement with such regimes is helping the country's economic, social and political development and is an eventual path to more democracy. The reality is that companies rarely care with whom they are doing business and begin to shy away from certain regimes only when they sense a business threat, such as the possibility of nationalisation in Venezuela.

Government trustworthiness

As a rule, companies should be at least mildly sceptical when listening to government promises. There are governments that mislead companies intentionally, and there are those that mean what they say but are unable to implement the promises. The best thing that companies can do is to study the previous record of government promises and understand the current political set-up. Even in countries with a good track record, the external affairs team should keep the pressure on with regard to changes that are desired and changes that have been promised but not delivered.

An economic crisis may not be bad for business

Bad and inefficient politics have contributed to many economic crises and many corporate frustrations. But many companies (not publicly, of course) love economic crises and devaluations. This includes companies that manufacture locally and export (now cheaply manufactured goods) mostly to the developed world and companies seeking to buy local assets.

Respect the power of provincial and city authorities

Regional governors and/or city mayors are usually important for business, sometimes even more than federal authorities. As ever, companies should have a clear and detailed understanding of the previous record of such individuals and act accordingly.

What's yours is now not

The risk of property being expropriated or nationalised was serious a few decades ago in a number of countries, but it has clearly diminished. Still, it should not be ignored. When times get desperate so can government actions, as the expropriation of property in Zimbabwe under Robert Mugabe has shown.

Barriers to trade

Although 150 countries now belong to the World Trade Organisation and regional trading blocs have flourished, some countries – both developed and emerging-market – are openly protectionist in certain ways. Currently the biggest issue in world trade talks is the reluctance of the United States, the European Union and Japan to reduce their massive barriers to agricultural imports. However, trading barriers are significantly lower than a few decades ago. Tariff barriers have been cut or removed in many instances, but the use of non-tariff barriers persists in ways that can be complex and infuriating. Examples range from overnight import taxes or import surcharges to imposing quality controls that are either prohibitively expensive or highly complex and time-consuming. All undermine smooth business and profitability and sometimes even price companies out of the market.

Although non-tariff barriers are more likely to be introduced in tough economic times, this may also occur when a local industrial or state lobby is strong.

Companies should understand how a government has behaved and how it is likely to behave in future. Certain signs can indicate an increased likelihood of protectionist measures. For example, if a country's current-account deficit is deteriorating, the government may act to reduce imports by, for example, introducing an import tax (which the WTO usually tolerates for a limited period in certain circumstances – typically a high current-account deficit or similar macroeconomic imbalance).

Pricing interference

Pharmaceuticals and utility companies are particularly exposed to governments seeking to control prices, but so are tobacco, oil and alcohol manufacturers. For example, when a foreign company bought an electricity distributor in Hungary in 2003, the government promised (and agreed contractually) that the investor would be able to gradually raise prices to market levels at a certain percentage a year. But for political reasons the government went back on its word and allowed for only half the agreed annual price increases.

Pharmaceuticals companies are already used to governments that tie reimbursement levels to the price of cheap generics.

Public administration and bureaucracy – more quid than pro

If you want to open a manufacturing plant (greenfield or acquisition) in certain emerging markets you will probably have to fly the members of the state environmental committee to inspect your plant in the West. They will also ask for large daily payments and some will insist that their wives (or "nieces") accompany them. In some countries you have to wait for months to get a stamp on an important document, an exercise that would take a few minutes, hours or at worst a few days in the developed world.

Even if corruption is eliminated, many bureaucracies are still inefficient, largely because of the quality of the people. Governments and the low salaries they pay are not magnets for top-notch individuals. Private businesses in emerging markets pay much better and usually attract the best people. Thus many countries end up with low-quality staff in key government positions. They may have good intentions, but often they are of little positive use to foreign companies. As a result, many firms setting up or operating in emerging markets put a lot of time and effort into educating bureaucrats and winning them over.

Inefficient and ineffective government

It is important to be aware of how much government inefficiency impinges on the local economy and diminishes the potential for growth. But even so there are many examples of manufacturing companies making good profits in countries run by hopeless governments. For example, if a country is widely perceived as risky, investors can enjoy preferential treatment. When Croatia had a government that few companies wanted to deal with, Ericsson invested some $30m in cash (and some $45m in kind) in manufacturing operations and in return received an exclusive long-term contract (worth at least $500m) to be the sole supplier to the local telecoms monopoly.

When considering more dangerous places, companies often argue that it is too risky to employ people on the ground. The reality is that locals live in dangerous and risky places anyway and are often keen to work. Besides, it is usually possible to find a local distributor.

6 Interpreting economic indicators

Academic economics ... is a primitive science, of course. If you want a parallel, think of medicine at the turn of the century.

Paul Krugman in 1994

Understanding how to interpret often confusing and misleading economic indicators is essential in getting to grips with an emerging market. This chapter explains the important economic indicators and how they should be interpreted for business purposes. It also highlights the dangers of taking indicators at face value and ignoring the drivers behind them, and it includes examples of how companies have been seriously misled in the past.

Economic performance can never be perfectly measured. Economic indicators do a good job in measuring it, but in most emerging markets the indicators are much less reliable than those for the developed world. Just walk through the streets of Cairo or Mexico City or any rural area in an emerging market and it is clear that unrecorded economic activity is rampant. Turkish or Ukrainian unofficial economic activities are probably as large as official ones.

Even statistics on the official economy are inaccurate, including statistics in developed countries. In developing countries, inaccuracy is typically of much greater magnitude. It is too expensive to collect information on all economic activity, so collection is based on surveys and sampling. As a result, accounts are full of estimates. Many governments distort samples and surveys to produce results that support their political agenda. In many countries there are significant flaws in the data compiling systems.

It is not only a question of lies and bad systems: there are genuine measurement problems. Measurement methodologies have traditionally focused on measuring the output of easy-to-measure physical goods. Few countries, especially in the developing world, bother to measure sectors which have boomed in recent decades, such as information technology, financial services, health care or entertainment. Even if countries try to capture these service industries, it is hard to define what one unit of production really is – which is easy to do if you want to know how many tractors a country produced in a given year. For all countries, accurate statistics are elusive because the share of easy-to-measure manufacturing is shrinking as a proportion of the whole economy. Technological advances often remain unmeasured, which suggests that GDP growth is regularly understated throughout the world.

Where statistics are shaky, economic forecasts are even more uncertain than usual. Remember that forecasters usually publish a main scenario, so it is important to question them about the risks to the scenario and to warn senior management about these before submitting the business plan.

Hints and tips

- Are the numbers you are looking at real (with the effects of inflation stripped out) or nominal (including inflation)? If they are nominal, look for real.
- Never judge a situation by a number or two. Look at the past trend and make sure you know what happened before and what is driving current numbers. For example, a country might record high growth rates in a particular year, but this could be because there was a slump in the previous year and the high growth represents catching up rather than a genuine improvement in standards of living.
- Will the data be subject to later revisions? GDP figures are nearly always revised.
- Will the data you are looking at be seasonally adjusted? For example, third quarter GDP growth may be boosted by a bumper harvest, but growth over the whole year may be much lower.
- Don't get excited if a country's GDP rises by 2%. If its population increased by 2.2% in the same period, per head GDP actually declined.

GDP

GDP forecasts are given great weight in many business plans. But this can be misleading. As *The Economist* has said: "GDP should really stand for Grossly Deceptive Product."

GDP: what it is and why you should be careful when using GDP forecasts

GDP is the total market value of all final goods and services produced within an economy in a given year. The quantity of goods is multiplied by prices. Say that an economy produced 50,000 tractors (at a unit price of $20,000) and 20,000 cars (at $25,000 each) in a given year. GDP is thus $(50{,}000 \times \$20{,}000) + (20{,}000 \times \$25{,}000)$

$1.5 billion. If the prices of tractors and cars grow next year, it will appear that GDP has increased. This would be a nominal increase in GDP.

To calculate real GDP it is necessary to keep prices constant, or in other words adjust for inflation. Take the cars in this example. In year 1 GDP was 20,000 × $25,000 = $500m. In year 2 production increased to 22,000 cars and the price increased to $26,000, giving GDP of $572m. It appears that GDP rose by 14.4%. But if prices from year 1 are used to recalculate year 2 (22,000 cars × $25,000), it is clear that real GDP rose to $550m and there was a 10% real increase.

To understand what drives growth or decline in GDP, you need to know who is buying the final goods and services that are produced. Either they are bought by consumers, firms or government, or they are net exports (exports minus imports).

GDP forecasts are an indication of growth in standards of living over the medium to long term. They are also a broad indication of comparative wealth around the world. But companies in the middle of annual budgeting and planning should use GDP forecasts with caution, for three reasons:

- Growth can be "driven" by strong exports or strong government purchases, but this will not help a company selling toothpaste, for example. It can happen that GDP grows strongly because exports are booming, while at the same time consumer spending is declining (perhaps there has been an increase in personal income tax or utility prices).
- The numbers can be insufficient or exaggerated. China, for example, is widely believed to exaggerate its GDP growth figures by 1–3%.
- For emerging markets in particular, GDP is a far from perfect measure of economic activity. It does not count any underground economy (grey or black economy).

An understanding of what drives growth in an emerging market is more useful for business planning than knowing the overall GDP growth number. More important is an understanding of the underlying reasons for growth in, say, private consumption or purchases by firms. Those engaged in budgeting should look for economic forecasters who can tell the story behind the numbers and explain what will drive growth in future.

But companies need to know more than economics for budgeting purposes. For example, Hungarian governments between 2000 and 2006 increased public spending hugely, thereby helping to boost overall economic demand and the sales of international companies. But this overspending by government resulted in a budget deficit and current-account deficit that were out of control, making it hard for managers to budget with any degree of accuracy, even though senior management is likely to be pressing for increased sales and bigger profits. Hence the need for managers close to the market to warn about the build-up of imbalances in good time, before austerity measures that will depress demand have been introduced by a government that has finally accepted it must change track.

In some countries GDP as a whole is a misleading indicator for business because of the disproportionate influence of certain sectors. Moroccan GDP, for example, rises and falls like a yo-yo depending on the fortunes of the agriculture sector. Oil-dominated economies go through similar peaks and troughs depending on the oil price. In these countries, when looking at GDP estimates, it is important to understand the significance of the dominant sector and how its potential volatility affects sales and business.

It is also important to remember that business and economic cycles in most emerging markets are stronger than those in the developed world. Economic busts can be far more devastating than anyone would expect (see Chapter 14). The same goes for economic booms. Emerging markets have the capacity (if economic policies are run well) to grow at least twice as fast as developed countries.

So what should companies in the planning and budgeting cycle do to avoid being misled by GDP statistics?

- Understand what is driving growth or decline as well as the dynamics behind each driver.
- Identify and monitor the factors that drive sales in specific sectors.
- Benchmark sales and sales projections with competitors.
- Make sure that senior managers are aware that GDP growth numbers can be misleading.

Doubling GDP

How do you calculate how long will it take (approximately) for GDP/standards of living to double from current levels? The mathematical formula is 70 divided by an average percentage growth figure for the coming years. For example, if you believe the Chilean economy will grow 4% per year (on average in the next few years), dividing 70 by 4 you arrive at the estimate that it will take 17.5 years for Chilean living standards to double (on average) from current levels. Nice mathematics, but who believes in long-term forecasts?

Current-account deficit

Another indicator to monitor is the current-account deficit. This can act as a warning, highlighting currency weakness or potential changes in economic policy that might affect business.

Current account

The current account is the sum of net exports of goods and services (exports minus imports), net income received from investments abroad (net profits, dividends and rents) and net transfer payments from abroad (things like workers' remittances from abroad).

How does a deficit arise and how might it affect currency values? A current-account deficit is the result of actions that create a demand for foreign currency. Take the biggest chunk of the current account, exports and imports of goods, and assume other components are zero. Imagine that for some reason (large wage increases or a boom in loans, for example) there is a large demand for imported cars in Poland. BMW's distributor in Poland, facing strong demand from customers, has to sell zlotys to buy euros in order to get more cars from BMW in Germany. Now imagine hundreds and thousands of local importers all doing the same because there is booming demand for imported products. What is the net effect on the local currency? The price of it (the exchange rate) can come under pressure as more and more people sell the local currency. This is of particular concern to companies operating in volatile emerging markets. Any loss of currency value can be sudden (see Chapter 14) and throw a large spanner into the works of what had been thought to be sound business plans.

In theory, the balance of payments must balance, so any deficit must be financed by capital inflows. These include foreign direct investment (FDI), international borrowing and the sale of foreign-exchange reserves.

If the current-account deficit exceeds 4% of GDP, it is in the danger zone, according to standard international benchmarks. In other words, there is an increased risk of currency depreciation. In practice, it is not so clear-cut. Many emerging markets go over the limit without any obvious effect, and companies should always bear this in mind.

One of the reasons is that central banks intervene. They sell foreign reserves and buy local currency to stop currency depreciation (or vice versa if they are fighting a rising currency). This is why it is important to look at the value of foreign-exchange reserves (gold and foreign-currency reserves held by the country) to gauge whether a high current-account deficit spells devaluation. The rule of thumb is that reserves should cover at least the value of three months of imports. If they do not or are declining, this suggests potential difficulties for any central bank wanting to intervene to support the currency.

Another buffer for current-account deficits is FDI. If investment flows are high and rising and cover a large proportion of the deficit, the currency is in no danger (unless market psychology says it is). Foreign investment is a healthy way to cover the current-account gap. It will probably lead to improved exports, which should over time reduce the deficit and lead to better, sustainable economic growth.

The other variable is the reliability of other capital flows: access to international borrowing at an acceptable price; workers' remittances, which play a huge role in economies such as Turkey and India; and other foreign-exchange earners, such as the Suez Canal in Egypt. It is important to know whether the imports that are creating an imbalance are largely consumer goods inflows or capital goods inflows. If a large proportion of the inflows are for capital goods it indicates that industry is retooling, which should result in higher exports over time. In other words, capital goods imports are healthier for economic stability than consumer goods imports.

Taken all together, a country with poor access to international financing, low inflows of FDI and low or declining foreign-exchange reserves is more likely to face a currency crisis if it has a large current-account deficit. But in many cases, even that does not have to push a currency into collapse. Many African countries, for example, fit the description perfectly but are kept afloat by donor and multilateral financing, often from the IMF and World Bank.

As with other indicators, it is important to know the story behind the current-account deficit in order to assess its true riskiness. But even if the analysis shows that the risks are not dramatic, high deficits often bring changes in economic policy that might affect sales. Central banks may raise interest rates, for example, to cut demand for imports (and so reduce the current-account deficit). Or governments may impose an import tax or import surcharge to achieve the same effect. Both measures can easily reduce sales in a country.

Short-term capital-account flows – hot money, hot flushes

Capital-account flows have become increasingly important as an indicator of potential dangers for local currencies in many emerging economies (see Chapter 14). The deficit on the capital account arises from actions that result in a growing demand for foreign currency. Hot money is a popular name for short-term capital movements. These include investments in liquid assets such as Treasury bills and bank deposits, but most economists now also include portfolio investment in stocks and bonds under the hot money label. A change in market sentiment from positive to negative can result in sudden outflows of these liquid investments and that weakens the domestic currency. Country managers need to observe hot-money inflows and evaluate the likelihood of sudden outflows. Some countries regularly experience large inflows while market sentiment is positive and then sudden outflows as it turns negative. These tidal movements can easily create a series of seemingly unstoppable crises, as any manager running Mexico in 1994 or East Asia in 1997 will tell you.

Budget deficits

The fiscal policies and budgets of emerging economies often attract headline attention. A deficit is when expenditure is higher than revenue and is reconciled by borrowing or, if the government is unable to borrow, by printing money. The latter is the road to hyperinflation. Managers need to be well aware of the government's ability to borrow in order to assess potential risk for hyperinflation.

Another potential danger of the budget deficit is that it accumulates and future generations will have to pay higher taxes to finance it. To assess this risk, look at the level of government debt as a percentage of GDP. Government debt is the sum of all government deficits over the years. A large accumulation of debt increases interest payments, which add to the budget deficit.

By boosting demand for money, budget deficits lead to higher interest rates and these "crowd out" private investment. Funds are redirected to the government, starving local businesses of finance with which to boost productivity and living standards. The size of the impact depends on various factors; for example, countries with a higher savings rate absorb deficits more easily than those with low savings rates.

To cover budget deficits, central banks sometimes buy government securities (new issues and existing debt issues). This is called monetising, but it is nothing more than the government borrowing from the central bank, or in effect printing money, since new money enters into circulation. It is important to look out for operations like these because they often lead to high inflation. In former Yugoslavia in the early 1990s it led to hyperinflation of several trillion per cent which could only be stopped by reducing the excessive budget deficit.

Off-budget funds are another favourite way of hiding deficits. Developed countries have them too, but they are common in most emerging markets, giving a prettier picture for the "official" deficit. To get the full picture, you need to add the official numbers and the off-budget funds to get a consolidated budget deficit figure. Off-budget funds may not be transparent. People who track countries on a daily basis can estimate what they might be (and their size), and some countries do say which funds are treated off-budget.

Government debt approaching 60% of GDP and rising is considered worrying for emerging economies. Developed economies often carry higher percentages and still avoid major difficulties. As a rule of thumb, the danger signals are rising government debt accompanied by low domestic investment by firms and individuals and rising inflation.

Headline news about budget deficits is often misleading. A country may have a budget deficit of 10% of GDP, but if government debt is low by international standards at less than 40% of GDP the deficit is not worrying.

Deficit creation is not always bad news. A temporary increase in public spending to pull an economy out of recession is fine, especially if the overall government debt is within acceptable international standards. International financial institutions often tell emerging-market governments to tighten their belts during a regular, cyclical economic downturn. But this generally makes the downturn worse, turning small economic downturns into large ones (see Chapter 14).

Many countries end up running deficits on both the budget and the current account at the same time. Watching for twin deficits – or their potential emergence – is useful for business planning. Governments facing this double squeeze are often forced into austerity measures: reducing imports, cutting fiscal spending, raising interest rates to reduce local demand, and so on. For most companies, this means a substantial reduction in sales for one or two years.

Inflation

The inflation rate is a measure of the percentage change in price levels in an economy. These days in developed countries annual inflation of 2–3% is considered acceptable. In times of high inflation people have an incentive to spend since money does not hold its value. However, as central banks raise interest rates to bring down inflation, it becomes more attractive for those who can to save. Prices change quickly, causing confusion about true value. The consumer price index (CPI) is the most common indicator used to follow inflationary trends. Like other indicators it is not perfect, being based on a basket of different goods and services used by a supposedly typical household – and this basket is determined by governments. If they want to show low inflation, for example, the basket may include goods supported by government subsidies. It is good to be aware of these games before relying on official inflation figures.

Inflation

Inflation can be demand-pull or cost-push. Demand-pull inflation is frequently referred to as "too much money chasing too few goods". Prices go up when demand exceeds availability. Demand (purchasing power) can be pushed up by a number of factors: a credit boom (more borrowing), tax cuts, increased government spending, or wages rising faster than productivity (maybe because there are labour shortages).

Cost-push inflation arises from price shocks. They can include sudden jumps in commodity and raw materials prices (as happens sometimes with oil), or a weaker domestic currency can make imports more expensive (as happened following the introduction of the euro).

Hyperinflation (a term widely accepted to mean inflation exceeding 50% per month) is a result of high money-supply growth (usually linked to an inability to borrow to cover a large budget deficit).

High inflation is bad for business. It distorts real values and corporate behaviour. Companies operating in emerging markets have developed sophisticated inflation accounting standards. But inflation is hard to predict and uncertainty about it discourages investments.

Interest rates

Central bankers pay a lot of attention to the inflation rate. If it exceeds the level of nominal interest rates, the real interest rate becomes negative. This discourages savings, which means there is less money available for lending and for spending on capital goods, which in turn might eventually lead to a fall in living standards. Occasionally, where an economic downturn coincides with currency strength (as in Poland in 2001, for example), central banks allow temporary negative rates in an attempt to reduce the value of the currency and stimulate economic growth. But in emerging markets the typical reaction to economic downturns is to raise interest rates sharply and suddenly (see Chapter 14). Before the easing of capital controls (see Chapter 14) it was unusual for currencies to strengthen during weak economic growth. But these days countries often raise interest rates sharply in a downturn, with the aim of keeping capital in the country and attracting speculative funds from abroad, which gives the local currency a boost.

This is the opposite of what happens in developed markets and the impact on business can be enormous. Central banks in emerging markets have a tendency to increase rates too much too quickly to calm the financial markets. To be aware of possible sharp interest-rate hikes, you need to develop a good feel for the psychology of the market and always distinguish between nominal rates (those quoted in the market) and real rates. Subtracting the actual inflation rate from a nominal rate will give you the real interest rate.

Exports

The structure of exports indicates the overall health of the economy. If an economy is heavily dependent on exports of commodities or semi-finished products, it is much more likely to be affected by swings in world prices and there will be little it can do to avoid a slowdown or even a crisis. Data on export structures are available for all countries and are a good indicator of sustainable economic strength. It is also useful to know where exports are heading. For example, if the United States is in trouble this is immediately felt in Latin America because North America is the most important import destination for most Latin American countries.

A useful indicator for companies to track is the value of exports from various areas of a country. This can expose unexpected pockets of hard currency. For example, contrary to expectations that "there is little outside of Moscow and St Petersburg", there are prosperous companies and consumers in Russia's oil and diamond exporting regions.

Official reserves and currency interventions

The official reserves of a country include all foreign currency and gold held by governments. Governments should have at least enough reserves to cover three months of imports. The reserves are used for currency interventions and to pay for any international obligations. Any rapid fall in reserves is a possible sign of intervention to stop the currency depreciating. A rapid rise in reserves may indicate that the central bank wants to stop the currency appreciating in value. Note that many countries in emerging markets overestimate the gold value of their reserves.

One important impact on business of a currency intervention that aims to stop depreciation (selling foreign reserves and buying local currency to increase the demand for the latter) is that the money supply shrinks, which may have an impact on domestic demand and liquidity and ultimately sales. But the amount of local currency in circulation will increase if the central bank is trying to stop the currency appreciating in value. To avoid the inflationary effect of a higher money supply, central banks "mop up" excess supply by selling government bonds to the public.

External debt and the ability to service it

External debt includes debt owed by both the private and the public sector. Deficits on the current account result in accumulation of external debt, the interest payments on which and the repayments of which can be financed only by income earned from exports. It is important to keep an eye on payment schedules. It is not difficult to identify the critical periods in the next few years when debt repayments will be particularly large. The next stage is to assess the ability of the country to meet such obligations (service the debt). There are many emerging markets with a potential debt repayment problem which could turn into a crisis.

7 Eternal dilemmas: market entry, corporate structure, marketing

We realise now that micro-managing from a distance does not work.

Sir Terry Leahy, CEO of Tesco

You own these businesses. Take charge of them. Get headquarters out of your hair. Fight the bureaucracy. Hate it. Kick it. Break it.

Jack Welch, former CEO of General Electric

Companies need a centre that is strong without being crushing and outposts that are true to themselves without losing our corporate identity.

Rod Eddington, former CEO of British Airways

Companies often assume that the product they sell so successfully in the developed world will sell successfully in emerging markets. In practice, this is only partly true. This chapter explains why and explores the latest successful and less successful market entry and marketing approaches employed by multinationals in emerging economies.

Glance at the market shares of many companies from country to country and you will see enormous differences. In some markets they are leaders; in others they are far behind their international and domestic competition. Even large multinationals, which are clearly market leaders in the developed world, sometimes fall far behind smaller international competitors and even tiny domestic companies in some emerging markets. How is that possible?

The explanation can be found in different approaches to market entry and market expansion. Companies such as Coca-Cola, Nestlé or Procter & Gamble, which have exceptionally strong emerging-market operations, demonstrate two crucial traits. First, they have strong commitment from the top to developing long-term dominance in emerging markets. Second, they focus on building up local infrastructure and brands at the time of market entry. They know that getting a strong local presence in place as early as possible lays the foundations for future business success. These two basic prerequisites for building a strong local business sound like common sense. So why do so many companies fail to do it?

As discussed in Chapter 2, the main reason is entrenched short-termist behaviour. The more short-termist the company, the more it is likely to trail behind international and local market leaders in emerging markets – and many trail big time. Most are disappointed and frustrated at the success of their smaller and otherwise weaker competitors who achieve excellent sales, market shares and profits. As emerging markets mature commercially, it will become harder to change market shares, as it is in the developed world.

Reasons for firms failing to secure a strong position in emerging markets include the following:

- No commitment from the top to long-term dominance of emerging markets.
- Minimal or no local presence to support marketing and sales.
- Leaving distributors to run the business on the ground.
- Fly-in, fly-out management of local markets (a regional manager who "lives" on the plane and manages distributors by visits only).
- Leaving distributors without or with little support.
- Limited or no investment in marketing/advertising.

This kind of approach will not work. The company will not develop a deep enough knowledge of the market and customers, and it will not build those crucial personal relationships with authorities, partners and customers. The company will have little control over its business. Sales will be limited by the capacity of importers and distributors (who often have a hard time raising finance at acceptable cost). They may also be limited to certain areas within a country, and it will be hard to develop a strong brand with widespread market reach. So how should it be done?

Local presence

Local presence is crucial to success. Companies need to have a local office focusing on marketing and sales, even when markets are small. Companies that invest in at least a one-man office usually do better than those that rely solely on distributors. How big the initial investment needs to be and when the move should be made are questions of strategy. Companies that focus aggressively on achieving market leadership admit that they "overinvest" initially, although they are aware of the potential retrenchment risk if the fixed-cost base becomes too large during an emerging-market crisis. These companies argue that slight overinvesting is better than underinvesting in local offices, especially while the market is in an earlier business-development stage.

Underinvestment leads to underpenetrating the market; in other words, not fully taking advantage of all the opportunities it presents. As a senior manager at Nike says:

> One of the frequent internal debates we have is whether we have penetrated the market enough or if we are still in the underpenetration stage.

A fear of underpenetrating the market is the driving force behind the over-investment philosophy. Regardless of how much good market research is done, it is easy to miss some of the business opportunities that exist. Underpenetration results in the competition grabbing more of the local market.

Other, less aggressive, companies wait until sales reach a certain (fairly low) level and then decide to set up a local presence. This can work well as long as the local presence is set up early enough. However, many companies wait too long to get their sales up before going local. Those that adopt this approach usually fall behind the competition.

Getting the corporate structure right

> We trained very hard, but it seemed that every time we were beginning to form into teams, we would be reorganised. I was to learn later in life that we tend to meet any new situation by reorganising – and a wonderful method it can be for creating the illusion of progress while producing confusion, inefficiency and demoralisation.

Attributed, almost certainly falsely, to Gaius Petronius, a Roman general who died in AD66, it is easy to imagine a regional manager in a large multinational saying these words. While some companies choose inappropriate corporate structures for the emerging-market region they are operating in, even more companies damage their businesses by restructuring frequently.

Some of those in emerging markets turn a full circle. They start heavily centralised to save costs and dip a toe into the market. Then they realise they need to be more decentralised to do business effectively. After a while, they start focusing on rapidly rising costs as the business grows, so they centralise again – all in less than five years. No wonder many regional managers complain that they have no time to run the business. Frequent changes in organisational structure are among the top time-wasters for regional managers. Sometimes the restructuring is a response to changes on the ground, but usually it is initiated by a change of corporate leadership or stock price pressures.

Before setting up a structure or restructuring the old one, companies should ask themselves a fundamental question: what is the structure that will best and fully address the opportunities that exist in the group of emerging economies that it wishes to "conquer"? Here are some recommendations.

Make sure that the CEO supports the emerging-market business
The head of global emerging-markets operations should be close to and supported by the CEO. This is the best way to give emerging-markets business enough push and commitment and to get a fair and proper hearing at the top.

Make sure that each region has its own boss
Each emerging-market region needs its own head manager reporting to the global emerging-markets director and/or the global emerging-markets business unit director. Emerging markets can be divided into three regions: Latin America; Asia (excluding Japan); and Central Eastern Europe, Middle East and Africa (CEEMEA). Some companies break these down further and have regional heads for central Europe, Russia and the CIS, China, South-East Asia, Middle East and North Africa (MENA), Sub-Saharan Africa, and Latin America. This breakdown is fine for a market approach, but the plethora of regional bosses generally makes it more difficult to get the region on to the radar screens of the CEO and senior management. If the regions are large, it is easier to get a proper hearing at the top. Central and eastern Europe, for example, represents some 4% of global GDP. But add to that the Middle East and Africa, and the market size of the region almost doubles.

Don't give a developed-market head the additional responsibility for emerging markets
Those in charge of developed markets (especially large ones) should not be in charge of emerging markets at the same time. For most companies, emerging markets represent low-volume and high-growth business, whereas developed countries represent high-volume and low-growth business. As highlighted in this book, the business issues in emerging markets are different, requiring greater flexibility and speed of decision-

making, more time, patience and perseverance. Because of this, many multinationals operating in Asia, for example, separate the Japanese operation from the emerging markets in the Asia-Pacific region. This is the right approach. The Japanese market is so huge in itself that the Japan manager barely has time to keep that market going, let alone focus attention on new developments in Vietnam or Indonesia. Equally, managers in charge of Germany and France should not be given responsibility to develop Russia or Romania. These markets should have a regional head. "Put any emerging market together with Germany and it will die," says a senior regional director of a major IT firm.

It sounds like common sense and American multinationals would not dream of having someone who runs the US market also in charge of Latin America. But if multinationals are in short-termist mode (and many are), they will try to save costs and ask their German manager: "Hans, east of you is a large region. Please go ahead and develop the business." This will not work. Hans's focus is Germany. This is where his performance is usually judged. He does not necessarily understand the central and eastern Europe region and its peculiarities, and he probably has neither the time nor the inclination to fly to Ukraine to set up a business. As a manager of a large industrial firm points out: "Our regional boss who also runs France thinks of central and eastern Europe only when he has time. And he never has time."

Choose a good location for the regional office
Think of placing a regional office in a hub that offers good tax savings from a corporate and personal standpoint (as well as good transport links or good quality of life). In Europe, for example, many multinationals choose certain Swiss cantons as a regional head office, saving millions in tax every year.

Consider clusters
Consider clusters rather than having each country manager reporting to a regional head (and also an emerging-market business unit head if there is a matrix structure). These clusters are subregions based on geographical proximity, culture, ways of doing business, commercial market maturity, common distributors, trading links or common language. Many firms, for example, have heads of areas such as North Africa, the Arabian Peninsula (or the Gulf), South-East Europe, or South Asia. Heads of subregions would have country managers reporting to them and they would report to the regional head (and also the business unit head in case of matrix structures).

Clusters within larger emerging-market regions can operate well, providing something of a halfway house between centralised and decentralised operations. They allow companies to keep a clear focus on local business opportunities, while avoiding the high fixed costs associated with multiple full-service subsidiaries. Typically, clusters will provide shared services for back-office functions such as finance, HR and IT support. Increasingly companies have started relocating shared service units for developed regions in emerging markets too.

Another advantage of clusters is that it gives smaller countries a proper hearing with regional management. If they are presented as a group, their size and sales growth rates attract attention, reducing the risk that they will be neglected when it comes to allocation of resources.

Give managers operational freedom

Country or cluster managers need considerable freedom to operate, hire the right people and decide how budgets are spent. They should be held accountable for the performance in their area. Head offices should not stop a local manager from acting in a way that he thinks will be good for the business. For example, they should not insist on keeping the head-count at a certain level if the local manager thinks hiring an extra person will bring in new business. Head office should simply say: "Go ahead and hire if you are convinced this will help your business; you know it is your neck on the line if you can't show results." Importantly, senior management should understand that it may take several years for the results to become apparent.

Don't centralise the marketing and sales functions

The centre must say what the brand should stand for in principle and provide basic brand guidelines, but the universal brand message needs to be adapted to the specifics of an emerging market. Centralised marketing may save costs, but it is also likely to limit sales.

Marketing in emerging markets – global versus local

Every major multinational can tell at least one story of a marketing fiasco in an emerging market, and the reason is usually the failure to adapt the product, brand image or advertising to local tastes and sensitivities. It is dangerous to assume that the product you have is truly global. Nestlé's yoghurt tastes sweeter in the Middle East and Nescafé instant coffee varies in strength and bitterness from market to market. Even Coke tastes a bit sweeter in Asia. And what MTV shows in India or Brazil is very different from what it shows in the United States.

67

Localise

The key to designing a successful marketing approach is to adapt all elements of the marketing mix to the local market. The main points to bear in mind are as follows:

- Your products and brands are probably not known. Even if they are, are they perceived in the way you want the customer to perceive them?
- Emerging markets offer opportunities for new positioning. If your product is positioned in one of the lower market segments in the developed world, the lack of recognition and loyalty for that brand in emerging markets offers an opportunity to position it at a higher end and earn a higher margin.
- You will not know what customers want and need unless you ask many of them in different market segments. Research until you drop.
- That the product is foreign is not necessarily an advantage. In some markets, such as India, it is often a disadvantage.
- If market research shows you do not have a suitable product for the local market, consider whether it would pay to design new products (or reintroduce ones that are no longer profitable in developed markets).
- Most buyers are likely to be price-sensitive, some extremely so. For many, bargain hunting is a way to survive.
- Some buyers will be very well off and a middle class is growing in emerging markets – but it is typically more price-sensitive than the middle class in the developed world, even though people in the West have become much more price conscious.
- Nestlé has 8,000 brands but only one-tenth are registered in more than one country.

Customers may not be susceptible to promotional messages that work in developed markets. They are influenced by local cultures, which shape their habits and preferences.

Next look at the product mix and pricing. One of the worst mistakes a company can make is to assume that its products and brands, part of everyday language in developed markets, are known in the local market. It is more likely they will not be known, and a great deal of effort will need to be put into building brand recognition, brand comprehension, brand image, and brand loyalty and trust.

It is also wrong to assume that global premium brands will be seen as superior to local ones. When Kraft Foods acquired a company in central Europe, for example, its plan was to keep selling the acquired domestic brands for a while but gradually phase them out as sales of Kraft's premium brands took off. As time went by the opposite happened. Local buyers were reluctant to spend money on the more expensive premium brands but liked the better quality Kraft brought to local brands. Sales of these started to grow more rapidly than those of the new premium products. When times are tough, consumers not only become more price-sensitive but also experiment less with their limited funds. They stick to trusted brands.

Many companies have now abandoned the idea of just selling their global brands. Instead they introduce a variety of products for multiple domestic market segments from the cheapest to the most expensive, embracing a mix of global and local products. This trend, especially the launching of cheaper products, is likely to accelerate in the future.

Product adaptation does not always have to be based on one market (unless it is a large one). There are bound to be similarities among similar market segments in, say, Brazil, Uruguay and Chile. Companies are therefore trying to adapt as much as possible on a regional basis to avoid losing economies of scale. Some successful companies have now adopted an approach of being as regional as possible and as local as necessary, cleverly building on the old cliché of "think global, act local".

Although it is possible to launch and sell regionally adapted products and still position them as international ones, advertising in most emerging markets is still predominantly local. Numerous studies have shown that dubbed advertising is culturally insensitive and irritates local pride. In many countries companies are even localising at a provincial level, taking into account cultural differences between different regions. And it is important to remember that although individual achievement may be prized in the West, in Asia it is collective achievements that are valued more. This has significant implications for the advertising approach.

It should go without saying that packaging has to have local language on it, but some companies still ignore this basic cultural adaptation. Even package sizes need to be different in certain markets; for example, consumer goods companies package detergents in smaller packs in poorer markets, and some sell tiny packages of cosmetics in very poor parts of Asia or Africa. This may put pressure on margins, but it may be necessary to capture that market segment. In some countries the focus is on selling larger packs at discount prices. In countries like Turkey, for instance, where there is a history of currency crises, buying big packs has been a way for consumers to "hedge" the currency.

Understanding the local competition is crucial to success. "It is a nice fight between international competitors," says one experienced senior manager, "but the locals are formidable." Many large multinationals simply ignore domestic competition in their market entry or market expansion planning. This ignorance is based on arrogance and a feeling of superiority. It is a big mistake to think that domestic competitors will be easy to deal with. They may be protected by the government; they may produce more cheaply; they may be financed by capital that had previously been invested overseas; they are often willing to pay bribes to win deals; or they may be simply happy with lower profit margins. Domestic companies can be sophisticated and well run. Many also poach western executives, quickly learn from sophisticated foreign companies and are skilled copycats.

One of the side effects of tough domestic competition is something often not anticipated by multinationals: price wars. These have destroyed a number of otherwise good business plans, particularly for latecomers to the market. The stronger the market position, the easier it is to survive lower prices. Coming late to a market can increase this kind of price-related vulnerability.

8 Reaching the local market

We found that making the product available to every potential customer – and controlling that process well – has transformed our fortunes in developing countries.

Senior manager, fast-moving consumer goods company

Poor distribution networks and difficulties in making products available locally are major factors in the lack of success of many companies in emerging markets. This chapter looks at distribution: where companies most commonly run into problems and what they can do about them. Making products widely available is a daunting challenge in most emerging markets. Distribution networks are often fragmented, inefficient and full of potentially bankrupt partners. The rewards are rich for those who get it right, and huge sums are lost by those who get it wrong.

To get it right, several important principles should be followed.

Working with a distributor
Select the distributor carefully
Typically, there will be no shortage of companies wanting to distribute your products, but the selection process should be careful and thorough, involving a long list of important steps. These include:

- interviewing potential candidates;
- visiting their premises;
- checking their financial background with banks and credit-rating agencies (keeping in mind that this is no real guarantee);
- testing their technical expertise in sales and marketing;
- checking word-of-mouth recommendations;
- talking to retailers and end-buyers about them;
- checking the background of their relationship with retailers and end-buyers;
- checking their ability to provide customer and after-sales service;
- checking their nationwide reach.

The more information you get, the easier it should become to pick the right partner.

Ensure as much control as possible over the distribution network
This is best achieved by having local staff who work closely with the distributor. Attempting to control things from a distance does not work. Some companies take full control and handle distribution themselves, using their own fleet of vehicles. Others place their own staff within the distributor's organisation, which offers advantages if it is run well. Another option is to include a "key person clause" in the distributor contract, guaranteeing that one of the distributor's staff will deal exclusively with your company on a daily basis. Because this can be costly for the distributor, it can make sense (and increase the sense of control) to contribute to the salary costs of that person.

Communicate clear goals to the local distributor
Distributors are often in business to make a quick profit and are not always concerned with the broader goals of proper brand building, the appropriate pricing strategy or the continuous maintenance of brand and product values. They may jump from distributing TV sets one day to detergents the next. But local distributors should know what your long-term strategic goals are. If they see they have a lucrative future by distributing your products, they may adapt their behaviour to suit your longer-term strategic business goals.

Never let the distributor define and build your brand
A distributor's suggestions may be clever and useful, but it is your company, ideally through your local organisation, that has to take responsibility for marketing and positioning and building your brands. Any marketing done by a distributor must be fully in tune with your overall marketing message. Remember also that distributors are often reluctant to distribute goods that require too much "push" (requiring extensive salesforce activity, for example). They prefer to work with companies that have invested in "pull" strategies (increasing consumer demand through, for example, advertising and other brand-building activities). A commitment to concerted and continuous brand building will help in finding and retaining the best distributors, and in making the business grow.

Control pricing carefully
Pricing is a frequent cause of disputes. In emerging markets, a problem can be that resellers seek to sell products at a higher price than the company believes is appropriate for the market. Combating this is time- and resource-consuming, even when you have a strong local sales

and marketing organisation. Possibly the best strategy to avoid pricing problems is to make the public aware through advertising what the price benchmark is. If people know what the price should be, they will try to avoid sellers who attempt to charge more. Colgate advised consumers to come directly to the company if they were unable to buy the product at the recommended price.

Keep distributors under pressure to improve performance

It is important to keep distributors on their toes and focused on ways to deliver. This can be done through short-term contracts, setting sales targets and then requiring strict and frequent reporting. Distributors must not be allowed to become complacent and take your business for granted.

Provide training for distributors

Training helps to integrate a distributor's organisation and staff into your own. Technical and product update training is essential, but it is important to look at other areas where distributors have weaknesses (typically financial reporting and control, and often marketing and sales). Companies sometimes ask distributors to pay all or part of the costs of such training sessions – but it is best for a company to pay all the training costs if it has confidence in a partner who is keen but financially weak. There is always the danger that individuals you have paid to train will leave and take their skills to other companies, but on balance it is a risk worth taking. Some companies insist that distributors keep newly trained individuals in certain posts and sometimes offer slightly better terms if people are kept in the post for which they were trained for a certain period of time.

Develop strong personal relationships with the distributor

To develop a constructive and productive relationship with a distributor, local presence is a prerequisite. The ultimate goal should be the creation of a sense of genuine partnership: a win-win relationship. This is not something that any company, regardless of its status and skills, can achieve overnight. It takes a lot of time and energy, but building up both the tangible and intangible benefits of a commercial and personal relationship will, if skilfully done, pay off.

Managing the risk

Manage your receivables

Managing receivables is even more essential in emerging markets than it is in developed markets, but rigidly sticking to terms that require prepayment in hard currency can stunt business development, especially once competition heats up and in markets where credit lines are tight and expensive. Successful emerging-markets players relax credit terms as trust develops, using their own research and experience to determine when and to whom to extend credit. But in volatile countries where the risk of crisis is high (especially a risk of banking system or currency collapse), it is sensible to be extra cautious. Only an experienced local team's closeness to the customer and market enables the appropriate balance to be struck on the basis of knowledge, trust and instinct. To diversify risk, many companies like to work with several distributors. If one collapses, at least not all of their outstanding receivables go with it. Despite the precautions, all companies will experience losses at some time and somewhere in the distribution channel, so they should have provisions and buffers in the budget in case money is lost. Many companies have adopted a rigorously prudent accounting practice of booking income only when the money they are owed is safely in their bank account.

The risk sometimes lies not with the distributor but with the distributor's bank. During economic crises, there is more chance of banking collapses. It is essential to have people monitoring the stability of the banking system, in particular the banks through which distributors work. Millions of dollars of outstanding payments can be stuck in a collapsed bank, resulting in serious losses for those who have left themselves exposed to such a risk. This is why many companies work with several banks to diversify their risk of a bank collapsing.

Be ready to support distributors

This is particularly important if your distributors do not have access to capital through domestic or international loans. The cost of capital is high in most emerging economies and to establish and run a successful business, companies will often need or be asked to provide assistance to local partners. This can range from co-funded promotions involving anything from advertisements to trade fairs to help in securing credit lines. Most companies are reluctant to directly finance their distributor. Those that do see it as a necessary and temporary measure aimed at building the business. Others simply take their local distributor to their bank and say: "Give this guy a loan. We trust him. He will be working with us for many years to come."

Make sure the contract is sufficiently detailed

The following are some of the items that a contract with a distributor should contain:

- duration of the contract (limited to maintain pressure on performance);
- prices;
- terms and conditions of sales;
- rights to visit distributors' premises and inspect the accounts;
- protection against delivery delays (for example, if a product gets held up at a border);
- marketing and facilities expenditure;
- a cancellation clause (what constitutes a breach of the contract and how it will be dealt with);
- an agreed place for arbitration.

Some companies include buyback agreements in the contract, giving them control of inventories should, say, the currency be devalued. Remember that judicial systems even in developed emerging markets are overburdened, slow and often corrupt. Many companies insist that arbitration abroad is the only way to resolve commercial disputes.

Important things to remember

Be flexible and adapt to local circumstances

In emerging markets it is important to be creative in the way you do things. If there are no distributors that have national reach, for example, why not invest in your own fleet of vans where drivers not only physically distribute but also take cash from small retailers. Many consumer goods companies have used this approach successfully. Although it appears expensive, the returns on such an investment have been good. If there is a problem with finding a good distributor on the ground, why not ask a distributor from a developed country to set up a distributorship for you? Ford did this in Bulgaria and became a market leader.

Caterpillar is another company famous for relying on its strong global dealer network to grow its business. However, because it could not find suitable dealers in Russia, it decided to handle distribution itself until suitable partners were found. An alternative is to buy a distributor and oversee and guide its operations. It is important to be decisive: you cannot afford to let your business be dependent on incompetent or under-financed distributors. You do not necessarily need to remain in charge of distribution, but you must take steps to make sure that you have efficient distribution.

Emerging-market offices should regularly talk to each other and share knowledge. An approach tested in one country, such as sharing warehouse space with other companies or setting up supplier alliances, might offer useful lessons to offices in other countries.

Consider combining several options to cover all market opportunities

Some companies, such as IT firms, sell their products and services through multiple channels. They sell directly to customers, to distributors, directly to dealers and through a select group of agents covering different areas of the market. This can be complicated, but if the set-up avoids overlap and it is clear who targets whom, it can work well. If your distributor does a good job but cannot reach all customers, add more distributors in areas beyond your distributor's reach. Many companies prefer to keep this option open and therefore do not enter into exclusive contracts with distributors.

Handle key accounts yourself

These customers are too important to be left to distributors.

Don't ignore the rural customer

Forgetting about rural consumers can be a big mistake. In India, for example, Coca-Cola initially ignored the huge rural market and focused on cities. As a result, the company (unusually) lagged behind Pepsi in terms of market share. In an effort to regain market share, Coca-Cola, among other things, bought a large chunk of domestic refrigerator production at a huge discount, which it passed on to small retailers in remote villages.

Consider franchising or flagship stores

Franchising or flagship stores are strategies that work for such sectors as food, clothing or cosmetics. Franchising allows producers to create a retailing concept without jeopardising the product's image, which can be preserved through the careful choice of premium locations, employees, interior design and merchandising displays. One of the problems in getting the franchising concept up and running in many emerging markets is that local banks are unwilling to finance local franchisees. Another common problem is that the franchising concept is not fully understood by local entrepreneurs. Franchisers must communicate relentlessly what the concept is and how it should be executed. They should make sure that contracts spell everything out in detail and that there is a clear exit strategy should things not work out.

Setting up your own shops to penetrate the market gives you control over all aspects of the business: the state of facilities, behaviour of staff, point of sale promotion and merchandising. The downside compared with franchising is cost, but flagship stores are often profitable ventures and good brand builders.

Keep a close eye on global retailers

As international retailers move into emerging markets, the distribution landscape changes dramatically. For a transition period, large consumer goods companies usually benefit from losing the middleman, but once retailers start getting entrenched the price squeeze begins. Companies have to be on top of the game and adapt as the rules change.

9 Manufacturing in emerging markets

We will keep moving our manufacturing to cheaper locations.

Gerard Kleisterlee, CEO, Philips

This chapter looks at why companies decide to relocate their manufacturing operations to cheaper locations and how they do it. It also outlines the many different types of tax and other incentives that companies can negotiate for when setting up manufacturing sites in emerging markets.

A manager employed by a large French multinational says:

> *The only reason why we still manufacture our goods in France is because our CEO, who is French, does not want to be seen as someone who destroys French jobs. But I don't know how long we can maintain profitability medium term. Most of our competitors have already set up manufacturing in cheaper locations.*

The French company's dilemma demonstrates that, on the one hand, global competitive pressures are forcing companies to lower their manufacturing costs, while on the other hand, there are emotional pressures pushing in the opposite direction. Furthermore, labour laws in western Europe make it expensive to shut down manufacturing facilities. Many senior managers have private reasons for wanting to stay put, and may justify the status quo by claiming that manufacturing in emerging markets is risky. But how risky is it really?

Companies that have many manufacturing facilities in emerging markets claim that the benefits far outweigh the risks and frustrations, provided the location is selected carefully and that entry into the market has been thoroughly prepared. Some aspects of manufacturing in emerging markets are complicated, but most of the worries people have are unjustified or exaggerated.

Take product quality, for example. Many of those who have set up manufacturing operations in emerging markets such as central and eastern Europe claim that the quality of their output exceeds that achieved in Germany, Italy or the UK. Productivity may be lower for the country as a whole, but this is because published figures reflect average productivity, including state-owned enterprises. If a multinational trains its own people to use its technology and implements top-notch manufacturing processes, it will quickly reach internal productivity benchmarks and far surpass national productivity levels.

For many emerging markets, the commercial evidence is clear: it pays to manufacture there and it is possible to manufacture good-quality products far more cheaply. For example, a large Japanese consumer electronics company says that manufacturing costs in emerging markets it has operations in are 35–40% lower than in developed markets.

The growth in free-trade agreements and the reduction in trade barriers around the world have made it viable to set up manufacturing operations in all kinds of places. For example, a growing number of Japanese companies now manufacture for the EU market in central and eastern Europe. But companies need to be careful about the realities of free-trade agreements when making decisions about locating manufacturing operations. Many of the agreements do not work in practice as they are supposed to in theory.

There is no doubt that more manufacturing from the developed world will be transferred to emerging markets. The question is how quickly this will happen and where the investment will go. Will it be concentrated in a few "stars" or will it be more widespread? Will it continue to shift to even cheaper locations as labour costs rise?

Many multinationals are in the process of rethinking their global manufacturing strategies. They want to reduce the number of manufacturing sites globally to a minimum. If most of the world is going to become a large free-trade area, then unless, say, transport costs would be prohibitive (as they would for a cement manufacturer), it makes sense to make a product in as few locations as possible. By benefiting massively from economies of scale, the plants will significantly reduce cost per unit. This is probably the next big global manufacturing trend, and it is likely to accelerate as trade becomes genuinely freer. At the same time, it has huge implications for governments in emerging markets.

Once a decision has been made to move manufacturing operations to a cheaper location in an emerging market, two crucial further decisions that have to be made are where and how – for example, through a joint venture or acquisition (see Chapter 10).

Choosing a location

The process for selecting a manufacturing location involves:

- determining project criteria (see below), assumptions and requirements;
- producing a list of potential locations;
- analysing in detail each location according to your criteria;
- producing a shortlist of locations and evaluating them further by, for example, interviewing real-estate agents and construction companies, assessing the availability of suppliers, assessing other companies manufacturing there, evaluating infrastructure development plans, validating desk research findings, discussing incentives at different government levels;
- visiting sites, interviewing and starting negotiations.

Of the developing countries not suitable for manufacturing, some lack such basic infrastructure as reliable power supplies and have too few sufficiently skilled workers; some are plagued by armed conflict and so security issues would be overwhelming; and others may have such disadvantages as trading arrangements that hinder exports. But there are many excellent, inexpensive places around the world in which to locate manufacturing operations.

Criteria for choosing a manufacturing location
- Which firms have set up operations and what are their experiences?
- What is the ease and cost of shipment to desired export locations, and how good is the transport infrastructure?
- Are there signed free-trade agreements? Do they work in practice? What other agreements are being negotiated?
- Which suppliers (domestic and foreign) operate in the country? How good are they? What are their experiences? Will your existing suppliers support you if you switch to this location?
- What investment incentives will be available?
- How easy will it be to set up operations and run them from day to day?
- What are labour costs likely to be? What is the availability of both skilled and unskilled local workers? What is the unemployment level in the region and the country as a whole?
- How easy will it be to obtain land and other permits?
- Will it be possible to operate seven days a week, 24 hours a day in flexible shifts?
- What is the strength and attitude of trade unions? Will you be

able to hire workers on individual contracts? Will you have the flexibility to hire and fire workers according to demand?
- Are there any special economic zones with tax and customs benefits?
- Will it be possible to get cheap or free land and reduced prices for services such as electricity and water?

Incentives and privileges

Companies are naturally coy about the importance of investment incentives but, whatever people will say on the record, they clearly do influence investment decisions.

Multinationals are often unaware of how many privileges they can extract from governments. The law may not be clear on what incentives are obtainable in practice and many firms now negotiate investment incentives with officials beyond what the law appears to allow for. One senior director of a well-known European multinational said its strategy regarding investment incentives was simple: "Apply, complain, negotiate, and if it does not work move to a new country where it will." Of course, many countries offer packages and special economic zones that are sufficiently attractive without the need for tough negotiations.

Below are some examples of what multinationals have been able to get from many governments:

- Tax breaks of 10–15 years (usually conveniently counting from the first year of profit). Needless to say, creative transfer pricing (the prices at which subsidiaries of the same firm move goods across national boundaries), for example, can delay that first profitable year for quite some time. (For example, a multinational company with operations in an emerging market buys some goods or services from its own plants elsewhere. These are often overcharged to the emerging-market operation and thus reduce the profit and delay tax payments to the host country.
- Duty-free import of any machinery.
- Tax or other incentives at regional or provincial level (including any local tax breaks).
- Free or cheap land.
- Free or cheap connections to water and electricity supplies and subsidised running costs.
- Necessary infrastructure around the factory. Japan's Matsushita, for example, persuaded local authorities in the Czech Republic to build a road from its factory to the main road.

- ◪ A brownfield site (an empty, abandoned building, which can be used either immediately or after some refurbishment).
- ◪ Employment grants for each created job (some countries offer €5,000–10,000 per person).

Companies should not of course base their investment decision solely on the investment incentives they are offered or can negotiate. All the important criteria must be taken into account. But if you have shortlisted several locations with similar advantages, then why not go "tax shopping", focusing on both national and local authorities.

The negotiating position of governments has been weakening as the competition to attract foreign direct investment has grown stronger. Investors are now likely to say: "If you don't want to give us this incentive, there are countries that will be happy to do so."

It is hard for a government, looking at a high unemployment rate and a vulnerable current account, to say no. The multiplier effect of one large multinational manufacturing facility is powerful, bringing in more investors (as suppliers) and boosting the local supplier and servicing industry. This is why governments are willing to give incentives to powerful multinationals to invest in their countries. Success feeds on success. Economically, the impact of FDI on developing economies is enormous. In Poland, for example, the top five regions (coincidentally those that attracted the largest amount of FDI) grew eight times faster than the bottom five (that had virtually none) in the first ten years after the collapse of communism. Differences in unemployment in such regions are enormous, ranging from 5–6% in the most developed regions to over 30% in the least developed ones.

Many governments do not truly understand the way in which big foreign investors decide where to manufacture. Companies like IBM hold sessions with government officials to explain how multinational companies make investment decisions. This helps create greater understanding between a company and a government and is likely to result in proposals that work for both. Governments that still feel they are in a position to bring in new investors without incentives are likely to find that their economic growth is slower than that of countries that provide incentives to attract foreign firms. Russia, for example, has attracted only a fraction of China's investment, despite its large market and low labour costs. This is partly because the federal government does not offer incentives for foreign investors, and its attitude to them is, at best, lukewarm. Negative perceptions of the market among senior managers have not helped (see Chapter 17).

Several multinationals with manufacturing operations in emerging markets have suffered from adverse publicity, mainly on the grounds of such matters as working conditions, the use of child labour and environmental issues. Taking steps to avoid such criticism in future is now high on the agenda of most big firms with valuable brands. But it can be difficult to make sure your emerging-market operations stand up to ethical scrutiny – and so it is crucial that you do your utmost to ensure your business operations are seen as socially responsible (see Chapter 13), whether you run things yourself or outsource to subcontractors.

Subcontracting is increasing in certain industries. A number of pharmaceuticals companies use high-tech Turkish companies to manufacture their products while they focus on marketing and sales. Good subcontractors are not easy to find in emerging markets. They also need to be supervised, monitored and controlled in order to avoid bad publicity for the company that uses them. The best way to monitor outsourced manufacturing sites is to place someone in the factory to check that the required standards in such matters as employment are being met. Nike suffered serious damage some years ago after it was discovered that its outsourcing partners used child labour.

10 Making acquisitions work

Buying multibillion-dollar companies in the United States is a breeze compared to buying small companies in emerging markets.

Senior director, Kraft Foods

Everything is worth only what a purchaser is willing to pay for it.

Publius, 1BC

This chapter looks at the important lessons of acquisitions and joint ventures in emerging markets and considers what successful companies have done to avoid acquisitions and joint ventures going wrong.

Buying companies in emerging markets can be like walking through a minefield. But, surprisingly, many companies start rambling through it without a mine detector. Acquisitions often fail to add value in the developed world, as numerous studies have shown. Making them work in emerging markets is even more difficult.

Growth by acquisition is quicker but riskier than organic growth – investing in and developing existing businesses and launching new businesses. Companies need to evaluate whether an acquisition is more cost-effective than organic growth for achieving a desired market position. It should offer clear advantages over achieving the same objectives through organic growth. Many companies feel that if there is no brand name, market share or strategic competitive advantage to purchase, then it is probably better not to take the risks involved in an acquisition.

Observations of many deals in emerging markets indicate that organic growth/greenfield investments have had a significantly higher success rate than acquisitions. Therefore companies should think hard and see clear advantages before embarking on an acquisition in difficult markets. For years, many companies preferred to go for growth through acquisitions, but after so many disappointments the strategy is changing. In the 2006 Economist Intelligence Unit *CEO briefing*, only 14% of executives see mergers and acquisitions (M&A) as a central part of their growth strategy. Organic growth is now the generally preferred route, coupled inevitably with more "upward" and "downward" innovation (see Chapter 1).

At the same time, the number of cross-border acquisitions has been growing. Some 60% of all acquisitions conducted every year in the world involve an international transaction. Many such deals are still in the developed world but the number of acquisitions in emerging markets is growing steadily. This applies especially to larger, strategic emerging markets where domestic competition is strong and "annoying" as one experienced executive put it. He also said: "It's hard to compete against some of those local guys, so we gain a lot by buying them."

Acquiring companies in emerging markets is complex, and it is dangerous to underestimate this. Most companies make mistakes in the acquisition process and it is estimated that more than half of all acquisitions fail to add value for two fundamental reasons: poorly executed due diligence before the purchase; poor management during post-acquisition restructuring. Some mistakes cause almost irreparable damage to the business; others are less lethal but cause disruptions, delays and temporarily disappointing results.

A decision on whether an acquisition is the right way to go and at what price should be based on comparing the two options. First, determine the cost of setting up a new operation and achieving new sales from scratch. Second, look at the cost of making an acquisition and any post-acquisition restructuring. These estimates are not easy to make.

Types of acquisitions

- ◪ Vertical acquisitions: the acquired company is either a customer or a supplier of the acquirer.
- ◪ Horizontal acquisitions: an acquirer buys companies in the same industry to achieve better market position and gain economies of scale.
- ◪ Concentric acquisitions: an acquirer buys additional product lines or technologies to share resources (for higher profitability).
- ◪ Conglomerate acquisitions: an acquirer expands the total portfolio of businesses.
  Source: Rock, M.L., Rock, R.H. and Sikora, H., *The Mergers and Acquisitions Handbook*, 2nd edition, McGraw Hill, 1994, p. 5

When considering an acquisition strategy in emerging markets, companies should ask several fundamental questions:

- ◪ Do we, as a company and a group of individuals, know how to acquire successfully, especially in emerging markets?

◪ Do we have dedicated internal resources (time, knowledgeable people, money) to seek out and engage in cross-border acquisitions?

◪ Are we aware that there may be potential problems with acquisitions in the market we are looking at?

◪ Are we aware that we need to spend significant time and money to identify potential problems before making a purchasing decision?

◪ Are we aware that our usual investment bankers may not be the best advisers, especially if they do not have a long-standing local presence in the market under consideration, and that we should consider working with well-informed locally based (domestic or international) advisers?

◪ Are the managers we value most and most want to retain for or against acquiring? This is important because internal resistance may undermine an acquisition.

In emerging markets the goal of acquisition is often geographic expansion as well as strategically limiting the manoeuvring space of key international and domestic competitors. Whatever the aim, in emerging markets it is essential to be vigorous in seeking out opportunities and taking advantage of them. There are not many great acquisition targets in individual emerging markets and the competition to buy them can be fierce. It is often the fast firms that buy companies, not the big ones, so you need to identify and approach the best targets early. It is best to have a dedicated acquisition team or teams, which can give you a competitive advantage. Assigning a manager with other duties to lead acquisitions often results in a lack of necessary speed and dedication. Needless to say, local presence is a great help.

Having a constant eye open for targets pays, especially in countries where governments sell their state holdings through quickly announced tenders. Deadlines for submitting bids can be short, leaving little time to conduct due diligence properly. Being on top of developments and fostering good relationships with governments and managers of target companies will increase the chances of submitting a bid on time (without plunging into the unknown). This is another argument in favour of having strong local presence. Worthwhile acquisition targets in emerging markets are those that hold good market shares and good brands, and whose processes and earnings can further be improved with better management skills and focus and/or injections of new capital investment. Most acquisition targets in emerging markets need thorough restructuring and, in particular, the introduction of more efficient management systems. This is both an opportunity and a threat, and should be approached in that fashion.

Companies should avoid looking at just one country. Regional or global acquisition teams should have an overview of several countries within particular trading blocs (where exporting does not encounter obstacles) in order to be able to spot opportunities quickly.

Experience in the developed world has shown that acquisitions within the same industry often offer the best chances for success. Diversification through acquisition can be an effective strategy, but is a risky one to pursue in more challenging markets. Synergies typically play a crucial role. A company that acquires a firm in a familiar industry can use its experience and expertise to integrate it into its worldwide operations. Lack of familiarity with the industry can prevent the successful integration of the target company's operations with those of the acquiring company.

After a company decides that it wants to acquire, rather than grow organically, it should:

- establish acquisition criteria;
- identify candidates;
- perform due diligence and valuation;
- negotiate the purchase;
- restructure and integrate.

Establishing acquisition criteria

Once a company decides it has the capability to make acquisitions and run the acquired business successfully, it should determine its acquisition criteria and, more importantly, keep them in mind. Too often companies pay much more than they wanted to. After all the work that has gone into the process, the thinking is that an additional 10–20% will not kill them. Moreover, acquisition teams become so close to the potential transaction that they are willing to overlook certain criteria. The project has become "their baby" and they do not want to see it fail. Some managers decide on acquisitions because of their own private interest and the money they can make. It is therefore not surprising that much research on the success of acquisitions shows that they often fail to bring value to shareholders.

The criteria should describe the ideal candidate and can be used as a benchmark against which to measure acquisition candidates. It should start with external criteria that cover the political, economic and business environment. These are covered in more detail in the checklists in previous chapters, but they should address the following kinds of questions:

- Political situation: what is the political risk we will be willing to live with?
- Economic situation: what is the economic risk or economic situation we will be willing to live with?
- Government regulations: will the government enable us to compete fairly and without interference?
- Trade constraints: can we rely on the free-trade agreements that are in place?
- Infrastructure: will it be possible to ship goods out of the country efficiently and at minimum cost?

Internal criteria, focusing on the acquisition target, should consider tangible and measurable benefits. Below is a selection, but each company must create its own list based on its specific needs:

- Market share: what is it now and what position would we like to capture?
- Existence and method of distribution: how much should the distribution network be developed?
- Price: how much money can we spend on an acquisition?
- Cost of labour: what is the maximum cost of labour we will be willing to accept?
- Strengths: what competitive strengths would we consider attractive in an acquisition target?
- Weaknesses: what weaknesses of an acquisition target will we be willing to correct? What weaknesses will stop us from acquiring?
- Quality: does the product have to be of exportable quality?
- Trade unions: how strong are they and are we prepared to work with them?

Identifying acquisition candidates

Identifying acquisition candidates that meet the criteria is time-consuming and some aspects of the search are complex. It may be easy to find a list of potential targets and to analyse external criteria, but it is difficult to get to grips with the internal position of potential candidates. Even financial statements, in general, should not be taken at face value; the quality of financial information in emerging markets is often suspect. To avoid unpleasant surprises, use many sources to verify internal information, especially during the due diligence process.

In the developed world firms may look at a large number of companies in order to identify the most attractive. In emerging markets, the choice is much smaller except in a few large countries. Background research can provide an initial list of candidates in a specific industry. It is also quite easy to identify successful exporters, which gives a good indication of hard-currency earnings and the relative competitiveness of the goods they produce.

Far more difficult to find is relevant and accurate information about the economics of and the competitive forces affecting the domestic industry, without which you would never make an acquisition in the developed world. For some products, for example, it is virtually impossible to find reliable consumption data; and different sources often state substantially different numbers. To make things worse, domestic companies in emerging markets are often secretive about their operations. Few are listed on stock exchanges and even in the case of those which are, the exchange will usually be more loosely regulated than in the developed world, with the quality of disclosure being much poorer.

The process of identifying candidates and doing due diligence on them has to be heavily reliant on contacts. Getting senior and other relevant managers or owners of potential candidate firms to co-operate is essential. Techniques for getting managers on your side include:

- promising them that they will keep their jobs and remain an integral part of the company (many companies promise to keep old managers as honorary presidents or consultants, often increasing their pay and giving them bigger offices, which makes them feel more important – but they do not give them any decision-making power);
- promising them higher incomes and a better future;
- taking them to corporate headquarters to explain strategy and impress them;
- taking them to see successful acquisitions in other countries.

All such actions are a great help in building mutual trust and understanding. These trust-building measures may become a decisive factor in the due diligence process in emerging markets. A local management that is supportive and gives clear signals of co-operation will make this process much more revealing, and therefore more effective.

Performing due diligence and valuation

The due diligence process involves intensive fact-finding about and thorough analysis of an acquisition target. All due diligence actions aim to answer three critical questions:

- Is the target really as attractive as it appears on the surface?
- Will it fit well into our sales and profit growth plans?
- Can it be restructured and managed in a way that will help us profitably grow the business?

A large amount of information needs to be processed and understood to answer these questions.

Performing thorough due diligence is crucial for the success of any acquisition in emerging markets. This may seem obvious, but as in the developed world, it is surprising how many companies carry out half-hearted due diligence, sometimes even after the deal has been done "to verify what was bought". No wonder surveys reveal that a majority of acquisitions fail to meet set objectives and do not create shareholder value.

A plan for how the due diligence is to be conducted should cover the following:

- **Who will do the job?** Who will be the members of the team and outside researchers/consultants, and how will they communicate with each other? Who will be responsible for which due diligence activities? Always make sure that senior management is closely involved. It may be tempting to let a management consultancy and/or an investment bank take the lead, but this is an easy way to lose the feel for the deal. Most due diligence processes leave unanswered questions, and the proportion of "unknown" at the end of the process is much larger in emerging markets. So inevitably a large part of the final decision has to be based on the feel – a qualitative characteristic. If senior managers are detached from an investigation and lack first-hand contact with the deal, it will diminish the company's ability to make a sound purchasing decision.
- **Sources of information.** What approach will be used for the investigation? Which sources will be used? Are these all the sources that can be used, or are there other excellent sources that you do not know about? To get the most objective picture

of the candidate, talk to customers, distributors, industry experts, think-tanks, suppliers, trade unions, management, workers and competitors.

◪ **Key information.** Which information is the most crucial for making the decision? Is it possible to find multiple sources to verify this information? Which information is merely "nice to know"? Do not waste time and resources on this type of information, but if it is easy to get, then get it to give a more complete picture. Remember that the quality of information is more important than the quantity.

There are general checklists of information necessary for any due diligence process, but each acquisition requires its own specific checklist too. The list of specifics to investigate in emerging markets is particularly long, and many items are notoriously hard to investigate and understand. In theory all information should be analysed in depth. In practice this is hard to achieve in emerging markets. Lawyers and investment bankers claim that companies rarely feel they understand as much as they would expect, based on their experience in the developed world. This can be discouraging, but companies should still aim to carry out the most in-depth investigations possible. This will give them the best chance of evaluating the strengths and weaknesses of the target in respect of existing and potential competitors and therefore give them confidence to proceed (or not) with the acquisition. Most importantly, a view will emerge on what the potential earnings may be and, ultimately, on how much to pay.

A target evaluation typically comprises the following broad areas:

◪ strategy and background;
◪ markets, products and marketing;
◪ distribution and sales;
◪ financial audit;
◪ manufacturing and technology;
◪ environmental audit;
◪ legal audit;
◪ organisational structure and human resources.

Companies should also supplement the above with a thorough understanding of the checklist in Chapter 3.

Strategy and background

This part of the evaluation should focus on describing the acquisition target in the past and the present, as well as its strategy. It is important to know the company's strategic strengths and weaknesses.

Markets, products and marketing

A buyer obviously needs an in-depth understanding of the business's products (or services). It is also crucial to determine the market share potential of the business's products, particularly when buying market share is the primary motive for the acquisition. In doing this, market developments and trends should be taken into account.

Here is a selection of important questions a buyer should answer:

- What is the product portfolio and what are its market shares? How have market shares moved up or down in the past and why? What are the USP (unique selling proposition), pricing history and profit margins? What will drive demand for products and their prices in the future? What is the risk of price wars?
- What is the product positioning? How is it perceived by customers and how has it influenced sales levels in various market segments?
- How do competitors, distributors and consumers perceive the product and its quality? Conduct primary research and detect any dissatisfaction and negative brand perceptions early.
- If we could improve the quality and service of the product(s), would that have a positive impact on potential earnings?
- How has the market segment in general behaved in the past and what is driving demand? Is this market segment under pressure or shrinking relative to other segments? Is it cyclical and how long are the cycles? Which market segments are actually growing?
- Will we need to upgrade quality and how expensive will that be?
- Can we and should we use that facility to develop and manufacture new products for various market segments that are growing?
- How large should marketing and advertising expenses be to accelerate demand and earnings in the future?
- Is the domestic industry in question profitable? What have the profitability cycles been in the past and what are they likely to be in the future?
- Are there any complex measures in the customs system of the target country that will inhibit imports or exports?

Distribution and sales

Efficient distribution is a big competitive advantage in complex and rapidly changing emerging markets. Distribution networks are grossly under-developed in virtually all emerging markets. Although many are developing fast, it can take years if not decades for them to match those that are found in the developed world. Therefore it often makes sense for companies to acquire an enterprise that has a distribution network in place.

Even if it does not have warehousing facilities and a fleet of vehicles, an acquisition target should have in-depth knowledge of the distribution system and the options and methods open to it and used by its competitors. It should also have a pool of sales people who are familiar with local distribution problems and have good contacts with customers.

Financial audit

Financial projections should be based on careful analysis of what assumptions are sound and of the drivers of demand. Future earnings potential is what matters. Before any financial projections are created, all the due diligence issues should be examined. When examining the business's financial statements, buyers should keep in mind that these are frequently ambiguous and unreliable and that accounting standards often differ from international norms. Buyers should make their own assumptions about the expected future earnings performance and cash flows from an acquisition rather than rely on what the seller tells them.

The financial audit should help in assessing the value of the business, but there will almost always be disagreements between buyer and seller as to what the company is worth. Past performance is not a useful indicator for business valuation in emerging markets, so buyers try to make price a function of the business's earnings potential. Sellers rarely agree with this valuation approach and often put high values on past sales and, often stretching credibility, on their fixed assets.

Price is not necessarily the principal issue in reaching agreement on an acquisition. Treatment of management and workers often plays an important role, as do promises of further investments and on-the-job training programmes. Determining market value is not easy for a number of reasons:

- **Lack of reliable information.** To go over some things mentioned above, many companies are not listed on any stock exchange so valuing them is similar to valuing a closely held business in the developed world. There is often no central authority that can provide any meaningful information on the company's standing. Even if a company is listed on a stock exchange, not all exchanges are well regulated. Attempts to compare a company with others are equally problematic. In many emerging markets, it is difficult to obtain financial statements and even when they exist they are likely to be flawed.

◪ **Irrelevant past earnings.** Earnings forecasts should be crucial in value determination. But getting a true financial picture of the past on which to base forecasts is tricky. Past earnings are distorted by competitive market conditions that will or may have been less competitive than they are now. Larger state enterprises are often sole producers or virtual monopolies as a result of government protectionism. After privatisation, barriers to entry and good government connections fall by the wayside. The implications for future cash flows are enormous. It is essential to investigate how much the company's earnings may be boosted by monopoly privileges, low-interest loans, privileged access to government contracts, subsidised rents or other government help. By removing these factors from cash-flow calculations, a more realistic picture emerges, often turning a money-spinner into a potential money-loser. This sounds sensible, but how do you go about evaluating the cash-flow generating ability of companies that have never operated without subsidies or subtle government protection? All you can do is carry out due diligence and detailed analysis of the industry, trade trends, quality of products, competition and other fundamentals in order to fully understand the drivers of future sales.

Since official financial information is of limited value, it is important to tap managers at all levels and workers for accurate information about the state of an enterprise. They will be well acquainted with the problems of distribution and supplies, the state of machinery, and to some extent their customers and end-users. One investment banker maintains he can get more out of one meeting with an enterprise's production manager than many meetings with the general manager; this is something to keep in mind.

◪ **Overvalued assets.** Many buyers have found that balance sheets reveal little useful information. The problem is that assets, especially equipment, are often overvalued in a firm's official financial statements. In many countries, assets also often have longer lives and lower depreciation rates than in the developed world. You may find that certain assets have never been depreciated. It is a particular problem in former communist countries, where central state funds were disbursed based on the size of assets. But assets are worth only what they are able to produce and this should be the basis for valuation. If they can only produce an outdated product poorly, they are worthless – a fact that local companies find hard to believe.

◪ **Accounts receivable and accounts payable.** It is crucial to check whether receivables listed are enforceable. In many countries the quality of the courts is poor and trying to enforce payment of receivables through them is often impossible. In some countries it is useful to check whether the companies were allowed to or whether they have written off any doubtful receivables. Another option is to try to negotiate a purchase without taking over the receivables. Signed contracts promising new production orders are another potential trap. They should not be accepted at face value; investigation should be made into how likely they are to materialise. The system of inter-company invoicing and recording of receivables is slow and inefficient in some emerging markets. Unpaid invoices pile up and demands for payment become impossible to enforce.

◪ **Inter-enterprise debt.** Given tight credit conditions and high interest rates in many emerging markets, local companies have difficulties in obtaining bank loans. By using private connections, enterprises borrow from each other but some then default on payments. Extreme care should be taken during due diligence to try to determine the level of inter-enterprise debt. Many such debts are never recorded on a balance sheet. One company was hit by millions of dollars of old debt several months after a purchase in Bulgaria. Another component of inter-enterprise debt is inter-company borrowing. In some instances it is not only money that is owed. One company was stunned when approached by a nearby company demanding 100 workers for a month. It had previously lent 100 workers to the acquired company and now wanted the favour returned.

◪ **Tax and social security liabilities.** An important part of the financial audit is to check for any tax liabilities and for the impact of tax payments or non-payments on financial statements. Many firms have discovered that their acquisition targets had not paid tax or social security for years, thus creating a large potential liability and inflating their results. Some firms have been pursued by the tax authorities after the acquisition to pay the back tax. The risk of this happening should be avoided by thorough due diligence.

- **Politicisation.** Business valuation is not purely a financial issue. It often requires sensitivity to political issues, for example when buying a state-owned company or when local public opinion is hostile to foreign takeovers. Some companies have done "face-saving" deals with local governments and privatisation bodies, whereby a higher sale price is publicly announced and creative ways are found to convince the government to put some of the money back into the company after the transaction is completed.

If there is a suspicion that hidden liabilities are there but they cannot be detected, a buyer should insist on paying in instalments over several months or even years, so that they can hold back payments if some nasty surprises emerge.

As the number of acquisitions in emerging markets increases, multinationals are using market comparison values more and more. They increasingly use prices paid for previous acquisitions as yardsticks to enable them to come to a figure for the acquisition currently under consideration. Investment bankers generally compare acquisition deals by looking at an entire region because of similarities between countries and industries.

Companies whose senior management is supportive of long-term business development are sometimes prepared to pay well over current value. They are more concerned about what the purchase can bring in terms of long-term earnings streams and what it means strategically – if it captures, for example, an important local brand and so limits the competition's room for manoeuvre.

Nevertheless, a buyer should try to create a business plan based on future profit estimates, taking all the uncertainties involved into account, and measure it against the price being asked for the business.

The value of a candidate as a going concern depends on future cash flows and earnings, discounted back to the present using an appropriate discount rate. When trying to determine the appropriate discount rate, it is necessary to make adjustments for distortions created by monopolies, subsidies and past (perhaps now irrelevant) trading relationships. This is of course a subjective process, but some provisions should be made. Further problems arise when trying to make realistic assumptions on future performance. This is especially hard when trying to predict a target company's sales and profits in five years' time. Emerging markets can change rapidly for a number of reasons, such as the threat of economic crisis, changing consumer habits and new domestic or international competitors.

Manufacturing and technology

The main goal of this part of the investigation is to estimate the investment that will be required after acquisition to integrate the acquired business into a global manufacturing system and to achieve desired standards of productivity and quality. An assessment should also be made to determine the ease and cost of expanding the facility for any future increases in demand.

The investigation should answer some of the following questions:

- What are the current manufacturing processes and the capacity and state of equipment? How productive is the facility?
- How are supply channels organised? What has been the behaviour of supply channel participants? What are the current supply problems?
- If there are any problems with the supply of components, can these be solved? What is the local supplier base of manufacturing components like? Will we have to persuade our global suppliers to invest nearby?
- What are the availability and prices of raw materials? How are those likely to behave in the next five years?
- Are there R&D facilities and researchers that could be integrated into the buyer's regional and global strategy?

Environmental audit

In some sectors, this audit should be the first due diligence step. Companies often find environmental damage on site. The audit should establish the extent of damage and, more importantly, indicate how the liability can be contractually avoided. Several companies have made acquisitions and have later been asked by local authorities to clean up the damage that was there before the purchase. Buyers should make it clear before the purchase that they will not be held responsible for any existing environmental damage.

Legal audit

A legal audit typically includes such things as the following:

- ◪ **Ownership structure.** It is sometimes tricky to find out who really owns a company. Some buyers have negotiated for months with people who claim they own the business but in fact do not.
- ◪ **Restitution.** Restitution claims on property should be checked, especially in countries with a socialist legacy. If a claim comes after an acquisition, this can create serious problems. For example, in Hungary one buyer could not raise local financing until the restitution claim was resolved, which took many months.
- ◪ **Corporate agreements.** Close examination of the various corporate agreements is important. For example, you may find that certain deals among shareholders shed a new light on management decisions and appointments, or sharing of profits.
- ◪ **Labour contracts.** A careful review of labour contracts is essential. For example, managers may be entitled to large payments upon termination of their employment and may receive huge bonuses regardless of the enterprise's performance.

Organisational structure and human resources

It is important to understand the existing management structure in order to change it successfully. Former communist countries had inefficient management structures. There was widespread overmanning, no sense of the concept of customer satisfaction and a reluctance among workers to take responsibility. The due diligence process must look at the costs and requirements of reorganisation, since without substantial reorganisation most acquisitions are doomed to fail.

It is also important to know who the important people in the organisation are, at both management and supervisory level. Will there be extra costs if these people are kept on? Are they likely to leave? What would keep them with the company? Acquisitions often fail because some key employees are unwilling to work with new employers and decide to leave. If a new structure and systems are imposed, will these be in sharp contrast to the existing systems in the target? If significant work has to be done, this will have to be planned for and executed during the post-acquisition restructuring.

Investigate how the target company is winning business

When buyers analyse a target company's sales they may appear to be strong and growing steadily. But buyers should check how the sales are actually made. Many companies, especially those involved in business-to-business or business-to-government operations, have discovered during due diligence that their targets win business by paying bribes – and it is a fair assumption that if such corrupt payments ceased, the business would decrease, or even disappear.

Assess the role that personal relationships play
Many companies have found out too late that the strong sales of the company they have acquired were the result of close personal relationships between the former owner or his sales staff and clients. When an international company takes a firm over, the people who have nurtured these relationships may well leave, which can leave an acquisition that seemed so promising looking distinctly shaky. Again, this is a matter of due diligence. If those sales relationships are seen as crucial, the company should either seek to recruit the people who have those relationships and follow the organic route to growth, or devise a strategy to keep them in the event of an acquisition which would involve talking to them well in advance to determine what would persuade them to stay.

Negotiating terms of purchase
After carrying out due diligence, the acquisition team usually has a reasonably good idea of what it would be willing to pay for a business. Buyers now need to be patient and persistent, because negotiations in emerging markets frequently take far longer than expected. In some cases, it can take more than a year to conduct due diligence thoroughly and as long again to negotiate a deal. In other cases, negotiations involve competing domestic parties, including various ministries or different governmental bodies. Or the target's management, favourable to an acquisition, may be forced by outside pressure to resign before a deal is concluded, sending negotiations back to square one.

Delays can create serious problems. The acquisition target may lose value after the bid is submitted and while negotiations are going on. When buyers lower their offer to reflect the change, government officials may insist that the previous bid is binding, thus lengthening negotiations for several more months. To avoid this problem, buyers should include a clause in the contract allowing the final price to be renegotiated in specified circumstances.

The power of lobby groups should not be underestimated during both due diligence and negotiations. Many deals are politically sensitive and governments are usually under pressure from the public not to sell the "family silver" too cheaply. It is worth spending time to find out how ministries and privatisation agencies are connected to the target enterprises; in many cases, the people in charge are "old buddies" or have some kind of connection through a seat on the supervisory board. If they receive a fee as a member of the supervisory board, they are generally not keen to do anything that could lead to a change in the status quo. One Coca-Cola manager who negotiated numerous deals in emerging countries argues that non-stop lobbying, political connections and persistence are some of the key skills needed to get through the negotiation process successfully. He says:

> You have to be networking all around, with all the key players,
> and all the time. This builds key relationships, which are critical
> if you want to get something done.

A well-judged accompanying public relations campaign is important. Many investors find all sorts of negative rumours circulating in the local press once their acquisition intentions become public or even, worryingly, before that. Most centre on how the company is planning to shut down the plant and dismiss most of the workers. This puts further pressure on the authorities and complicates the negotiation process.

The corporate communications division, with the help of an established locally based PR agency, should draw up a campaign to start as early as possible, even during the due diligence process. The goal is to pre-empt negative publicity by focusing on positive issues such as maintaining employment and promising a good future for the whole enterprise and the region. Donations to a local school or hospital will also help to gain acceptance in the local community (see Chapter 13).

Bad press usually originates from labour leaders in the target enterprise so it is crucial to identify and communicate with key workers (many enterprises have this on their due diligence checklists). A lack of employee support may not destroy negotiations, but it is now widely believed that gaining this support early during due diligence is good for fact-finding and for final negotiations. Getting the target's management on the buyer's side is also important. Not many governments are willing to do a deal if management and employees are not keen on the sale (especially in cases of sales of state property).

Eyes on the ball, ears to the ground

One of the challenges throughout a negotiation process is keeping track of where the deal is in the decision-making pipeline, and then maintaining contact with the appropriate officials and managers. This can be done only if there are people who can keep their ears to the ground and their eyes on how things are progressing. Important papers can get lost in bureaucratic channels or new competition can enter the market. These are not things that you find out about in good time without a local presence.

Before submitting a bid for a state-owned company, the investor needs to be aware of the government's goals. It is useful to know where the proceeds from a privatisation sell-off will go as this can shape motivations. Some governments are interested in price, especially if the money will go directly into the budget. Others are looking for a buyer with a good track record of managing acquisitions while minimising lay-offs, and which has big investment plans or a strong emphasis on production for export. Since negotiations often extend over many months and conditions change, companies need to be alert to changes in government attitudes; for example, if unemployment starts to rise, a government may well start to pay more attention to the employment side of the negotiation.

Below is a list of some of the non-price evaluation criteria that will be in the minds of those selling government-owned companies:

- Willingness to provide employment guarantees for a certain period of time.
- Enhancement of the export earnings potential.
- Improvement of the technological standards.
- Readiness to reinvest profits.
- Readiness to use local suppliers or bring in other foreign suppliers as new investors.
- Immediate and future improvements of environmental standards.
- Guarantee of future investment plans.
- Taking over old debts (and lessening the pressure on the state budget).

How large a stake to buy?

Although there are exceptions, in emerging markets you should never buy into a domestic enterprise unless you acquire control. Without control over the daily operations of the enterprise, all restructuring efforts are likely to be severely hampered. But, where political sensitivities or the size of the local company make buying a majority stake impossible, there are other ways to gain operational control. One is to have a majority of seats on the management board despite a minority or non-controlling stake. Needless to say this is hard to negotiate. Another is to use so-called management contracts, where the minority shareholder (buyer) is hired as manager for a specified period, usually until it can purchase a majority stake.

Sometimes companies buy minority stakes, but this is usually only the case when local companies are truly large and very strategic, such as large oil companies in Russia, or in countries where it may be legally impossible to buy a majority stake in all businesses or in those deemed strategic. The goal is to use the involvement in the company to learn more about the potential purchase of a majority stake and in the meantime earn some profits/dividends.

Restructuring and integration

Post-acquisition restructuring in emerging markets is costly and time-consuming. Integrating different working attitudes and cultures is always difficult, but most emerging-market businesses require a substantial overhaul if they are to become an integral and successful part of the buyer's company. This is why many companies investing in an emerging market opt for a greenfield investment.

One of the most complicated issues in post-acquisition restructuring is trying to increase productivity. This typically involves laying off many employees, so the first stage has to involve a positive public relations campaign and communication with opinion leaders among the workforce. If they turn against the deal after it is completed, the company can suffer immense difficulties. One large American multinational bought a local manufacturer and then struggled to make efficiency gains in the manufacturing process. After some investigation, the company learned that several foremen were ignoring any orders from above and telling workers to do things in the old way. When these individuals were identified they were not laid off. On the contrary, they were told they were doing a good job and were sent, with their families, for a year of intensive training in the United States. By the time they returned they had become champions of the corporate agenda and the need to increase productivity.

In many countries acquisition contracts stipulate no lay-offs for a certain period, usually ranging from one to three years. Multinationals may be opposed to such agreements, but many recognise that they are an important way of showing sensitivity to local public opinion and therefore agree to them.

Keeping a factory overmanned for some time may seem wasteful but it has some advantages. It helps avoid negative publicity. It allows time to help those who will be laid off – for example, through offering incentives to those who volunteer for early retirement. Wages are generally low in most emerging markets so the overall cost is rarely prohibitive in the scheme of things. But buyers should be aware in advance of closing the deal what the cost will be. You may find scores of workers listed as employees in the books who were registered merely to have time counted towards their pension and to receive social and health benefits. Thorough due diligence should identify the number of such workers.

Another reason for giving short-term employment guarantees is that many firms need time to restructure the acquired business. This allows them to assess individual employees and decide which ones they want to keep and which they do not need when the guarantee has run its term.

Spinning off certain functions is a way to improve efficiency and eliminate headcount. Acquisition candidates may own their own kindergartens or fire brigades, or are so vertically integrated that the buyer would never want to engage in all the activities involved. Some spin-offs are small and easy; for example, vehicles can be given to workers from the fire brigade to start their own business. Other spin-offs are more complicated but always possible.

Another way to win over the public and workers is to create good outplacement and retraining programmes for those who are not wanted. The message is clear: "We are not just kicking you out, we will help you acquire new skills and we will try to help you find work elsewhere. Also, once we reach our productivity targets and if production starts to grow, we will need new people and you will be the first ones we will look at." Such an attitude boosts the morale of those who stay because everyone likes to work for an employer who cares.

Ask any M&A consultant why acquisitions often fail and one of the top three responses will always be poor post-acquisition restructuring and integration. Integration is a complex procedure. It involves keeping all acquired employees focused, making sure the best people have good incentives to stay and identifying early any potential personnel conflicts. It also involves merging organisational cultures and structures and engaging new employees in new activities. A skilled integration manager should work closely with an external human resources consultancy specialising in integration issues, of which one of the most critical is to make sure that staff in the acquired company fully understand the objectives of the acquisition, the plan for the future and how it will be implemented.

Acquisitions in emerging countries: some lessons

- Acquisitions in emerging markets depend on due diligence being conducted thoroughly, so be prepared to invest time, money and human resources in this. Expect due diligence to take much longer than for an acquisition in the developed world.
- Acquisitions in emerging markets make sense if there is a significant market share or brand to buy. They also make sense if they give access to a new market segment or strategically limit the activities of your fiercest competitors (international or domestic).
- Approach a potential target's managers and get them on your side. In many cases, only managers have real inside knowledge of the enterprise they work in.
- Looking for the fundamental drivers of future earnings is much more important than number crunching. (See Chapter 3 for help on making good guesstimates about future earnings potential.)
- Use the best characteristics of investigative journalism during the due diligence process. Talk to workers, customers, distributors, suppliers, other companies in the industry, ministries, independent industrial experts and market research agencies. Any one of these may reveal information that makes all the difference to the attractiveness of the acquisition.
- Expect due diligence and negotiations to last a long time and be prepared for setbacks. Persistence and patience pay off.
- Set up acquisition teams to constantly search for suitable targets.
- Identify a target's weak points, and make use of them during negotiations.
- Check every number in the financial statements and treat all numbers with caution.
- Have people on the ground from the beginning of the due diligence process. Don't expect things to happen if you are trying to buy "from a distance".
- Focus on real future earnings potential rather than any fixed asset values and adjust earnings potential to the point in time when any direct and indirect government support ends and when market conditions evolve.

Joint ventures

Companies should think not twice but five or six times before deciding to go into a joint venture in any emerging market. The verdict on joint ventures from those who are involved in emerging markets seems to be: only go into them if you have no other choice and/or if you really know how to manage them. Managers with experience of a joint venture often say that it was beset by friction between the parties. Various surveys have shown that over a ten-year period, barely 5–10% of joint ventures survive. Before taking the joint-venture route, ask yourself some questions. What can a partner do for us that we cannot do ourselves? Is what the partner offers really not achievable through organic growth or an acquisition? If we enter a joint venture, how easy will it be to turn it into a full-scale acquisition? What rules are there requiring local partners?

Joint ventures are never easy to manage, but there are added complexities in emerging markets. Below is a list of things that companies should pay particular attention to:

- **Financial problems.** Local partners may be less financially adept than the foreign partner. They may not have enough money to invest if the foreign partner wishes to expand and build more manufacturing capacity, for example. This limits growth opportunity and is the main reason why joint ventures fail.
- **Different strategic objectives.** The strategies and objectives of joint-venture partners are often not aligned. Just as many domestic distributors and importers import anything that will earn them a quick return, many domestic companies will go into partnership with anyone who brings them some technology and offers quick and painless profits.
- **Management clashes.** Different managerial styles and approaches are a frequent cause of problems. Work attitudes and the "way things are done around here" can cause enormous problems.
- **Cultural clashes.** This is a particular problem in emerging markets.
- **Lack of communication.** The two partners fail to communicate strategies and tactics to achieve joint-venture objectives. Before a deal is signed, it is essential to talk to the local partner about expansion plans and expectations.
- **Transfer pricing disagreements.** In the words of a manager of one firm that set up a joint venture in an emerging market: "We are wondering when they are going to realise that we are ripping them off with our transfer pricing." Well, sooner or later, most local partners learn the tricks and the trouble begins.

11 Dealing with corruption and crime

If the soul is left in darkness, sins will be committed. The guilty one is not he who commits the sin, but he who causes the darkness.

Victor Hugo

It takes a crook to catch a crook.

Franklin Delano Roosevelt, explaining why he hired Joseph K. Kennedy to head the Securities and Exchange Commission

Corruption and crime are constant problems in many emerging markets. In some countries the threats they pose can be serious, even fatal. This chapter outlines the types of corruption and crime that firms may come up against, and explains how to recognise and deal with them. It looks at international efforts to eliminate corruption and explains why so few companies are entirely clean (even if they insist that they are).

Corruption

Dealing with corruption is a daily task in all emerging markets, and the cost for both international companies and developing countries is high. Indeed, the World Bank warns that corruption is the greatest obstacle to economic and social development in developing countries. Numerous studies have shown a strong correlation between a high incidence of crime and corruption and low foreign direct investment. World Bank reports have repeatedly shown that countries with high levels of crime and corruption grow more slowly than cleaner countries, and their share of world trade and exports keeps shrinking.

Government projects may be awarded to incompetent contractors. Money changes hands but the work is never properly done. The country's infrastructure remains poor but its debt balloons. Corrupt regimes often cause economic crises in their countries. In Slovakia in the mid-1990s, for example, the autocratic leader appointed his friends to run state banks and large state companies. Loans were given to enterprises without regard to risk management. Most of the money ended up in companies where directors stripped assets and moved cash offshore to private bank accounts. Local legislation was so immature that technically many of these crony capitalist schemes were not illegal. The subsequent prime minister of Slovakia told an Economist Conferences government roundtable:

> We can't even start prosecuting. The law in those days allowed the scheme. Those that we'd like to prosecute, where we have some evidence of wrongdoing, live abroad in big houses.

Similar crony capitalism is often cited as one of the fundamental reasons for the Asian crisis of 1997, although this is not entirely correct (see Chapter 14).

Studies have shown that bribes increase the cost of doing business in emerging markets by 3–10%. If the country has a physical security problem (as in South Africa or some Latin American countries), the cost of doing business can increase by a similar amount. Table 11.1 on pages 113–15 reveals perceptions about levels of corruption in different countries. Some are less corrupt than others, and even in corrupt countries the corruption may be limited to a small number of institutions and individuals. It may also be seasonal, as some individuals try to get rich before their public post expires. It is not difficult to find out about and keep track of who these individuals are and what they demand. Some countries are rampantly corrupt; others may have less corruption but are harder to deal with because it is not so obvious. Second, it is possible to do business in emerging markets without paying bribes.

Many companies try to stay clean even if this means a loss of business. Some work with third parties and turn a blind eye to what those parties do. But executives can now be liable even for the actions of the third parties they work with.

American companies complained for years that European companies paid large commissions to those who secured contracts for them in various emerging markets. European companies say that they had to do it because American political clout could secure lucrative contracts for American companies. Until 1997, a number of EU countries allowed companies to treat commissions as a tax deductible expense for international contracts. OECD (Organisation for Economic Co-operation and Development) rules introduced in 1997 have in theory changed this, although in practice enforcement of the new rules by governments has been patchy.

Hypocrisy surrounds the issue of corruption. Before the Foreign Corrupt Practices Act (FCPA) came into force in the United States in 1977, the Securities and Exchange Commission (SEC) got over 400 American companies to admit to making multimillion-dollar payments to foreign governments directly and indirectly to secure business. Today, many American companies claim to be super clean and to stick to the letter of the FCPA, which outlaws bribery of government officials.

However, they may not be keeping to the spirit of the FCPA. Some companies sell their products to third parties who pay bribes in order to resell them to final buyers or further intermediaries. Thus American products may end up being bought by buyers who would never buy them without a bribe. It is unlikely that these companies do not know what their partners do to sell the products to the final buyers. As one executive says:

> I don't want to know how they do it. I get the money from their account in Geneva or the Cayman Islands, we ship the goods, and that's where my engagement ends.

Many companies use intermediaries to win tenders, and these intermediaries may pay bribes to secure deals.

This is a breach of the FCPA and the most recent anti-bribery legislation in the UK. Both laws require companies to know what their intermediaries do. Indeed, in a recent groundbreaking bribery case in Lesotho, a German company was charged for allowing a non-employed agent to pay a bribe to an official. By demonstrating that the intermediary's primary purpose was to pay the bribe to win the business and so avoid corporate liability, the judge wiped out the company's defence that it could not be responsible for third parties.

Managers engage in such transactions for a simple reason: they are under pressure to sell more and meet budgets. Cutting corners on the borderline of legality has become normal even for companies that claim publicly to be squeaky clean.

It seems that there is a possibility that even after 1997 well-known firms have been siphoning off funds into offshore accounts in order to use those funds to win business in emerging markets. If the allegations that have been made prove to be well-founded, any company involved could be prevented from bidding in public tenders in many countries and some senior executives may end up in jail. That would certainly act as a deterrent to business managers.

It is important to differentiate between facilitating payments and bribes, although not all legislation makes the distinction. The FCPA does, but the new UK legislation apparently does not. A facilitating payment is made to an individual who demands it for a service that a company would expect to receive without payment in normal commercial circumstances, for example for getting a stamp from a customs official. The FCPA says facilitating payments are made "for routine government action" and accept them as legal. But companies are obliged to report these payments to the authorities, their own company and their embassies.

This is one example of activities on the edge of legality that some observers regard as bribery. But reality is not so black and white. Many companies, including American companies under the scrutiny of the FCPA, engage in all sorts of activities that are not outright illegal and are intended to get things done in a corrupt environment. Companies sometimes put a corrupt business partner or government official on the books as a consultant. Or they ask them if their sons or daughters would like scholarships for top business schools. Or they invite them to Paris or New York with their families for several weeks of "business negotiations" and give them substantial daily payments. There is a thin line between an envelope full of money and more sophisticated methods.

One regional director offers some practical advice:

> It is possible to do straight business. You have to be ready to lose out on some big sales short-term. But in the end, straight business is better business. If you decide to pay bribes it is like dancing with a gorilla – what do you do when you want to stop?

Most legislative attempts to reduce bribes have largely been in vain. It is hard to police and catch those who do it. It is particularly hard to monitor remote subsidiaries of large American, EU and Japanese multinationals. Although FCPA and OECD anti-bribery legislation (the latter signed by 35 countries only in 1997 and in force since 1999) sounds encouraging, there seems to be little practical enforcement. According to a 2002 Transparency International survey of more than 800 businesses, the new OECD legislation is failing to make an impact, despite the fact that anyone found breaking the rules can end up in jail. In a rare publicised case, IBM's headquarters found that its subsidiary in Buenos Aires had paid some $4.5m to directors of the state-owned Banco de la Nacion Argentina (via a local subcontractor to whom IBM Argentina paid $22m) to win a contract to install IT systems. The value of the contract was estimated at $250m. Were it not for IBM's own internal controls, the case would never have reached the SEC. However, the fine imposed on IBM was only $300,000; that is, 0.12% of the value of the business it secured with the bribe. The reason for the low fine was the "strong corrective action taken by IBM".

The Economist, on March 2nd 2002, wondered if IBM would have had to report the case to the SEC if the bribe had been paid to a privately owned bank (since such payments are not covered by the FCPA). Until recently the number of prosecutions since the FCPA came into force in 1977 had been quite modest, but since 2004 there has been a significant increase. In 2004 and 2005 the US Department of Justice (DOJ) brought more prosecutions under the FCPA than it had in the preceding 20 years.

Apart from a few companies themselves reporting corruption to the SEC and internally punishing the managers involved, little policing and enforcement actually happens. With the emergence of more accounting scandals, SEC staff seem to have more pressing things to do than pay much attention to bribes being paid thousands of miles away.

UK legislation has been criticised as being full of loopholes, but new anti-bribery legislation became law on January 1st 2004.

Nevertheless, the most effective way to deal with the problem of corruption is through internal corporate controls. Companies should provide clear guidelines for managers who are asked to pay a bribe, including, for example, to whom they should report the incident and what procedures they should follow. Leadership must come from the top. The CEO should implement a zero-tolerance bribery policy and install systems to police and implement it. The message to staff in remote locations should be: "If you are asked to pay a bribe to secure a sale, and not securing it means missing your budget, don't be afraid to tell your partner to look for someone else who will pay the money."

Company leaders need to be aware that if they do not impose tough internal controls, the loss of reputation will affect the company far more than typically low fines for misconduct. Although companies can secure some short-term business through bribery, the loss of reputation will mean long-term damage. They should also be aware that the public increasingly knows what is going on. The World Bank features a list of bribe-payers on its website and does not allow them to bid for any new Bank-related projects.

What is corruption?

If an American congressman gets money from a corporation to lobby for certain corporate interests, this would constitute bribery in many EU countries. An Italian prime minister and a former German chancellor, let alone seven Japanese construction ministers, have been investigated for corruption.

The use of offshore tax havens – places where individuals and companies can manage and dispose of capital at minimum cost without political interference and punitive taxes – is denounced when rich Russians are involved. But the media rarely mention the fact that these were created by wealthy industrialised countries for corporate and private tax avoidance. Worse, many offshore havens are not even physically offshore. There are more than 100 of them with offices in New York City alone. Not surprisingly, many companies use the offshore accounts of their partners in emerging markets to do business and get paid quickly.

Crime: individual and organised

A regional manager for Latin America at a large consumer goods company says:

> *Some goods were always missing from our truck and sometimes the whole truck disappears. Now we employ armed security guards to look after the shipments. We had to do it since no insurance company would insure the load.*

Most security risks are manageable provided that there are clear and detailed security guidelines and precautions, and enough resources to implement them. In risky countries, all new employees should attend a personal security seminar. It is also essential to have a manual detailing security guidelines and procedures on how to prevent and deal with various security threats. This has become one of the most important internal corporate documents in many markets. Companies should develop such manuals systematically. Less experienced firms should learn from those experienced in emerging markets. It is surprising how many companies deal with security in an ad hoc fashion. These companies are clearly vulnerable.

Security guidelines must be detailed. They should cover such matters as what to do if a staff member and his or her family are threatened by local organised crime groups and list the blood group of all employees in case they are wounded. There are many instances in which local employees of multinational companies and their families have been threatened.

There is no doubt that the cost of doing business in many emerging markets is seriously inflated by the need to ensure the physical security of assets and people. Substantial amounts are budgeted each year for security. This is a necessity because investment in security is not only a protective but also a preventive measure. Companies that erect visible security obstacles around their facilities face fewer threats. Gangsters prefer the easy prey.

In a number of countries, it has become usual to drive around in armoured company cars and have bodyguards. If someone is kidnapped, it is wise to listen to the kidnappers' demands. A director of a German company was kidnapped in Russia. A ransom was demanded but not paid. The director was killed. When the German company sent a replacement, he was also kidnapped. A ransom was demanded and this time it was paid. The director was released unharmed.

Companies have come up with many ways of combating criminal threats. The fight against highway hijacking is turning into a mini industry: as well as employing security guards to follow convoys, goods are increasingly being marked with serial numbers so stolen goods can be tracked more easily. External affairs managers try to work closely with all levels of government and in particular interior ministries. New technologies are used too. A *Financial Times* report from Brazil described trucks equipped with devices that can shut off the fuel supply of stolen vehicles via satellite. But sometimes none of this is enough. Mini armies attack convoys and armed guards prove inadequate. Police officers may turn out to be not just part of the gang but organisers too. However, although the problem remains expensive and frustrating, it is ultimately manageable.

Organised crime is more difficult to deal with than visible security threats. It comes in many guises and is not always easy to recognise. Generally, domestically owned businesses are much easier to attack than multinationals. But organised criminals sometimes target multinationals for extortion and managers should be ready to respond.

One company was approached by what seemed like a well-dressed, legitimate group of local businessmen wanting to talk about co-operation. Gradually, the questioning went beyond matters concerning co-operation and the company grew suspicious. One way of dealing with such threats is to "kill" intruders with corporate bureaucracy. In this example the company brought in legal advisers who asked the intruders polite but legally loaded questions. The manager also kept repeating that on such matters they would have to check with headquarters and that this would take time.

Companies should also be careful when recruiting. Organised crime groups are well known for trying to place people in the target company. The legitimacy of degrees and diplomas should be checked, and security companies may be able to do other pre-hire checks. This is important, especially if the person concerned is likely to have access to certain accounts or banking links.

Table 11.1 **Corruption: business perceptions 2006**

10=least corrupt

Haiti	1.8	Guyana	2.5
Guinea	1.9	Honduras	2.5
Iraq	1.9	Nepal	2.5
Myanmar	1.9	Philippines	2.5
Bangladesh	2.0	Russia	2.5
Chad	2.0	Rwanda	2.5
Congo–Kinshasa	2.0	Swaziland	2.5
Sudan	2.0	Albania	2.6
Belarus	2.1	Guatemala	2.6
Cambodia	2.1	Kazakhstan	2.6
Côte d'Ivoire	2.1	Laos	2.6
Equatorial Guinea	2.1	Nicaragua	2.6
Uzbekistan	2.1	Paraguay	2.6
Angola	2.2	Timor–Leste	2.6
Congo–Brazzaville	2.2	Vietnam	2.6
Kenya	2.2	Yemen	2.6
Kyrgyzstan	2.2	Zambia	2.6
Nigeria	2.2	Bolivia	2.7
Pakistan	2.2	Iran	2.7
Sierra Leone	2.2	Libya	2.7
Tajikistan	2.2	Macedonia	2.7
Turkmenistan	2.2	Malawi	2.7
Cameroon	2.3	Uganda	2.7
Ecuador	2.3	Dominican Republic	2.8
Niger	2.3	Georgia	2.8
Venezuela	2.3	Mali	2.8
Azerbaijan	2.4	Mongolia	2.8
Burundi	2.4	Mozambique	2.8
Central African Republic	2.4	Ukraine	2.8
Ethiopia	2.4	Argentina	2.9
Indonesia	2.4	Armenia	2.9
Papua New Guinea	2.4	Bosnia	2.9
Togo	2.4	Eritrea	2.9
Zimbabwe	2.4	Syria	2.9
Benin	2.5	Tanzania	2.9
Gambia	2.5	Gabon	3.0

Serbia	3.0	Tunisia	4.6
Suriname	3.0	Latvia	4.7
Algeria	3.1	Slovakia	4.7
Madagascar	3.1	Czech Republic	4.8
Mauritania	3.1	Kuwait	4.8
Panama	3.1	Lithuania	4.8
Romania	3.1	Italy	4.9
Sri Lanka	3.1	Malaysia	5.0
Burkina Faso	3.2	Mauritius	5.1
Lesotho	3.2	South Korea	5.1
Moldova	3.2	Hungary	5.2
Morocco	3.2	Jordan	5.3
Trinidad & Tobago	3.2	Oman	5.4
Brazil	3.3	Botswana	5.6
China	3.3	Cyprus	5.6
Egypt	3.3	Bahrain	5.7
Ghana	3.3	Israel	5.9
India	3.3	Taiwan	5.9
Mexico	3.3	Bhutan	6.0
Peru	3.3	Qatar	6.0
Saudi Arabia	3.3	UAE	6.2
Senegal	3.3	Malta	6.4
Croatia	3.4	Slovenia	6.4
Belize	3.5	Uruguay	6.4
Cuba	3.5	Macao	6.6
Grenada	3.5	Portugal	6.6
Lebanon	3.6	Barbados	6.7
Seychelles	3.6	Estonia	6.7
Thailand	3.6	Spain	6.8
Jamaica	3.7	Belgium	7.3
Poland	3.7	Chile	7.3
Turkey	3.8	US	7.3
Colombia	3.9	France	7.4
Bulgaria	4.0	Ireland	7.4
El Salvador	4.0	Japan	7.6
Costa Rica	4.1	Germany	8.0
Namibia	4.1	Hong Kong	8.3
Greece	4.4	Canada	8.5
Dominica	4.5	Austria	8.6
South Africa	4.6	Luxembourg	8.6

UK	8.6	Singapore	9.4
Australia	8.7	Denmark	9.5
Netherlands	8.7	Finland	9.6
Norway	8.8	Iceland	9.6
Switzerland	9.1	New Zealand	9.6
Sweden	9.2		

Note: This index ranks countries based on how much corruption is perceived by business people, academics and risk analysts to exist among politicians and public officials.
Source: Transparency International

12 Human resources: myths and reality

Treat people as if they were what they ought to be and you help them become what they are capable of being.

Johann Wolfgang von Goethe

This chapter explores the issues of attracting, retaining and managing talent in emerging markets. It also analyses the pros and cons of using local staff rather than expatriates.

Experienced companies in emerging markets know that talented and reliable local managers are essential for success, and they try to remove expatriate managers as soon as possible. But finding and keeping such people in emerging markets is hard for one overwhelming reason: the pool of local talent is shallow. With typically strong demand and weak supply, it is no wonder that multinationals are forced to pay top salaries to local managers. Despite overall low labour costs in emerging markets, it is not uncommon for, say, a finance manager in Poland or Hungary to earn more than his peers in Germany or the UK.

Many companies are unwilling to adjust their global corporate pay scales to the local circumstances of supply and demand. But if a company refuses to pay the Hungarian finance manager more than its British one, it will have to settle for a person of average ability running its finances in Hungary. Another option is to fill the difficult positions with an expatriate, but this is generally even more expensive, considering all the benefits that are included in a typical expatriate package. Furthermore, it is only a local who will know the market best and will be able to establish something that expatriates often mismanage: personal relationships with customers, partners and government ministers and officials.

Expatriates, if needed, should be carefully selected. A successful manager in the United States does not necessarily translate into a successful manager in Turkey or India. During the selection process it is necessary to look for two important ingredients: international exposure and a passion for new environments and cultures. It is no use transferring an excellent American manager who has never travelled abroad and is not pushing for an international expatriate assignment.

Companies with large operations in certain emerging-market regions have started relocating experienced managers from one country to build up business in a less-developed market in the same region. The knowledge transfer often works better than with managers from developed markets, but companies need to be aware of cultural sensitivities. It may, for example, be acceptable to give an American manager a generous expatriate package, but giving the same package to a manager from a neighbouring country may cause problems. A solution is to introduce regional expatriate packages that cover relocation costs but offer fewer frills.

Once on the ground, expatriates are usually replaced too often. As soon as they settle down, develop some local relationships, start (maybe) speaking the local language and gain trust from local business partners and employees, they are sent to a new location. The process of integrating a new expatriate then starts all over again. Such rapid turnover of expatriate staff and lack of continuity are bad for business.

Many successful companies start with expatriates but set up a system of searching for a local replacement early on. Top local talent is trained to take over, with intensive mentoring and coaching. It is a paradox these days that expatriate country managers must train locals so they can eliminate their own position. In these difficult economic times many expatriates simply try to slow down the process of replacement. They fear (in many cases rightly) that once there is a capable replacement in situ, there will be nowhere for them to return or go to. Even if they do return to the home country, seasoned expatriates know that it will not be easy. Many say that working again in the developed world is boring and predictable. Some are unable to readjust to the old way of living. Most, of course, miss the generous expatriate packages and luxurious standard of living. It is not unusual to hear expatriate managers reporting to the top: "This local guy I've been training to take over is really great but I don't think he is ready yet. Here are the reasons why I think I need to stay here a little longer." Needless to say, in the more dangerous locations in emerging markets, expatriates on assignment often cannot wait to get out.

Once an emerging market starts developing, the supply of skilled labour improves. New universities offer new programmes which are better tailored to the real world and the needs of companies. With time, an increase in supply inevitably reduces the relative price of skilled managers. But in many markets, a shortage of skilled local labour continues for a long time.

Finding local managers

There is no magic formula for finding local managers, but the following methods may help.

Establish good links to universities

Many companies prefer to hire new graduates, who can be trained to be good corporate soldiers. To identify the best students and get to them early, companies set up links with universities, funding certain programmes and offering internships to students who have not yet graduated. Many successful companies fund scholarships for the most talented students.

Use locally based headhunters

Many successful companies rely on headhunters to find the best people. Locally based human resources consultants (not necessarily local companies) usually offer a better service than those trying to operate from a distance. Their local contacts are better and they are better able to assess candidates' skills for a specific local market.

Invest in corporate brand building

Like western products and brands, company names often mean little in emerging markets. It is important to do some brand building for the company as a whole so that talented jobseekers understand who you are and why they should want to work for you. The process of building a company name in a local market should not be underestimated. A manager at Diageo, the company formed by the merger of Guinness and Grand Metropolitan, tells the story of his empty stand at a Budapest jobs fair. Perplexed by the lack of interest, he collared a student and asked him what the problem was. "Why should I want to work for a Hungarian carpet firm?" the student asked. The manager realised that nobody knew what Diageo was. He went to a bar and brought back Guinness, Bailey's and Smirnoff and was soon surrounded by hundreds of potential applicants. (Whether this was a result of brand recognition or thirst is beside the point.) Because skilled talent is scarce, the best people are keen to work for companies with a good name and reputation. If your company name is not known locally, you will find it difficult to attract the best. Companies preparing for market entry and market expansion should see the cost of making potential employees aware of their brand and their products as a necessary investment and plan for it.

Hire from other multinationals

The downside for companies that train young graduates is that they often lose them to "poachers" from other companies. Extensive job hopping and poaching are the norm in many emerging markets.

Participate in job fairs

Job fairs and careers days present the company to young local people seeking work, and it is worth taking part in them. However, it is hard to stand out from the crowd, and the method is more reactive than proactive. There is a strong chance that the best candidates will have been pre-selected by proactive companies, leaving you with more average ones.

Retention strategies

Because the pool of skilled workers is shallower than it is in developed countries, retention strategies require a different approach. In many emerging markets, staff retention is a bigger challenge than staff selection. Some successful multinationals admit that local managers they are keen to keep in developing countries often enjoy far superior packages to managers at the same level in developed countries. As well as a salary that exceeds the local average for the post, for example, standard benefits will include performance-related bonuses, private health insurance and private pensions. These are often topped up with loans to buy or renovate homes (either direct company loans or through an outside institution, with the company often subsidising interest rates); share ownership (even if an employee at that level in the developed country would never receive any shares); company cars (again at a junior level); and membership of gyms and sports clubs. Employees take it for granted that the company will provide a clear career path, continuous training opportunities, mentoring and coaching, as well as allowing for a balance between work and private life.

It is important that senior managers know what local salaries and packages for skilled managers are before market entry. Clearly, there are markets where compensation for local managers will be a substantial cost, higher than in a developed country. Senior managers must be flexible and allow adjustments (if necessary) of global pay and benefits scales. Imposing a global scale on a heated emerging market is a great way to lose great staff.

Most companies acknowledge that it is dangerous to underpay relative to market averages, but most are wary of paying much more than the average. They feel it is dangerous to enter a pay race because there will always be a company that will offer something more (a bigger starting salary, a bigger bonus or a more generous private pension). Multinationals increasingly find that competition for skilled people comes from unexpected sources. In Russia, for example, large domestic firms in the hands of new "robber barons" now pay young MBA graduates twice as much as large multinational companies do. Many companies, unwilling or unable to pay such premium rates, now focus their retention strategies on other aspects of job satisfaction. There is a widely held view that it makes sense to conduct employee and/or job satisfaction surveys more often in emerging markets than in developed countries. With continued shortages of skilled workers, the wants and needs of those with the required skills change frequently, so it is useful to keep track of signs of job dissatisfaction.

Tracking salaries

Keeping track of salary movements is tricky. Levels change quickly, rocketing upwards in good times and sliding rapidly downwards in times of crisis. Wage levels often have nothing to do with broad economic indicators, such as inflation or GDP per head. At the same time, prices in the economy in general went up about 50%.

In countries with a history of economic crisis or those that are potentially vulnerable to devaluation, it is wise to avoid paying salaries linked to dollars or euros. When crisis strikes, the hard-currency link boosts fixed costs at a time of declining revenues (when converted into hard-currency earnings).

Important aspects of job satisfaction other than pay in emerging markets include the following:

- Career planning with a clear path, ideally in combination with international assignments and later permanent international responsibility.
- Training and development covering all aspects of business, including soft-skills training (such as communications, cultural training, leadership skills and stress management).
- Performance management, including coaching, mentoring, regular feedback, good communications and appraisals.
- Providing a good balance between work and leisure time.

13 Corporate social responsibility

With great powers come great responsibilities ... The inhibitions placed on
the irresponsible use of technology are weak, often half-hearted, and almost
always, worldwide, subordinated to short-term national or corporate interest.

Carl Sagan

Many companies have run into trouble as a result of criticism of their
standards of what in the jargon is termed corporate social responsibility (CSR); for example, over working conditions in their factories or the
use of child labour. This chapter gives practical advice on what companies
should be aware of and what action they should take to help improve the
bottom line and avoid damaging bad publicity.

"The sea is alive" said a print advertisement signed (in small print) by
Coca-Cola Beverages (one of Coca-Cola's largest bottlers). The text of the
advertisement told the story of a group of kindergarten children taught
by two young marine biologists, learning about animals living in the sea
and learning that the sea has to be kept clean to keep these animals alive.
It went on to say that the company supports ecological education and
any action that protects the environment. There were photos of children
sitting on the beach listening to the two young scientists in their wet suits.
None of the children was drinking Coke. The Coke logo was in fairly small
print.

This is just one creative example where CSR and brand building
become one. Those who see the advertisement get a "feel-good" sensation
about the company and the brand. It is also a clever, subtle way to sell
the product.

But how many companies really use CSR to help their business?
Imagine you need to fill your tank and there is a choice between several
fuel stations along the road. Would you avoid, say, Shell because the
company was accused by pressure groups of wanting to sink one of its
old oil platforms in the sea? Would you really care if the price of fuel was
cheaper at Shell than at other filling stations?

This is the kind of dilemma that many companies face. If they invest
a lot of money in CSR, will it really affect their business? If they invest
nothing in CSR, will it make any difference?

In emerging markets, many citizens are cynical about and sometimes hostile to "the big fat capitalists coming to exploit us". Many companies witness high levels of scepticism and hostility during and after market entry. Well thought through and active CSR with substance can prevent this.

In a 2003 survey of CEOs conducted by the consultancy arm of PricewaterhouseCoopers, one of the big four accountancy firms, 79% of respondents believed that CSR was crucial for profitability. This is an increase of some 10% compared with the previous year. Awareness of CSR at the top of the corporate hierarchy seems to be increasing. However, critics say that CEOs are just paying lip-service to CSR and that there is little substance in their actions. The reason is simple – there is no clear link between short-term profitability (an overwhelming concern to most CEOs) and spending on CSR.

Despite some improvements, many international companies still neglect CSR. Some have already suffered bad publicity, which has affected their sales, profits and share price. Companies that have ignored the environment or working conditions or working practices in their emerging-market operations (generally where manufacturing has been outsourced to local third parties) have suffered the most. For example, some multinationals were censured in the media when it was alleged that they were using child labour. International companies are now under the tough scrutiny of a plethora of organisations, pressure groups and anti-globalisation protesters.

Companies should have a clear strategy for implementing CSR, especially in emerging markets. It can and should be used to build brands, gain a good reputation and minimise the risk of bad publicity. Over time, such actions do have an impact on revenues and profits. If a company systematically builds a public image as a good corporate citizen, it will be in a better position to weather a storm of bad publicity. Furthermore, although surveys have shown that only 20% of consumers will punish companies that are not good corporate citizens by not buying their products, they also show that almost 80% of consumers are more likely to buy products manufactured by good corporate citizens.

To be effective, a CSR strategy must be supported at all corporate levels, most importantly the top. Many companies take a half-hearted approach to CSR, giving it a low priority or treating it as "window dressing". It is companies in so-called controversial industries, such as tobacco, oil or alcohol, which have as a group made the biggest advances in terms of internal "buy in" and getting all to recognise the strategic necessity of having an active CSR approach.

How to create a genuine CSR strategy

There has to be a clear commitment at the top, but not just a statement from the CEO. "Buy in" has to be genuine at all levels, and all business leaders should be involved in the creation of a meaningful strategy that will have an impact on the top and bottom lines. "I don't have time for this nonsense! I have a business to run," said a country manager of a large multinational when asked about CSR in his company. No wonder, perhaps. The economic environment is tough, and the pressures of keeping the business running are too high for managers to focus on what they see as the intangible and uncertain benefits of CSR. This is why many companies wanting to get a genuine CSR strategy off the ground have used the services of consultants specialising in change management.

Best practice is to have a dedicated global CSR co-ordinator working with marketing and PR teams or, in some cases, local people with responsibility for CSR (some tobacco companies have them). As consumers become more socially aware, they are increasingly linking a company's name and its brands to CSR. If a company has a bad image, this will rub off on its brands.

The pressure on companies to be good corporate citizens has spread to more and more areas. The *Financial Times* ("Bitter taste of success", March 11th 2002) reported that Starbucks was being pursued by the US Organic Consumer Association for paying low wages to coffee farmers in emerging countries. The association demanded third-party verified proof that the company does donate money to clinics, schools and credit schemes in coffee-growing communities and that it pays them more than the regular coffee market price. It also told Starbucks not to use milk with Recombinant Bovine Somatotropin (RBST), a growth hormone (although it is approved by the Food and Drugs Administration).

How should companies respond in such circumstances? Starbucks got it right by being diplomatic and not arrogant when responding to these accusations. The last thing a company should do is to make enemies in the community of pressure groups and protesters. Ideally, every effort should be made to listen to their concerns, to communicate and to come up with good arguments to explain why certain demands may be unreasonable. However, where demands make sense, companies can create joint initiatives with pressure groups, and by working as partners bolster the brand.

The benefits for companies that behave as good corporate citizens are clear. After the stockmarket bubble burst, many investors said they were only interested in buying long-term sustainable businesses with an effective CSR policy. There are already funds which invest in companies with good CSR credentials, and they have a growing following and are growing in number. There are also internal corporate benefits. Studies have shown that companies with strong CSR have lower staff turnover and this helps the bottom line.

Some companies still regard CSR as a costly exercise with no proof of tangible benefits. Yet those who do spend on CSR admit (off the record) that the amount they spend is a tiny fraction of their local profit in certain countries. Although it may be difficult to show that CSR boosts profits, particularly in the short term, it does – if it is genuine and well thought out – act as an insurance policy, providing protection against serious business risk. Managers may not like the CSR responsibilities, but it is important that they work closely with certain non-governmental pressure groups, whose influence should not be underestimated.

Other companies are suggesting a radical rethink of branding strategies around CSR issues. Global Legacy, an organisation run by Craig Cohon, a former Coca-Cola marketing executive, proposes that companies should view CSR as an active part of their marketing strategy. "Why not link brand to eradication of urban poverty or fighting against AIDS, for example?" Cohon asks. The same argument could be used for many other areas in emerging markets where the need for improvement is recognised, such as health, education, nutrition and water sanitation.

What a CSR strategy should contain

There are many things that companies do in emerging markets to show they care. These include:

- donating money and equipment to hospitals, universities, schools, kindergartens and orphanages;
- donating money and equipment for environmental clean-up programmes;
- financing vaccination programmes;
- creating scholarships for students;
- donating buses or ambulances to cities or trucks to local fire brigades;
- donating food and vitamin drinks to schoolchildren in poor countries;
- supporting local sporting events which might cease without corporate donations.

But companies need to think of new ways to link CSR activity with brand and corporate image. Bring in all employees to brainstorm. What is it that would really make a difference to the local community? What is urgent and badly needed? Do this frequently, not just once a year.

It is also crucial to make sure the public knows that you are good corporate citizens. Every time you do something, splash it all over the media. This can go further:

- Make the media aware of the financial contribution you are making to the country.
- Get journalists to talk to your blue-collar workers so they see you treat them well and pay fairly and on time.
- Tell local and international journalists how many jobs were created directly and indirectly because of your presence in the country. In case you need to lay off workers, create an outplacement and/or retraining centre to help them find new jobs.

One major area of pressure on companies in emerging markets is poor working conditions and child labour. Conditions must be acceptable, and this often means better than those laid down by law. This includes the conditions in operations run by subcontractors, which can be more difficult to control. Facilities should be inspected regularly. It is not enough for company representatives to visit a factory, check if quality and quantity are acceptable and leave. It is essential to talk to workers, hear their concerns and take action to improve things where necessary. Some companies have hired outside investigators to check how subcontractors treat workers and then acted on the findings.

This is how workers described working conditions to an investigative journalist in one of the Indonesian factories (apparently Taiwanese owned) working for a large American clothing company:

> If you want to go to the toilet you have to be lucky. If the supervisor says no, you wet your pants.

In another subcontractor's manufacturing facility, the women regularly worked 18-hour shifts without a break, journalists discovered. When a supply deadline approached, they were given amphetamines to drink, and they were fined for yawning in case someone saw them. Company inspectors were often in the plant, but the subcontractor fined workers for telling the truth.

This is the problem. Most companies have a code of conduct, which, on paper, protects workers' basic rights. But what happens in practice is too often very different, particularly in poor countries and in labour-intensive manufacturing. To prevent bad publicity, many newly socially aware companies now have full-time staff monitoring working conditions where manufacturing is outsourced.

Many economists argue that working in these conditions is better than having no job. "If workers are so unhappy, why do they work there?" they say. "Without foreign manufacturers, they would probably dig through the bins and starve. Now at least they can afford a less miserable way of life." There were sweatshops during the industrial revolution in western Europe and the United States, many argue, so why should it be different this time? Early in the 20th century, they say, it was still common to find child labourers in factories and on farms in many European countries, so why shouldn't a child in Indonesia work if this pays for the food for survival?

Whatever the merits of these arguments, companies should be cautious about the business implications of bad publicity. Not paying enough attention to workers' conditions could come to haunt them as public scrutiny intensifies. No one wants their brand identified with cruel working conditions.

14 Understanding and coping with emerging-market crises

The single most important thing that prevents us from meeting our targets in emerging markets is unpredictable devaluations.

Regional director, Procter & Gamble

Some of my markets are submerging, not emerging.

Regional vice-president, Bacardi-Martini

Think hard before you retrench in a crisis. If you stay you will have more loyal staff, be able to hire the best others lay off, and you will win new customers.

Regional director, Du Pont

In the 1990s crises hit Mexico (1994), Thailand and other Asian countries (1997), Russia (1998) and Brazil (1999). In the early 2000s it was Argentina's turn. Volatility is a characteristic of emerging markets. This chapter looks at the main causes and effects of such crises and considers the likelihood of them becoming less frequent and more predictable. Conventional wisdom suggests that companies should retrench during severe crises, and so retrenchment options are outlined. So too are the alternatives, with reference to companies that have reaped huge benefits by choosing to stay put or expand in times of economic crisis.

Crises in emerging markets are more frequent and more severe than in the developed world. But why do they happen? More worryingly, why do they spread so quickly, even to supposedly well-managed countries? What is the likelihood of a new crisis somewhere and where will it hit next? Managers living and operating in many emerging markets worry about these questions all the time.

Countries hit by a crisis suffer disproportionately, but the majority bounce back, many of them much faster than anyone would have expected.

Mexico

The Mexican collapse was serious. Economists who track recessions say this was one of the worst crises since the Great Depression in the United

States. Worse, the crisis spread to the rest of a traditionally volatile Latin America. What happened?

Foreign investors fell in love with Mexico in the late 1980s and early 1990s. The country's debt crisis was resolved. Mexico, the United States and Canada started to negotiate a North American Free Trade Agreement (NAFTA). The Mexican government was run by economists who were trained at leading American universities. Optimism and enthusiasm spread in the multinational business community as policies grew more liberal and macroeconomic stability seemed impossible to shatter.

But the seeds of instability were already being sown. The inflation rate stayed relatively high and, with a stable exchange rate, there was continuous real appreciation of the currency. As a result, Mexican exports gradually became less competitive. At the same time, as long-standing import barriers were dismantled and more multinationals started to push sales more aggressively (to buyers who felt richer because their currency had in effect become stronger), an import boom was inevitable. To add fuel to the fire, banks started to loan more and more money, which further encouraged demand for imports.

Economists started to worry that the situation was unsustainable and argued for a devaluation to restore competitiveness and push GDP growth higher than population growth. With foreign reserves decreasing, Mexico decided to devalue. But as Paul Krugman, a professor of economics at Princeton University, argued in his book *The Return of Depression Economics*, the authorities made several mistakes and failed to follow the golden rules. First, if a country decides to devalue, the devaluation has to be big enough to prevent speculators from betting on a further decline. Mexico devalued much less than economists and (nervous) markets expected. Second, after the devaluation, the authorities must appear fully in control of economic policies, or nervous investors might start to panic. As well as not following the golden rules, it emerged that certain Mexican businessmen were given inside information about the devaluation and that they profited from it. Soon foreign investors panicked, prompting a large flight of capital out of the country.

Once foreign portfolio capital starts stampeding out of a country (as later happened in Asia and elsewhere), it is hard to stop it. Panic sales of securities denominated in a local currency are quick, often irrational and ruthless, leaving the currency exposed to sharp falls. Investors all want out at the same time, as they try to minimise losses from a falling currency. The Mexican peso quickly lost half of its value. To convince investors to stay in the peso, interest rates reached almost 80%. Another problem fuelled the panic: Mexico had a large dollarised short-term debt and, with the peso weak, the debt ballooned.

Looking back, it is clear that a powerful force was at work, one frequently underestimated by economists obsessed with numbers rather than human behaviour: market psychology or market sentiment. "People value the comfort of the herd," wrote *The Economist*. Psychology would come to play an even bigger role in subsequent emerging-market crises, but in 1994 it received little attention in economic circles. Tellingly, in 2002 the Nobel prize for economics went to Daniel Kahneman, a psychologist, and Vernon Smith, an economist, for their work on market psychology.

Market sentiment on Mexico changed from enthusiasm to panic virtually overnight. When that happens, exchange-rate overshooting is inevitable (as masterfully explained in an economics paper written by the late Rudiger Dornbusch, when he was professor of economics at MIT) and rationality goes out of the window.

It is not just financial markets that are hit; the whole economy is too. In Mexico, sales – particularly those of multinationals – slumped together with the peso. The foreign banks that in the heady days had lent large sums to local banks and enterprises panicked too. They demanded immediate repayment and shut down new credit lines, exacerbating economic decline and accelerating the fall of the peso, which Mexican banks were forced to sell in order to repay their dollar loans. Many found they did not have enough cash so they made their local borrowers repay their loans.

The pattern has been repeated frequently since. In some cases, as in Argentina and Uruguay in 2002, consumers also panic and withdraw deposits. Whenever there is a run on a bank, the crisis becomes more entrenched and more difficult to recover from. Mexico avoided complete collapse thanks to financial support from the United States and the IMF. Companies operating in Mexico had a tough two years before it turned the corner to recovery. Had the United States not intervened, Mexico would probably have faced a repeat of its 1980s crisis, which lasted some eight years.

Managers running multinationals drew three worrying conclusions as the Mexican crisis unravelled and spread to the rest of Latin America. First, if it could happen in Mexico, which had a sound government and lacked fundamental economic problems, it could probably happen in any emerging country. Second, even an apparently firmly rooted positive perception of a market among media and analysts can change remarkably rapidly. Third, the policy mistakes that set off the crisis had a disproportionately negative effect, but the bounce-back came sooner than anyone anticipated.

These are the lessons of Mexico, but the Asian crisis in 1997 was even more complicated. Market sentiment was still to show its darker side.

Asia

The Asian crisis of 1997 was immense and unexpected. The way it spread from the small Thai economy to the rest of the region was frightening. Overnight, multinational companies went into crisis-management mode.

Pinpointing the reasons for the crisis is not easy. A number of South-East Asian economies had been growing rapidly for over two decades. Growth rates were so high that GDP doubled every decade in some countries. Most economists were entranced, but some questioned the growth figures and argued that the growth was based on bringing more people into the workforce and investing in physical capital and infrastructure. They found little evidence that productivity (output per unit of input) was going up in parallel. As economic theory argues, if growth is based only on growth in inputs, it is unsustainable, and the fast growth rates of the past, they concluded, are unlikely to be repeated.

Although this research offered a view on a future period of lower growth in Asia, there was no reason to suspect that this slowdown would cause a full-blown regional crisis. What happened? One explanation is crony capitalism, which exists in many other emerging markets. Crony capitalism is simple in its perversity and has many facets. For example, a group of friends or the family of the autocratic leader of a developing country gain control over state-owned banks which channel "loans" to other friends who, thanks to the loans, gain control over large enterprises. Assets get stripped and billions end up in private offshore bank accounts. Some of the money trickles back in a process called "the return of flight capital", but most of the capital does not return. "Loans" are not repaid; banks fail and are often bailed out by unsuspecting taxpayers. But cronyism is not a recent phenomenon and so it cannot explain why the crisis happened at that particular time and why it was so severe and so contagious.

Like Mexico, Thailand went from boom to bust in a very short period, through a typical currency crisis. Thailand shared in the emerging-markets enthusiasm of the early 1990s. The Latin American debt crisis was over, Mexico was a miracle, Asia was full of tiger economies and central and eastern Europe offered an unprecedented opening into a vast territory. Capital flowed happily to Thailand, mostly in bank loans and portfolio investment. But such portfolio capital can easily flee the country if market sentiment changes. As capital was flowing in, demand for the baht soared. The central bank, fearing that exports would suffer if the baht appreciated much in value, tried to preserve a fixed exchange rate. To meet the demand for more baht, it had to print more and sell it in exchange for foreign currency. No central bank likes a credit boom, but in this case it was particularly worrying. Domestic loans poured into the real-estate market, which was overheating. The central bank tried to reduce the money supply by selling government securities to mop up excess baht liquidity. But the scheme backfired. The new government securities were attractive to foreign buyers, returns increased and demand grew. The credit, imports and wage boom continued. The current-account deficit catapulted to levels that made markets nervous. It was then that crony capitalism kicked in, as corrupt banks lent recklessly to corrupt companies without caring about the risk. Foreign bankers made matters worse by continuing to lend to local banks, believing – correctly – that the government (with the help of multilaterals) would bail out such politically well-connected banks.

Observers became nervous. It was clear that if the boom continued it would inevitably drag the country into a currency crisis. When the first crony investments started to lose money, foreign lenders and institutional investors stopped pumping money into Thailand. The real-estate bubble burst and, as in Mexico, the boom turned to bust. Demand for the baht collapsed, and the central bank suddenly faced a different kind of problem. If it let the currency fall, it would worsen the indebtedness of local players because many owed foreign currency to their foreign lenders. A depreciation would also have serious implications for the real economy. However, if the central bank intervened to support the baht by selling its accumulated foreign-exchange reserves, it feared that the resulting reduction of the domestic money supply would make the recession worse (interest rates would certainly go up as a result).

Once a country faces a dilemma like this it becomes easy prey for currency speculators. Why not borrow baht, convert them promptly into dollars at a stable rate, sit on dollars, still owe baht, order a drink, sit on the beach, call a journalist friend to write a story that the baht is about to fall, wait for the baht to collapse, return the baht loan and walk away with a fortune.

At the same time, domestic businesses start to worry about a depreciation, so they carry out the same exercise as the speculators in order to pay back any dollar-denominated debt. In short, no one wanted to hold baht any more. When everyone could see that government intervention to support the baht was quickly exhausting the foreign-exchange reserves, the baht fell much more than expected and the government had to raise interest rates to persuade people to keep baht. So those with loans in dollars and in baht were affected: the former because the weaker baht made the dollar loans more expensive; and the latter because the interest rates on baht loans increased. With high interest rates and a weak currency, the recession hit the real economy and any multinational companies selling in the domestic market.

The Thai crisis started to spread to other Asian countries. Economic theories of contagion had always posited trade links as the main conduit. But the crisis spread to countries with which Thailand had few if any trading links. The main route for contagion was via western financial markets. Although it might be argued that a crisis in Thailand is no reason to pull money out of other Asian markets, many big banks and institutional investors in the West treated Asia as one emerging market (as they did with Latin America). They made little meaningful distinction between national markets and acted on a regional basis (which they are less prone to do these days). They also needed to compensate for losses in Thailand. Curiously, as the crisis spread within Asia, currencies in some central European economies also fell by 10–15%. The reason was similar: investors were looking at profitable markets and pulled out to cover for losses in Asia. Many simply said: "Forget about emerging markets. Just reduce exposure in all of them."

Would capital controls help avoid crises?

Why do all emerging-market countries allow hot capital (short-term portfolio investment, for example) to enter and exit so freely? Western European countries did not fully liberalise controls on capital-account movements (particularly short-term ones) for decades after the second world war. Most of them liberalised gradually after reaching a certain level of wealth and stability, and mostly only well into the 1980s and 1990s. In 1993 Maria Schaumayer, a former central bank governor of Austria, said: "The last thing we wanted to liberalise was international capital-account movements." Austria fully liberalised capital-account movements in November 1991, when it was already one of the wealthiest and most stable countries in the world. It liberalised its capital account fully only when its GDP per head reached some $24,000. In other words, many west European economies were able to develop without facing the risk that speculative capital inflows and outflows carry.

Would the crises in Mexico and Asia have been so severe without such large and volatile foreign capital inflows and outflows? Many economists argue that there would not have been a crisis were it not for panic hot-capital outflows. Countries – such as China, India, Chile and Slovenia – that had capital controls in place during emerging-market crises which might have spread to them stayed clear of contagion. So there seems to be some evidence that limited capital controls on speculative movements may act as a buffer against economic crises. According to Frank Rogoff, a former chief economist of the IMF:

> The IMF may have sometimes tilted too far towards benign neglect as countries prematurely liberalised markets for short-term capital movements, before the internal regulatory structure was in place to handle them.

But at the same time, he argues, it is becoming more difficult to enforce capital controls (even if they exist) and to some degree capital-account and trade liberalisation go hand in hand.

Among economists who question this view, the most prominent is Joseph Stiglitz, a Nobel prize winner, whose book *Globalisation and its Discontents*, published in 2001, summed up his disillusionment with the IMF/World Bank consensus. He argues that "excessively rapid financial and capital market liberalisation was probably the single most important cause of the [Asian] crisis". Did the fact that Austria had capital-account controls until 1991 hinder its record on trade, foreign direct investment (FDI), economic growth and wealth accumulation? Not really. So the question is why a developing country (which is far from being wealthy and stable) should allow any foreigner to buy or borrow its currency for a purpose that is not beneficial for the real local economy. In other words, why not have free capital movements in the case of productive FDI but only gradual lifting of controls on "unproductive" portfolio investment? These questions will continue to be debated for many years.

Financial market players claim that offshore schemes can easily disguise speculative capital as FDI and that local authorities would not be able to tell the difference. There are indeed many tricks, but when Malaysia controversially introduced limited capital controls in September 1998, they proved mostly effective even against such speculative transactions. Others claim that controls are a great way for a few local politicians to enrich themselves. This is true, but corruption exists anyway and using capital controls is just one of many ways for the powerful elite to get rich.

Elimination of capital controls does not eliminate corruption. It is worth remembering, however, that if emerging-market economies systematically reduced their financing requirements, they would be less exposed to these hot-money flows.

Much of the debate on recent crises has focused on how the IMF responded to them and if its prescribed medicine made them worse. The debate is a heated one, and it is interesting to reflect on how developed markets react to economic downturns. American companies would have been furious if the Federal Reserve had not reduced interest rates following the bursting of the stockmarket bubble and the subsequent economic slowdown. Those who live in the developed world take it for granted that central banks reduce interest rates in the face of a downturn. They also expect governments to spend a bit more to support recovery (short-term increase in fiscal spending) and to cut taxes.

But what did the IMF recommend when Asian economies were threatened by a crisis? It suggested raising interest rates and cutting fiscal spending (and even closing some banks). Credit-rating agencies (which have an influence on market perceptions) often take the same line. Fitch, for example, in its report on Mexico in late 2001, said that the country should consider cutting spending because it seemed its economy was slowing down. Would Fitch give the same advice to the United States? Ironically, Mexico's economy was responding to a sharp slowdown in the United States, its key trading partner.

Why does the IMF give advice like this, and what have been the consequences of such advice for the economies that implemented it? The IMF claims that when a crisis strikes, it is like a paramedic in a battlefield, trying to stop the bleeding. At such times, when capital wants to take flight, the primary aim is to restore confidence in the market to enable economic stability to return. So to preserve or restore confidence, the IMF orders remedies that go against the kind of Keynesian policies that are widely practised in the developed world. There is a lingering question in all this. Would there be a need to preserve market confidence (by raising interest rates sharply and cutting fiscal spending) if some capital controls on certain hot-money movements existed?

A paper entitled "Did Malaysian Capital Controls Work?", written by Ethan Kaplan and Dani Rodrik of Harvard University, appeared in 2001. It analysed what happened during the 1997 Asian crisis to South Korea and Thailand, which implemented the IMF's advice, compared with Malaysia, which introduced short-term capital controls on portfolio capital (not FDI or profit repatriation, for example). Importantly, the comparison was made at the moment the IMF's policies were implemented in other countries and Malaysia (which was continually slipping into crisis) introduced its capital controls. In their conclusions Kaplan and Rodrik state:

> Compared to IMF programmes, we find that the Malaysian policies produced faster economic recovery, smaller declines in employment and real wages, and more rapid turnaround in the stockmarket.

Incidentally, as well as implementing limited short-term capital controls, Malaysia reversed its initial response to the crisis which included raising interest rates and cutting spending.

South Korea and Thailand (both of which followed IMF advice) saw their economies begin to recover once confidence was restored, but their recovery took longer. Many argue that the severe slump they suffered might have been avoided if limited capital controls had been in place, preventing a sudden flight of short-term capital. China, despite high levels of corruption and an imperfect banking system, avoided the Asian crisis. You could not buy the local currency unless you had a good reason to do so.

The debate on capital controls is lively, but a consensus is emerging that certain capital controls were lifted too soon. Jeffrey Sachs of Harvard University argues that interest rates should not have been raised and that this would have resulted in only modest devaluations. Furthermore, not introducing draconian measures overnight would have caused less panic and that in itself would have stopped the currency slide at a better level.

Something similar happened in Brazil in 1999 proving Sachs's point (which is standard in the developed world). As markets started to lose their "confidence", the authorities devalued by 8%. This was not enough to reassure nervous investors and eventually the central bank stopped intervening. The currency stabilised spontaneously at a somewhat lower level and the stockmarket jumped by a third. Suddenly, investors started to believe in Brazil and the prospect of lower interest rates, which would drive recovery. Two days later, the IMF insisted to surprised Brazilian officials that to achieve real restoration of market confidence, interest rates should be raised further. The next day the Brazilian government announced that it would not lower interest rates and the currency plunged. In *The Return of Depression Economics*, Krugman says:

> What seems to have happened is that Washington officials had

become so committed to the idea that one must always raise
interest rates to defend the currency that they could not bring
themselves to consider the alternative.

But even small devaluations in some countries can create enormous problems. For example, in many countries a fall in the currency feeds the inflation rate as people (who are used to currency instability) "think" in hard currency. Also, in cases when there are large foreign currency debts, a devaluation increases the debt and creates all sorts of economic problems.

The IMF usually advises countries to undertake certain structural reforms as a precondition for financial help. It is impossible to find a country in the world that does not have some sort of structural problem – look at the Japanese banking system or EU labour laws, for example. But a growing number of economists argue that although it is important to solve structural problems, this can be done more easily in an environment that does not create sharp recessions as a result of high interest rates, severe cuts in spending, higher taxes and orders to shut down certain banks. Moreover, insisting on structural reforms as part of a short-term package creates unrealistic deadlines, making market players even more nervous.

So why were capital flows liberalised so soon in so many developing countries? Some blame the influence of Wall Street bankers, who saw an opportunity to make money. Some even claim it is part of a western conspiracy to economically control (recolonise) the developing world.

Whatever the explanation, many are irritated by the IMF's double standards. Turkey, which rarely fulfils any promises it makes to the IMF, was regularly receiving substantial amounts of bail-out money. Meanwhile, other countries of less geopolitical importance to the United States were refused funds, even though their record in implementing IMF programmes was similar to or even better than Turkey's. Sometimes the IMF refuses immediate relief to certain countries because of corruption (as it did Kenya before the 2003 elections), but it gave $10 billion to Indonesia in November 1997 after the Asian economic crisis.

What about the future?
Shocks
It is unlikely that things will improve in the foreseeable future. In free-trade talks with Chile and Singapore in 2002, the Bush administration said that it would penalise these countries if they ever used capital controls.

Jagdish Bhagwati from Columbia University and Daniel Tarullo from Georgetown University call this "a discouraging triumph of ideology over experience and good sense". In large part because there has been no real change in how financial markets behave, how the IMF behaves, how the American Treasury behaves and how hot money moves in and out of so many countries, there will be more crises in emerging markets. In such circumstances, it is most unlikely that governments will change the way they respond (or are forced to respond) when a crisis is in the offing or actually occurs.

Rebound
In most cases, markets will demonstrate their resilience and bounce back after a crisis.

Opportunity knocks despite the risks
Emerging markets are exceptionally profitable if the business approach is sound and geared towards long-term investing for sustainable profit growth.

What happens when a market collapses?
Crises happen expectedly and unexpectedly, but whichever is the case, companies should have, at the minimum, an idea of how to react to them.

When a crisis does hit, most companies automatically engage in a strategy to "protect the bottom line" and cut fixed costs, especially staff. After all, in the developed world, it is common practice to lay off people during an economic slowdown and start hiring again when things improve. But most emerging markets bounce back fairly quickly after a crisis and radical cost-cutting can leave a company too weak to take advantage of the upturn and at the mercy of braver competitors who use the crisis to build up market share cheaply.

The Russian example
In early September 1998, a few weeks after the Russian rouble crash, when most western companies were cutting staff and bemoaning their losses, a Moscow-based manager of a European multinational had started to interview people for several hundred sales positions. He expressed his delight:

This is my chance to get a better market position. All our publicly

> *listed competitors will go through their regular knee-jerk reaction*
> *and make cuts across the board. Their bosses demand they*
> *protect the bottom line for this and the next quarter immediately.*
> *Our owners don't care about the next few quarters.*

The next day a general manager in charge of Russian operations for a publicly quoted multinational said:

> *I got a call last night from headquarters and the big boss said*
> *I knew what I had to do. I tried to ask if I could keep certain*
> *individuals but he interrupted and said that the budget is the*
> *most important thing at the moment.*

The decision was disappointing but did not surprise him. When told about the company starting to hire during the crisis, he said: "That's what I would do if this were my company."

Most Russia-based managers of publicly listed companies that year were reluctant to implement a knee-jerk reaction from the top but had little choice. One manager said:

> *When this crisis is over, and it will be over sooner than people*
> *think [which proved correct], I will be without some great, well-*
> *trained people and there are so many things I'll have to do all*
> *over again. Time and money will be lost. Worse, our market*
> *position will surely suffer.*

The Russian market started to recover less than a year later. By then, privately held foreign companies and domestic companies had strengthened their market positions. Local companies also benefited from a switch to cheaper local products by impoverished consumers. In these companies, which had maintained or even increased staff numbers, staff loyalty rose, turnover increased and market share jumped.

By contrast, those companies that had cut staff and costs did not have the human resources needed to take advantage of new business opportunities. When they started to hire, after spending a long time convincing headquarters it was a good idea to do so, the cost was high (as usual) and the quality of those who applied was not as good (on average) as those they had got rid of. Furthermore, they had acquired a reputation for not being loyal to their staff – and reputation matters when you are trying to attract able and qualified staff from a shallow pool of talent and experience.

Squaring the circle

Even if the pressure to cut costs cannot be avoided, companies should consider these options:

- ◪ **Redeploy staff.** Some companies send skilled, trained executives to other growth markets around the world or to headquarters until the crisis markets show signs of bouncing back. To enable this kind of movement, companies with operations in crisis-prone emerging markets should have a system which allows quick global reaction to a crisis.
- ◪ **Cut pay not staff.** Ask staff if they would take a pay cut instead of facing lay-offs. It is important that staff understand the pressure from the top and that the pay cut will last only until sales return to pre-crisis levels. In Russia, white-collar workers often approached their management with this kind of proposal and in many cases it was accepted. Hire and fire policies are culturally unacceptable in many emerging markets.
- ◪ **Cut alternatives to staff.** Look at other ways of cutting costs before laying off staff. Renegotiate the rent, for example, or move to a cheaper location. Remove the hard-currency link to locally paid salaries of white-collar employees.

During crises, companies are under pressure to raise prices, but doing this to, say, negate or reduce the effect of a devaluation will not work because consumers will not be able to pay the new prices. Conversely, maintaining local prices after a devaluation is dangerous because it is likely to mean selling at a loss and it may set a precedent with regard to prices. Finding the balance is hard and varies according to the sector.

Some companies argue that crises turn out to be positive for their operations, making them lean and mean, and providing an opportunity to get rid of average and bad performers. Maybe – but at what cost? In emerging markets, it is better to hire the right people in the first place and focus on steady growth. When a crisis strikes, consider buying or acquiring local firms that have suddenly become cheaper. Or consider acquiring more land, especially if you are planning to expand manufacturing in the medium term.

Is the next crisis just around the corner?

It has been hard for institutional investors to earn decent returns in recent years. The bursting of the stockmarket bubble in the late 1990s and early 2000s created a tough market for investment in equities, and returns on government bonds or cash in safe havens have been low. To generate good returns, institutional investors have put money in more risky investments, increasing their exposure to emerging-market risk to the highest level since the 1997 Asian crisis. This explains why the prices of emerging-market securities have risen in recent years. It also partly explains the unusually big rises in commodity prices, from oil to copper. In 2006, the yield spread of emerging-market debt over American Treasuries reached its lowest level since 1998. Meanwhile, many emerging-market governments have been borrowing in hard currency because of low interest rates on the world's major currencies, especially the yen and the Swiss franc.

This poses two major threats to economic stability. First, institutional investors' positive sentiment towards emerging markets might reverse. If this reversal is sudden and panicky (which can be expected), the outflow of portfolio investment will destabilise some emerging-market economies. The contagion may also spread regionally and even globally. The rush to exit from what seems a bit of a bubble would be triggered by enthusiasm about investment vehicles in the developed world or their safe-haven status at times of market uncertainty and turmoil. Second, increases in interest rates in developed economies would increase the cost of debt servicing for the emerging-market economies that have increased their borrowing to unsustainable levels, hitting those with high debt burdens and no capital controls first.

Companies operating in emerging markets should be aware of these risks and monitor them. Countries with high current-account deficits, high debt burdens (especially short-term external debt), high public debt and high budget deficits are more exposed to outflows of hot money than others. These are the key indicators of the potential risk.

However, in recent years the number of emerging countries that are likely to suffer major crisis as a result of hot-money outflows has fallen. Many countries, particularly in Asia, learned some hard lessons during the 1997 crisis. They have built up external surpluses and prudent fiscal policies which should help to shield them from negative market sentiment. Many countries have also built up record levels of foreign exchange reserves which has a twofold effect. First, it will enable central banks to intervene and protect their currencies in case of major panic about emerging markets. Second, it reduces their dependence on the IMF and other borrowing. The 2006 "mini" emerging-market crisis proves the point that the emerging world is now much more stable than it was 6–10 years ago. When investors suddenly started to pull out of emerging markets in the spring of 2006 there were notable encouraging differences from previous crises. First, the crisis was largely limited to countries that have twin deficits and/or large debt burdens being ramped up as a result of speculative inflows. Second, it showed that the scale of crisis was much lower. In the past, the Turkish lira would have dropped 50% or more; this time the fall was closer to 20%. Third, it showed that portfolio investors and speculators are now much more selective. They do not think of emerging markets as one any more.

All this is encouraging, but in the case of widespread panic it is hard to guess how people will behave. This is precisely why companies should not be complacent. Past crises have always appeared suddenly and with unbelievable speed. As the crises of the 1990s show, even well-managed markets can suffer steep currency depreciations once market panic starts. Managers operating in markets that are dependent on overpriced commodities should warn their senior managers of possible reversals of fortune. Furthermore, any country with high deficits, debts and overvalued currencies should be treated with special care, especially when budgeting.

PART 2
THE OUTLOOK FOR DIFFERENT MARKETS

15 The global economy

This chapter aims to provide an assessment of trends and risks in the global economy that will allow executives to benchmark their business activity and help them reduce expectations at corporate board level which are invariably unrealistically high.

Globalisation

In the past globalisation was mostly confined to free trade in goods and services, but since the bursting of the technology bubble in 2001 the transfer of jobs and skills across borders has gathered pace, as western companies have sought to reduce costs by such strategies as outsourcing or offshoring. This will greatly reduce the number of low value-added manufacturing jobs in the developed world and will also have an effect in the services sector. In 2006 Jean-Marie Folz, CEO of PSA Peugeot Citroen, remarked that he did not "see us ever building a new plant in Europe again". Peugeot Citroen has invested heavily in Slovakia, where average annual salaries are much, much lower than in western Europe.

The offshoring of jobs is often attacked by politicians, labour unions and in the media, but more western jobs have been lost in the past decade as a result of recession and technology-driven productivity than through offshoring. Furthermore, it can be argued that offshoring benefits the developed economies because it helps companies become more profitable and therefore more able to employ more highly skilled staff. Supporters of this argument claim that for every US job that is offshored, 1.4 jobs are created in the United States. But outsourcing and offshoring have not been without their problems and some firms have ended up bringing jobs back home. A likely trend is an increase in near-shoring, especially in manufacturing. For example, US firms may increase manufacturing operations in Mexico, and western European firms may set up in central and eastern Europe.

In the past decade China has become the factory of the world and India, with its well-educated, English-speaking, technologically adept workforce, has sought to become the world's back-office. These developments have brought prices down and boosted the spending power of western consumers. As China, Russia and central and eastern Europe follow the market route to development there will be a huge expansion of their middle classes with money to spend. This will both boost their local economies and provide an opportunity for western Europe and the United States to make products for those markets.

This will require increased investment in R&D, skills training and education, where many countries in western Europe have fallen behind. The 2000 European Union Lisbon summit set itself the task of making the EU the world's most competitive area, but there are few signs of that happening. Some 400,000 European science and technology graduates now work in the United States and only about one-third plan to return to Europe, and much of Europe's pharmaceuticals industry research has moved to the United States.

Europe does have a competitive advantage in mobile phones, semiconductors, medical equipment and aeronautics, but it is less strong in more advanced, fast-growing fields such as biotechnology, biopharma, IT and instrumentation.

Why emerging markets are better and what drives them

In developed markets it has become hard for companies involved in selling goods rather than services to achieve revenue growth of more than 1–4%, which is why so many are turning to emerging markets. In 2004, for example, in China and Russia firms were achieving 20–35% revenue growth, in Turkey 10–35%, and in places like Iran and Dubai 10–25%. For profits earned in currencies that have held up well against the currency they will be converted to for group accounting purposes, the picture is even rosier.

Emerging markets have been benefiting from a number of factors: high import demand from China; higher commodity prices; higher oil prices (for the oil producers); a falling dollar, which has helped the competitiveness of markets whose currencies are pegged to the dollar; and low global interest rates, which have reduced the cost of debt servicing. Many emerging markets have implemented structural reforms and reined back their budget deficits, and few retain unsustainably high currency pegs; indeed, several have benefited from "weak" currencies to boost their exports. But the increases in interest rates and lower commodity prices would bring about a less benign environment.

Emerging markets are sure to play a more important role in the business of global multinationals. Countries such as China, Russia, India and Brazil, followed by Turkey and perhaps one day Iran, will be (and in some cases already are) the engines of corporate growth. By 2015, China and India will account for 25% of world output in real terms and by 2025, 50% of world exports will come from emerging market economies, compared with only 10% in 1980 and 25% in 2004.

Which way are the big global markets heading?

The global economy recovered fairly quickly from the downturn of 2001, but many companies outside the "easy" sectors of finance, energy and military equipment found themselves under constant pressure to produce better results.

Global growth should fall from 5.3% in 2006 to about 4.5% during 2007–10 as a result of slower growth in the United States. It should not fall much further thanks to continued strong growth in emerging markets, such as China, Russia, India, Turkey, central and eastern Europe, Brazil and parts of South-East Asia, and increased demand from oil producers.

Rising interest rates and the slowing housing market reported in 2006 should help bring US GDP down in 2007 before it picks up again to between 3% and 3.5% in 2008–10. The euro area economy will remain sclerotic: growth in 2006 may have crept above 2% for the first time in five years, but for the next five years it is likely to average around 1.9%. The underlying reason for the upward blip in 2006 was enhanced German consumer spending driven by the World Cup tournament and perkier spending in anticipation of the VAT tax hike of January 2007 as consumers stocked up before prices increased. Growth in the other major developed economy, Japan, picked up sharply from 2004 but peaked at

Table 15.1 **GDP growth forecasts, 2006–09**

	2006	2007	2008	2009
US	3.4	2.5	3.0	3.2
Euro area	2.6	2.2	1.9	2.1
Germany	2.7	2.3	2.0	1.9
Italy	1.6	1.3	1.5	1.5
France	2.0	1.8	2.1	1.9
UK	2.7	2.4	2.3	2.1
Japan	2.5	1.8	1.4	1.2
India	9.2	8.4	8.0	7.5
China	10.7	10.0	9.4	8.5
Brazil	3.6	3.7	3.5	4.0
Russia	6.5	6.2	6.1	5.9
Turkey	6.1	5.2	5.2	5.3

2.8% in 2006. The outlook for the next five years in Japan is likely to be average annual GDP growth of around 1.7%.

Table 15.2 **World summary, 2001–10 (%)**

	2001	2002	2003	2004	2005	2006	2007	2008	2009	2010
Real GDP growth[a]										
OECD	1.1	1.5	1.9	3.1	2.6	3.0	2.2	2.5	2.5	2.5
Non-OECD	4.8	5.2	6.9	8.4	7.7	7.9	7.5	6.9	6.4	6.2
World	2.6	3.1	4.1	5.5	4.9	5.3	4.7	4.7	4.5	4.6
Regional growth summary										
North America	0.8	1.7	2.5	3.9	3.2	3.3	2.5	3.0	3.2	3.0
Western Europe	1.9	1.5	1.6	2.7	2.0	2.8	2.3	2.3	2.4	2.4
Transition economies	4.2	3.8	5.8	6.6	5.5	6.6	5.8	5.2	4.5	4.4
Asia & Australasia	2.1	3.1	4.1	4.9	4.9	5.3	4.9	4.2	4.0	4.0
Latin America	0.3	−0.4	2.1	5.8	5.0	4.5	3.7	3.5	3.6	3.7
Middle East & North Africa	3.4	2.1	5.0	6.2	5.7	5.6	5.1	4.5	4.3	4.2
Sub-Saharan Africa	3.1	3.7	4.8	4.9	5.3	5.7	5.1	5.1	5.3	5.7
Inflation (av)										
OECD	2.1	1.4	1.8	1.9	2.2	2.7	2.5	2.2	2.1	2.0
World	3.0	2.5	2.9	2.8	3.1	3.5	3.3	3.1	2.9	2.9
Trade in goods										
Developed countries	4.1	1.7	2.7	7.5	5.8	7.3	5.8	5.9	6.0	6.0
Developing countries	−11.6	8.8	12.5	18.4	11.7	13.1	10.9	10.9	11.0	11.0
World	−0.3	3.7	5.6	10.9	7.8	9.3	7.6	7.7	7.9	7.9

a At purchasing power parity exchange rates.
Source: Economist Intelligence Unit, 2006

Rich and poor

Companies in the United States and western Europe became cash rich thanks to strong corporate profits stemming from cost-cutting implemented in 2001–05. This cost-cutting has focused on slimming down the workforce, pay freezes and even pay cuts. In developed countries, real wage levels for many are not growing. Companies may be rich, but many of those who work for them feel no better, or even worse, off.

The curious thing is that so many companies do not really know what to do with their new-found riches: most have been paying off debt, buying back stock or putting the money into government bonds – boring for sure, but better than embarking on ill-considered and expensive mergers.

Few companies are reinvesting in their businesses. The world's 40 largest multinationals now employ an average of 55% of their workforces abroad and earn 59% of their revenues outside their domestic markets. In France and Germany, only 45–50% of staff are employed in the home market. In the United States, consumption is fuelled by credit not by growth in real wages. In Germany, real wages are falling. Only 33% of German firms' total turnover is generated in the home market, compared with 80% in Japan and 70% in the United States (although this figure falls to 55% for larger American companies).

What US companies earned from interest on money sitting in the bank doubled in the two years from 2004 and could account for as much as 3.6% of earnings for American industrial companies (excluding cash-rich banks). Put another way, their cash holdings of $650 billion in 2006 represented 7% of the companies' stockmarket value, the highest level in 20 years; for IT companies the proportion was 13% of stockmarket value.

The corporate profit outlook

Economic well-being depends largely on companies making healthy profits. Average year-on-year profit growth in the United States was running at 16% in 2005, with military equipment producers, energy companies and banks enjoying the highest growth. Companies in other sectors were mostly reporting profit growth of less (often much less) than 10%. This compares with average corporate profit growth in 2005 of 12% in Japan, 6% in Germany and 3–4% in the UK and France. With growth rates quite low in Europe, they are unlikely to go much lower and may even rise by one or two percentage points.

The reasons for profits coming under pressure are clear:

- rising interest rates;
- high oil prices;
- high commodity prices;
- rising employment;
- workers demanding higher pay.

And so there will be even more pressure to squeeze costs in budgets.

Profits in the United States will be buttressed by a weaker dollar enhancing exports, and all companies will boost profits by outsourcing to emerging markets. French and German companies now make 60% of their profits outside their home markets.

Rising interest rates

Increases in interest rates will slow growth and depress corporate profitability in markets such as the United States. They will also reduce international liquidity and raise the financing costs of many emerging-market economies such as Turkey.

One impact of rising interest rates was a slowdown in the so-called international "carry trade" whereby those such as investment banks and hedge funds borrow short at cheap interest rates and lend long at higher ones and/or speculate in purchasing emerging-market debts and/or commodities and oil. Carry trade has certainly been one factor in the global oil-price hike (and may account for 20% of the price rise in 2003–06) and any future slowdown in oil prices may be attributable in part to this trend abating. The carry trade becomes less attractive (that is, more risky) when people want to borrow and speculate at a time when US interest rates have risen from 1% to over 5%. The mini global crisis of May 2006 was almost entirely the result of investors moving to dollar safe havens as US interest rates rose to 5.25%, and the Bank of Japan announced an increase in the bank rate from zero to 0.25%.

The Fed and the Bank of England have been responsible for the most aggressive interest policy. Both argue that they are raising rates to combat inflation, but they are also seeking to slow down the housing and credit booms in both countries and avoid a house-price crash.

Betting the house

House price rises are the main reason why the total value of US household assets has increased by $6 trillion. Americans have felt richer and have been on a long spending spree. In the period 2001–03, consumer spending rose 3% per year in the United States and kept the economy afloat, whereas the rate of growth in the euro area was only 1%. Household debt in the euro area is the equivalent of 80% of personal disposable income, but the figure is 120% in the United States and 140% in the UK.

Europe has less-developed credit and mortgage systems in place, and remortgaging in many European countries is an expensive option. Consumer spending in Europe is mainly driven by income trends, whereas in much of the Anglo-Saxon world (the United States, the UK and Australia) it is driven by asset prices and personal debt. House price rises also explain some of the distinctions within Europe, where the French and Spanish economies are noticeably stronger than those of Germany and Austria. House prices have risen steadily in France and massively in Spain, whereas in Germany and Austria they have been flat for the past decade or even fallen in real terms.

The US dollar outlook

In 2002–04 the markets favoured a strong dollar because US growth was superior to that of the euro area or Japan. In this period there was little interest-rate differential and euro-area interest rates were often higher than US ones. But they were not attractive enough to compensate for the growth differential. During 2004–05 the markets again preferred the dollar over the euro and yen on account of US growth levels, and at this point US interest rates were also rising.

No matter what hits the US economy, the dollar seems to be able to sustain a higher exchange rate level than in theory it should.

Why is the dollar so strong?

During 2003–06 the dollar fell by about 25% and it is likely to stay at $1.25–1.35 to the euro. But given its record trade and current-account deficits, and its high budget deficit, the dollar ought to be much weaker. A large part of the reason it does not crumble is that Asian central banks hold more than $1.5 trillion of US assets, accounting for more than 50% of their total assets. They do this to prop up the dollar so that their own currencies stay relatively weak. This allows their exporters to sell aggressively into the American market at "cheap prices/exchange rates". It is not just the Chinese but most of the major Asian central banks that do this. The risk they run is that they would be obliged to sell dollars to buy their own currencies if domestic inflation started to rise rapidly. If they did this, the dollar would plunge.

Other reasons for the dollar holding up are that US GDP growth is above euro-area and Japanese levels, and US interest rates are higher than in the euro area and Japan.

There has also been an increase in inward investment into the United States. Private investors have been investing in dollar assets, attracted in part by the US mortgage market, which has been driven by a booming real estate sector.

The dollar was also given a helping hand by the 2005 Homeland

Investment Act, which temporarily reduced the tax on repatriated US corporate profits from 35% to 5.25%. The total impact of this in 2005 was to be an extra $150 billion in repatriated earnings. But most companies can no longer take advantage of this reduced tax rate.

In the long run, however, the US current account is unsustainable. If the dollar fell gradually and steadily over, say, 18 months to $1.50 to the euro it would not be a problem, and indeed it would benefit the United States and the global economy. The longer the dollar stays strong and the current-account deficit increases, the more risk is being stored up for the future.

For the moment it seems likely that the financial markets will take the view that America's relatively high growth rate and interest rates mean that they can put any concerns about the budget and current-account deficits to one side. As long as America is getting $2 billion of net investment per day, the message is "don't worry, be happy".

Also for the time being, Asian central banks seem content to continue to collude in keeping the dollar up to encourage their own exports. However, one major risk is that high oil prices will eventually push inflation up, forcing the sale of dollar assets. This will be fine if it is controlled and does not involve a "rush to the door".

There are many reasons why the dollar should fall, but a plunge in its value, which China could provoke by cutting itself free from dependence on it, would have devastating consequences.

The dollar's euro effect

What is perhaps remarkable is that the weakening of the dollar has not hurt European corporate performance more than it has. This is because 20% of the top 500 publicly quoted European companies' sales come from exports to the United States or from US subsidiaries. But earnings growth has been maintained or increased often as a result of cost savings.

It seems that European companies can live with a dollar/euro exchange rate of up to $1.30–1.35. Supporting this view, a survey in 2005 of German manufacturers put the pain threshold for 90% of companies at an exchange rate of $1.30.

European companies without manufacturing subsidiaries in the United States have been hurt the most. DSM, a Dutch chemicals group, reckons that a 1% move in the dollar value has a €10m impact on profits. The company has the worst mix: 80% of sales in dollars and around 70% of production in the euro area. SAP America has complained that as its results are measured in euros back at German headquarters, it has to grow by 20–25% in the United States just to stand still.

One feature of business has been that many European companies have not wanted to be priced out of the US market by exchange-rate fluctuations. During 2004, many chose to cut their prices to compensate for the exchange-rate price increase, thus retaining their market share in the important US market. But price cutting to compensate for exchange-rate increases, which are getting worse, is not a sustainable strategy. European companies may find themselves priced out of the US market, or they may have to find ways to live with a rate stronger than $1.30 to the euro.

Oil and commodity prices outlook

The global oil price outlook

The global oil price is likely to be $60–70 a barrel until 2008, after which the price is likely to fall but remain over $50 a barrel. The downward trend is predicated on slightly weaker global growth, and therefore less demand for oil, and an improvement in deliveries and supplies from new fields. But this consensus view could prove wrong and the price could remain above $70 per barrel if China, India and other emerging markets, along with the United States, continue to guzzle oil at high rates. Geopolitical risks in the Middle East could also ensure high prices.

Previous oil price spikes in 1973 and 1979 stemmed from supply shortages, and the price tumbled when supply was restored. Current high prices are driven by demand, especially from the United States, China and India. This is underlined by the fact that the annual rise in oil consumption in 2004 was the largest in 20 years. A weaker dollar also has an effect on the oil price, and OPEC has been taking a harder line on the dollar price per barrel. There is another supply problem on the demand side: little space capacity in either production or refining.

Oil prices in real terms are, however, not so bad: the 1980 equivalent price would be over $90 a barrel. Furthermore, developed economies use 5% less oil per dollar of GDP compared with the 1970s. The problem today is that China, India and other developing economies are not nearly as energy efficient as the big oil users of three decades ago.

The inflationary impact of oil prices affects global GDP growth. The IMF calculates that a $10 rise in the price of oil equates to a 0.6% fall in global GDP in the subsequent year. This would have meant a 2% fall in global GDP in 2006–07, whereas only a 1% fall is estimated.

Factors that may lead to lower oil prices include:

- ▣ the possibility that demand will not increase but stay steady;
- ▣ increases in Venezuelan oil streams;
- ▣ the development of new fields and pipelines, ensuring more volume from non-OPEC sources including Kazakhstan, Azerbaijan, Canada and West Africa;
- ▣ Iraq's oil coming back on stream;
- ▣ lower dependency on oil in the developing world – oil's share of OECD imports in value is now 4% compared with 13% in 1979; the United States uses 50% less oil per unit of GDP than it did in 1973 as its economy has moved from manufacturing to services.

Over the longer term things get hazier. By 2013, the world will be consuming 20% more oil than today, with consumption rising from 77m barrels per day in 2003 to 90m barrels per day in 2013. Demand for oil in China will rise significantly (China became a net oil importer in 1993) and US demand is expected to increase by 25% in the next 15 years. This, too, need not entail a sharp price hike as by then Iraq's fields should be fully on stream along with other new ones.

Non-oil commodity prices
Demand from China in recent years has driven up most commodity prices – both food and non-food – by about 10% a year. The outlook for non-oil commodities including food for 2006–09 is that they will stay broadly where they are today. But there is a 15% chance they will rise 10% from current levels, a 10% chance they will fall 5–15% and a 5% chance they will rise 15% or more.

Inflation
The oil price rose from some $28 per barrel in 2004 to about $70 per barrel in 2006, but for most of that time the inflation rate in developed economies barely moved upwards and in many emerging markets it fell, thanks to a tightening of economic policy with regard to budget deficits. At the end of 2006 top-line inflation in major developed markets ranged between 2.2% and 3.8%, with core inflation at 1.5–2.5%. There are several explanations for this apparent contradiction.

The world economy is nothing like that of 1973 and 1979, when big hikes in oil prices led to inflation and stagflation. Oil now plays a smaller role in GDP growth and it is a smaller element in trade flows. Furthermore, major economies are more oil-efficient.

As business turned downwards in 2001, most global corporations introduced severe cost-cutting programmes. The pressures on business stemmed from years of globalisation, price competition, deregulation and tightening in the retail sector, together with e-commerce and price transparency, deflation in many markets and low inflationary expectations.

Few companies today feel comfortable passing on price hikes to their customers, and consumers have come to expect cheap prices. Low inflation has meant that workers are not demanding high wage increases – indeed companies in Europe and Germany, such as Volkswagen and Siemens, were able to reduce wages in 2004–06 by insisting on longer hours for no increase in pay.

China plays a dual role in global inflation: it both helps raise and slow inflation. Global inflation rises because China's booming economy sucks in energy supplies and commodities, which is one factor behind the surge in commodity prices. By contrast, China helps bring down global prices by manufacturing cheap products that are then exported. For example, in 2004 Wal-Mart purchased $15 billion worth of products from China. These were invariably cheap consumer goods which were sold at cheap prices in Wal-Mart's stores. Those cheap prices helped keep US inflation down and encouraged American consumers to spend.

The US economy

The US economy has helped underpin western economies since the global downturn of 2001, but it remains uncertain how much Europe can absorb US exports driven by a weaker dollar. Japan may be able to take more exports from the United States, but its recovery is likely to be short-lived. Furthermore, America's GDP growth is likely to drop from 3.5% in 2006 to below 3% in 2007 and then average about 3.3% over the next three years. The reasons for a future slowdown are fairly clear:

- 35% of US growth stems from military spending and it is doubtful that this will be maintained;
- 20% of growth comes from consumer spending directly linked to the tax cuts of 2003–04;
- 20% stems from other consumer spending driven by massive levels of personal debt backed by housing remortgages.

Most of the growth has come from government consumption and consumer spending. Corporations have held back from investing and hiring, partly because they have taken advantage of the technology investment of the 1990s which means they have needed fewer workers. They have also been "offshoring" jobs.

However, against a background of rising productivity and booming house prices, those in jobs have been spending, with the result that the US savings ratio of 1.5% of disposable income in 2003 was close to its historic low. In the 12-year period 1992–2003, US consumer spending rose by 55% compared with 23% in the euro area and 16% in Japan. Total household debt leapt by $900 billion in 2003, almost twice as much as in 1999, a strong economic year. With record low interest rates and low bond yields, such levels of debt were less expensive and less risky. But of major concern now is the extent to which American household income is leveraged against a background of booming government deficits and rising interest rates.

The policies of Alan Greenspan, head of the Federal Reserve until 2006, helped mitigate the economic downturn of 2001–03. But to lessen the pain of the burst bubble of 2001 and to avoid recession he may have helped to create another economic bubble (built on debt and a real estate boom).

US companies have cut their borrowing substantially in recent years (unlike consumers) and are relatively cash rich, but the fragility of markets, at home and abroad, make it hard to decide what to do with the money. Some have chosen nothing more exciting than buying back their equity or are simply sitting on the cash pile. Others have invested in emerging-market operations.

US households save less than 2% of their disposable income compared with 12% in the euro area; and total household debt in the United States equals 84% of GDP, whereas it is relatively low in the euro area at 50%. But since 2006 business-to-business spending has picked up.

Most earnings growth in the United States is in the energy, military and banking sectors, and when they are removed the figures drop from 25–30% to around 5%. This is another reason CEOs are looking beyond the home market.

Europe

The problems of the euro area are its macroeconomic, fiscal and monetary policies. Real interest rates are too high, fiscal policy is too tight and labour markets are too rigid. Consumer confidence is fragile, and those worried about their pensions will be increasingly reluctant to spend. Domestic demand is weak as governments have to retrench on spending to meet the targets of the euro area's Stability and Growth Pact, and the euro is likely be too strong for European exporters to sell their way out of trouble. On top of this, the EU spends half its budget on subsidising farmers through the common agricultural policy.

The outlook for the euro area remains sober, despite a pick-up in 2006.

Germany

German economic and commercial risk has worsened with the new coalition government, thanks in large part to VAT increases in 2007 which could prove detrimental to growth and confidence. The CEO of Procter & Gamble stated in 2006 that he anticipated little growth for his company in Germany and the EU-15 in the next few years; other companies such as Unilever, Nestlé, McDonald's and Heinz are saying much the same. In 2006 Heinz sold its west European assets in frozen foods to reinvest the revenue in emerging markets. Major beer companies report the German market as flat with little growth future.

The problems for Germany, and in large part for Italy and France, are:

- weak domestic demand;
- low inflation;
- consumers waiting for prices to fall in a deflationary environment;
- a savage price discount model in the retail sector (see below) which passes pressure up the supply chain;
- few companies confident enough to pass on price rises to customers;
- high unemployment;
- high labour costs and related employment costs;
- increasing cost of capital;
- low commercial confidence in the business world.

Business confidence in Germany has taken a knocking. German banks have languished while major Austrian banks (Bank Austria, Erste Bank and Raiffeisen) have seen their share prices double in recent years and have benefited from the surge of business and their investment in central and eastern Europe.

In addition to the problems listed above, two long-standing reasons for Germany being in this state are the €1.5 trillion cost of rebuilding east Germany and the rate at which the D-mark joined the euro.

The "Aldi" discount retail model has been widely adopted and companies are wary of passing on price increases. Germany is now home to half of Europe's 28,000 discount retail outlets and their market share of total retail sales has risen to 36%, compared with 13% in France. Insolvencies among retailers are high and profits are low; even Wal-Mart has not yet reported profits from its German operations.

Investment weakened in Germany in 2002–06 as outsourcing accelerated. At the start of 2005 some 40% of companies in the German auto sector had offshored production to Asia or, more often, to central and eastern Europe. Of the 60% of companies which had not, some 80% were considering doing so. Many US companies located in Germany have been cutting staff and investment; they see Germany more as an end market for products manufactured elsewhere.

German companies began to return to profit in 2004 after three bad years, but this profitability was usually achieved through cost cutting. In 2006 German companies started to reinvest at home, and despite the low starting point this has helped domestic investment.

The main threat to the German economy is rising interest rates set by the European Central Bank (ECB). The German government seems to be following the ECB's rigorous line, which is likely to set back recovery. The government has set itself the target of bringing the budget deficit down to 3% in 2007 through tax hikes and spending cuts. It is a policy that could make a delicate situation worse.

On the plus side, Germany is the world's largest exporter of visible goods (with more than 10% of global manufactured goods), although China looks set to surpass it in 2008. Moreover, its export strength has not been achieved through exchange-rate fluctuations but through its high-quality manufacturing and engineering skills. Unit labour costs have fallen sharply, making Germany more competitive than other EU markets and as competitive as the United States. German companies are making more profits, and most big banks have their cost structures under control. Companies such as Deutsche Telecom, Deutsche Post and SAP are global successes (the weaker spot is among mid-sized service and financial companies). Skills and education levels are high.

But no country can run a decent economy without solid domestic demand and strong household consumption. In developed countries, domestic consumption usually accounts for between 60% and 70% of total GDP; Germany finds itself at the bottom of this scale while the UK is at the top.

Italy
Italy is the new sick man of Europe, with stagnant demand, weak exports, a large public debt and a large budget deficit. Public debt is 105% of GDP,

compared with 65% in Germany and France. Indicators on confidence and manufacturing and services output have been falling.

Italy's slow growth stems from the lack of structural reforms. The country is too dependent on small manufacturing companies involved in textiles, furniture, food processing and white goods. Such companies need a low cost base, and in the past whenever there was inflation the lira was devalued; under the euro regime this is no longer possible. Unfortunately for Italy, these companies, which in the past had competitive advantages and produced high-quality goods, now face intense competition from lower cost firms in central and eastern Europe and China. Small manufacturers do not have the scale or the cash to invest in R&D and investment to compete with their lean, low-cost competitors abroad. Expenditure on R&D is half the EU average. Labour costs are high: between 2000 and 2005, wages in Italy rose 40% more than in Germany.

Given the small (often family) firm structure of Italian manufacturing, companies are reluctant to save costs by outsourcing and offshoring production. Corporate governance has also proved a problem in Italy, with a number of high-profile scandals in recent years. It is this and uncertainties about the tax and legal systems that deters foreign direct investment (FDI): between 1993 and 2002 FDI totalled $73 billion, compared with $394 billion in Germany and $322 billion in France.

Italy also suffers in the modern internet age from poor education levels compared with other European economies and the keen workers of central and eastern Europe.

Given current EU policies, and the country's particular problems, it is quite likely that the Italian economy will continue on much the same course as it has in recent years.

The UK
Britain's economy has been remarkably resilient over the past decade, much of the boost coming from private consumption stimulated by strong credit expansion and a surge in the services sector. Whenever tax revenues fell below expectations in 2000–05, the government would intervene in spending increases which were also part of a concerted plan to invest in health and education. Manufacturing, however, has weakened, as have exports. A balanced budget in 1998 turned into a deficit hovering around 3% in 2006. GDP growth fell from 3.2% in 2005 to less than 2% in 2006, but it should stabilise at about 2.3% for several years.

There are concerns that the housing bubble will burst and the

Table 15.3 **European economic indicators, 2004–10 (annual % change)**

	2004	2005	2006	2007	2008	2009	2010
GDP							
Germany	1.3	0.8	2.7	2.3	2.0	1.9	2.1
France	2.0	1.4	2.0	1.8	2.1	1.9	2.2
Italy	1.1	0.1	1.6	1.3	1.5	1.5	1.6
Sweden	3.1	2.4	3.0	2.6	2.3	2.4	2.2
UK	3.2	1.8	2.7	2.4	2.1	2.5	2.2
Spain	3.1	3.1	3.3	2.8	2.8	2.5	2.1
Fixed investment							
Germany	−0.2	−0.2	5.6	4.1	4.4	3.5	3.1
France	2.1	3.0	3.5	3.2	2.5	2.3	2.3
Italy	1.9	−1.0	2.5	2.6	2.3	2.2	2.2
Sweden	5.5	8.9	8.3	6.7	3.8	3.0	2.3
UK	4.9	2.5	2.1	2.7	2.6	2.3	2.4
Spain	4.9	5.4	6.3	5.5	2.8	3.0	3.0
Private consumption							
Germany	0.6	−0.1	0.9	0.7	1.2	1.5	1.4
France	2.3	2.0	2.6	2.4	2.1	2.4	2.3
Italy	1.0	1.0	0.9	1.1	1.4	1.4	1.2
Sweden	1.8	2.2	3.0	3.8	3.1	2.5	1.7
UK	3.6	1.7	2.0	1.5	2.2	2.7	2.8
Spain	4.4	4.2	3.1	3.3	2.4	2.2	2.3
Real hourly wages							
Germany	−1.6	−0.5	0.0	0.4	0.7	0.7	0.7
France	0.6	0.6	0.8	1.2	1.3	1.5	1.5
Italy	0.6	0.8	1.4	0.8	0.5	0.8	0.8
Sweden	2.3	2.3	1.8	2.2	2.0	1.3	1.2
UK	3.1	2.3	2.0	1.8	2.2	2.3	2.3
Spain	0.5	0.5	0.6	0.6	0.4	0.4	0.5

stockmarket will stall or fall, but overall the outlook for the UK economy and business is better than for most other EU countries.

Japan

In 2005 – unless the figures are revised downwards as they have been in the past – Japan grew the fastest of the G7 economies, excluding the United States. Public debt may be more than twice the country's GDP, but booming exports to China have boosted the labour market, personal incomes and consumer spending in Japan. The recovery of domestic demand has been critical in giving companies the confidence to increase capital investment and hire more workers. The demand for workers has pushed up wages, which in turn has nudged up inflation. An increase in demand for mortgages has led to a pick-up in bank lending. Workers with more money are boosting personal consumption, which had increased by 3% at the end of 2005, the year Japan reported growth in retail sales for the first time in nine years.

Japanese companies make much more of their revenue in the domestic market than from sales abroad. This means the home market is more important for them, and they have been more willing to reinvest their growing profits at home than their counterparts in the United States and Germany.

Exports were moving upwards again in 2006, but imports were not growing as much. This could mean that the recovery is based more on services, where import demand is relatively low, than on the manufacturing sector.

The economy is likely to grow below its potential. Tax rises introduced in January 2006 have helped slow consumer demand and rising interest rates will take some of the steam out of corporate sector growth. Consumer spending will be hit in the coming years as the government starts to address the budget deficit: Japanese citizens will spend more on their pensions and consume less – and the world's fastest ageing population will put even more pressure on the already high budget deficit.

The Bank of Japan raised interest rates to 0.25% in mid-2006 as inflation had started to resurface. It is likely to be around 0.5% in 2007 and around 1.0% in the following 2–3 years. The growing economy and the end of deflation have prompted the bank to end the emergency monetary policy which it started in 2001 and which entailed pumping liquidity into the market. The danger is that the bank will raise interest rates too quickly, as it did in the 1990s, and cause another recession. The threat is heightened by the fact that the government has been tightening the fiscal side.

Growth is still too dependent on exports to potentially volatile markets in Asia. Between 2001 and 2005, exports to China accounted for 30% of Japan's total export growth. Furthermore, Japanese companies often invest inefficiently and require on average 70% more capital than US companies to produce the same output value.

One sobering thought about Japan is that its public debt, at 215% of GDP, is more than twice the size of Italy's.

16 The business outlook

This chapter examines current and future business trends and issues in some of the major emerging markets, focusing on countries with the best potential in the next few years.

Central and eastern Europe

Central and eastern Europe comprises:

- **Central Europe**

Czech Republic	Slovakia	Poland
Hungary	Slovenia	

- **South-eastern Europe**

Albania	Croatia	Serbia
Bosnia	Macedonia	
Bulgaria	Romania	

- **the Baltic states**

Estonia	Lithuania	Latvia

- **Russia** (covered separately in Chapter 17)
- **Other republics of the former Soviet Union** (also covered in Chapter 17)

Armenia	Kazakhstan	Turkmenistan
Azerbaijan	Kyrgyzstan	Ukraine
Belarus	Moldova	Uzbekistan
Georgia	Tajikistan	

Turkey is included in the Middle East and North Africa region (see page 174), but western companies usually include the country in their central Europe operations.

Winners and losers

The largest markets by volume but with slower business growth are the Czech Republic, Hungary, Poland and Slovakia. Poland is regarded as the most important market overall because of its large population. Business in Hungary has been tough, and as a result of austerity packages will remain tough at least until 2008.

Romania is the best south-eastern Europe market and sales growth in Serbia was good in 2006, but this small market carries high political risk.

Table 16.1 **Central and eastern Europe: GDP, 2004–10**
(real annual % change)

	2004	2005	2006	2007	2008	2009	2010
Albania	5.9	5.5	5.0	6.0	6.0	n/a	n/a
Armenia	10.5	14.0	13.4	10.0	7.5	n/a	n/a
Azerbaijan	10.2	26.4	34.5	23.5	14.6	9.9	7.4
Belarus	11.5	9.2	9.9	6.0	5.0	n/a	n/a
Bosnia	5.8	5.0	6.0	5.5	6.0	n/a	n/a
Bulgaria	5.7	5.5	6.4	5.3	4.5	4.0	3.3
Croatia	3.8	4.3	4.7	4.5	4.2	4.0	4.0
Czech Republic	4.2	6.1	6.1	5.0	4.0	4.5	4.0
Estonia	8.1	10.5	11.4	9.2	7.4	5.9	5.6
Georgia	5.9	9.3	8.0	6.5	7.3	n/a	n/a
Hungary	4.9	4.2	3.9	2.5	3.0	3.7	3.8
Kazakhstan	9.4	9.7	10.6	9.0	8.3	9.8	10.1
Kyrgyzstan	7.1	–0.2	2.7	4.0	4.5	n/a	n/a
Latvia	8.6	10.5	12.1	9.2	7.5	6.2	6.0
Lithuania	7.3	7.6	7.5	6.5	6.4	6.0	5.9
Macedonia	4.1	3.8	3.0	4.0	4.2	n/a	n/a
Moldova	7.4	7.5	4.0	5.5	5.0	n/a	n/a
Poland	5.3	3.5	5.8	6.1	5.0	4.4	4.1
Romania	8.4	4.1	7.7	6.1	5.4	5.0	4.2
Russia	7.2	6.4	6.7	6.2	5.7	4.8	4.5
Serbia	8.4	6.2	5.4	5.6	5.4	5.0	5.0
Slovakia	5.4	6.0	8.2	7.0	5.4	5.1	5.6
Slovenia	4.4	4.0	5.2	4.2	4.0	3.5	3.6
Tajikistan	10.6	6.7	7.0	7.0	7.2	n/a	n/a
Turkey	8.9	7.4	6.1	5.0	5.5	5.3	5.0
Turkmenistan	9.0	6.0	6.0	10.0	7.0	n/a	n/a
Ukraine	12.1	2.6	7.1	6.0	5.7	6.0	6.3
Uzbekistan	7.7	7.0	7.2	7.4	7.2	n/a	n/a

Table 16.2 **Central and eastern Europe: foreign direct investment, 2004–10**
($bn)

	2004	2005	2006	2007	2008	2009	2010
Albania	0.34	0.26	0.33	0.40	0.40	n/a	n/a
Armenia	0.22	0.26	n/a	n/a	n/a	n/a	n/a
Azerbaijan	3.56	1.68	1.69	1.60	1.60	1.50	1.65
Belarus	0.16	0.31	0.22	0.90	0.95	n/a	n/a
Bosnia	0.67	0.52	0.42	1.60	0.70	n/a	n/a
Bulgaria	3.46	3.87	5.17	3.50	2.25	2.10	2.05
Croatia	1.23	1.78	2.20	2.50	2.73	2.50	2.45
Czech Republic	4.98	10.97	6.02	6.50	6.50	4.50	3.50
Estonia	0.97	3.00	1.58	1.25	1.30	1.38	1.40
Georgia	0.50	0.45	0.89	0.40	0.45	n/a	n/a
Hungary	4.52	6.86	11.00	4.65	4.73	5.83	5.33
Kazakhstan	4.16	1.98	6.14	6.20	7.00	8.00	6.50
Kyrgyzstan	0.18	0.04	0.08	0.21	0.20	n/a	n/a
Latvia	0.64	0.73	1.63	1.00	0.85	0.65	0.60
Lithuania	0.77	1.03	1.81	1.00	1.05	1.20	1.15
Macedonia	0.16	0.10	0.35	0.25	0.25	n/a	n/a
Moldova	0.09	0.20	0.22	0.24	0.27	n/a	n/a
Poland	12.89	9.60	14.70	12.00	11.00	10.50	9.50
Romania	6.47	7.90	11.50	9.80	7.20	7.00	7.00
Russia	15.44	14.82	33.00	28.00	26.00	25.50	27.00
Serbia	0.97	1.55	4.39	4.60	2.00	1.80	1.80
Slovakia	1.12	1.91	3.90	1.99	2.05	1.49	1.47
Slovenia	0.83	0.54	0.73	0.82	1.39	0.73	0.66
Tajikistan	0.27	0.03	0.08	0.10	0.12	n/a	n/a
Turkey	2.88	9.81	20.62	19.00	20.00	21.00	20.00
Turkmenistan	0.35	0.30	0.30	0.32	0.33	n/a	n/a
Ukraine	1.72	7.81	5.20	5.20	4.80	4.60	4.80
Uzbekistan	n/a	n/a	n/a	n/a	n/a	n/a	n/a

The biggest and best east European market by far in 2001–06 was Russia (see Chapter 17) and this will remain the case for some years. It is "the elephant in the lounge" and is becoming the biggest volume market for a growing number of companies.

Strong performance

Against a sombre global outlook, the countries of central and eastern Europe (CEE) are reporting solid results compared with other emerging markets and developed ones. This has led companies to pay much more attention to the region. The danger is that companies which already have a presence there will expect too high a return from the region.

Central and eastern Europe has been one of the strongest performing emerging-market regions since 2000 and is likely to continue to be for the rest of the decade (see Table 16.4 on page 168). Foreign direct investment in the region reached $106 billion in 2006, compared with just $30 billion in 2001. Even if there was global economic crisis, the CEE region should come out of it reasonably well and better than other regions. This is because it has the following advantages:

- **Strong GDP growth.** During 2003–06 central and eastern Europe enjoyed average annual GDP growth of just under 5% which looks like continuing at round about that level up to 2010.
- **Underlying strong currencies.** Nearly all the major central and east European currencies have appreciated strongly in recent years, giving them a cushion for times of weakness. The main currency factor over the next few years will be euro entry, tentatively scheduled for 2008 for early EU entrants and 2010–12 for later arrivals. Most governments will want to ensure that their currencies adopt a conversion rate before entry which is low enough to ensure that the euro does not destroy growth. This will be quite a challenge as most currencies in the region are appreciating because of convergence trends with the EU. Hungary's currency is the most vulnerable, hence the austerity measures introduced to reduce the budget and current-account deficits.
- **Political stability.** Politics have become "normal" in central and eastern Europe, with the exception of Serbia and parts of the Balkans such as Macedonia. "There are not many al-Qaeda networks in Budapest," said one executive.

Table 16.3 **EU enlargement post 1995**

2004 (May 1st)	Czech Republic, Cyprus, Estonia, Hungary, Latvia, Lithuania, Malta, Poland, Slovenia, Slovakia
2007 (January 1st)	Bulgaria, Romania
2010	Possibly Croatia
2012	Possibly Macedonia
2015	Possibly Turkey

- **The EU as a guarantor.** The reality or prospect of EU membership (see Table 16.3) boosts growth prospects in the region by anchoring reform and stability, and providing the right climate for increased trade and investment. EU entry also provides reassurance to western companies that whatever concerns they have over such things as the legal framework and corporate governance should diminish.
- **Falling inflation.** In the 1990s inflation of 7–9% seemed entrenched, but now the outlook for the core markets (Czech Republic, Hungary, Poland and Slovakia) is for sustained lower inflation as EU convergence continues. This is not to say that inflation will not "bounce around", and certainly there is potential for a rise in Poland, Slovakia and Hungary, but any upward move is unlikely to be sustained.
- **Rising labour productivity.** Higher growth and falling inflation are largely the result of rising labour productivity in many markets.
- **Improving banking sector.** Weak financial sectors caused severe problems in most of central and eastern Europe in the 1990s, but most of the banking sector (over 90% in most countries) has now been acquired by western financial institutions and the "banking risk" in the region has largely evaporated. Most western banks have now cleaned up their balance sheets and are competing with each other to lend. Credit expansion in central and eastern Europe is among the highest in the world and western banks doing business in the region are reporting excellent profits. The major reason HV Bank of Germany bought Bank Austria in 2004 was to acquire its central and eastern European business. HV Bank was in turn bought by Unicredit, an Italian bank, in 2006, again mainly on account of this business.

Table 16.4 **Sales growth of western companies in central and eastern Europe,**[a] **2005–10 (%)**

	2005	2006	2007	2008	2009	2010
Manufacturing & industrial	16	15	13	12	11	9
Food & beverages	9	8	8	7	5	5
Consumer goods	12	12	9	8	7	7
Information technology	11	13	9	7	10	13
Pharmaceuticals & health care	16	15	12	12	11	10

a Organic sales growth in core CEE markets and south-eastern Europe, excluding Russia and Ukraine.
Source: Based on corporate anecdotes and authors' estimates

In doing business in the CEE region, especially in central Europe where top-line sales are slowing, it is important to manage expectations downwards. Senior executives should bear in mind that the region accounts for only 4% of global GDP, a figure that will rise to only 5–6% over the next 15 years (Latin America accounts for 10% of global GDP and Asia Pacific for 26%). For most average multinationals the CEE region usually represents about 3–5% of global sales and 13–16% of west European sales. Western market leaders in the CEE region may report slightly higher percentages.

The problem in some markets is that they are simply too small and companies meet a "natural" sales-level barrier.

One manager in the consumer goods sector said:

> We are doing very well overall. Hungary is particularly strong for us. In fact we have 4m customers in that market out of 10m and there is not much more we can do with our existing products and prices. The long-term challenge for us and others is to get to that poorer, more rural 6m customers. It will require a big shift in our marketing and I'm not sure we are up to it, nor our western competitors.

These comments are relevant also to Poland and the Czech Republic. Often individual markets for a multinational company can be broken down into the capital city and perhaps one or two other population centres. As one European telecoms vice-president noted: "Warsaw is a market within a market." The challenge and the real remaining growth potential in the core markets will come increasingly from relatively untapped subregions within each of the more prosperous markets.

A regional manager of a European industrial company notes that although there is still good organic and geographic sales growth to achieve in the region, another method to obtain good returns is to go deeper into the existing customer base:

> We are selling well to them but we should now expand the portfolio of products we sell to these existing customers and offer increasingly higher-value products ... which I'm pleased to say they are pushing for in any case.

The message is clear and sensible: aim to get more money from new clients and more money from existing ones in a maturing market. And there is still more potential out there, even as competition builds up. A regional manager of one of the world's large IT companies notes:

> We have an excellent existing business and the outlook is very good too. Piracy issues are improving in a couple of markets and helping top-line growth, especially in Russia. For every 0.1% improvement in piracy, we gain another $10m.

The impact of EU enlargement on business in central and eastern Europe

It has been estimated that EU membership will add an extra half a percentage point a year to the GDP of the new member states (see Table 16.3 on page 166) in 2007–11.

The benefits for business are significant:

- There will be more legal and tax transparency.
- The risk assessment for the region is falling and this will continue, entailing savings in financing and insurance.
- Many import tariffs will disappear, making western products more affordable.
- Customs problems will largely be eradicated, but poor infrastructure will continue to make just-in-time deliveries difficult.

For the first 5–10 years, it is likely that the rich will become richer and the poor will become poorer as the IT, financial and services sectors do well but mining, agriculture and heavy industry are restructured. The same applies to local companies: the least competitive will fail but the more competitive will seek to expand their existing business in the region and to enter markets in western Europe.

EU enlargement will change the shape of European business, and the process has already started. Extremely low-cost production will continue to move out of central and eastern Europe to cheaper labour-cost markets in Asia. But new investment is moving from western to central and eastern Europe. Western companies with production facilities in the region will seek to consolidate or restructure them. A regional production plan that made sense in 1999 may not now. Some countries, such as Spain, may become large exporters of FDI, investing in the developed markets of western Europe. In a few years' time more companies from the CEE region will be exporting capital to the West.

Many western companies are reassessing their business interests in central and eastern Europe, asking such questions as: How many staff do we have, how many representative offices, how many legal entities, how many production sites? Are they adequate? Should we invest more? Western and CEE companies will consider partnerships and alliances in Europe. There will also be an increase in mergers and acquisitions as companies fight for market leadership. Those entering the market late will pay higher prices for acquisitions as all the blue-chip players were bought long ago or are fiercely independent.

Labour costs are likely to remain low – behind those in Spain, Portugal and Greece – for at least a decade. This makes central and eastern Europe attractive as a low-cost production location within Europe. Costs for managers, office staff and technically skilled staff have already risen, and this trend will continue. Some companies will consider bringing back expatriates on short-term contracts to fill key posts as wage costs for local middle managers approach those of expatriates.

Why things are getting tougher in central and eastern Europe

- **Competition.** Since 2002 competition has increased sharply and will continue to do so. Poland is for many companies, including Nestlé and Unilever, the most competitive market in the whole of Europe and for some the most competitive globally. In several CEE markets in 2003 there were a dozen or so western and domestic players in any product sector. This number is starting to decrease as the market leaders flex their muscles and other players are marginalised, take up niche positions or leave the market. Consolidation is a clear trend in the retail, beer, paper and energy sectors, and others will follow.
- **Market structure.** The structure of the market is changing and

companies have to adapt. For example, fast-moving consumer goods (FMCG) companies have established a presence in the capital cities and wealthier areas. Now the challenge is to extend sales into rural regions where people's disposable income is lower.

◪ **Retailing.** Retailers have flooded into CEE markets and oversupplied Poland and the Czech Republic. In earlier years they went for growth and market share, whereas now they need to focus more on margins or it will be unprofitable to stay in the market. This is putting the squeeze on western consumer goods companies whose products they sell.

◪ **Cyclical problems.** There are usually one or two markets going through cyclical crises at any time. In 2000–03 it was Poland's turn, and the Czech Republic and Hungary each experienced a 2–3 year economic decline in the 1990s. Hungary is again experiencing a crisis which is likely to last until 2008. Regional managers in emerging markets invariably have at least one market in their portfolio which is experiencing cyclical problems.

◪ **Western Europe.** Slow growth in Germany and other west European countries will affect demand for exports from the CEE region. Germany, for example, takes 31% of Czech exports. Although EU GDP growth picked up to 2.5% in 2006, it will stumble along at only 2.2% on average for the next few years. Despite this, CEE markets' sales to the EU are good, thanks to high productivity levels in the region. This is why vehicle producers are setting up in Poland, the Czech Republic and Slovakia.

◪ **Budget deficits.** This was a major problem in 2002–05. In 2002, most of the main central and east European countries had budget deficits well over euro entry targets. Cutting the deficits entailed spending cuts or tax increases, or a combination of both. As it turned out, by 2005 most governments were able to get their budget deficits down to either below 3% or not far from it thanks to higher than expected corporate and personal income tax revenues, stemming from good growth levels. (The major exception has been Hungary.) This was accompanied by tighter government expenditure which meant fewer sales to government. Most markets now have their fiscal houses in order so sales to government will be better than could have otherwise been expected in 2007–11. However, growth in sales to government will lag behind that of sales to consumers and manufacturing sales to business. Generally, the CEE markets have gone for lower direct and corporate taxes, although electorates have proven reluctant to endorse full flat-tax regimes (for example, Poland and Slovakia). But they have been keen to use indirect taxes, especially duties on tobacco and alcoholic beverages which have hurt sales in these sectors. Indirect taxes have hurt sales overall but this has been compensated for by an increase in consumer credit.

How companies are responding

The response of companies has been to expand into other emerging markets such as Russia, Ukraine, south-eastern Europe, Turkey and South Africa, and to cut costs. A number of companies working in central and eastern Europe report that in order to keep up margins, costs are being cut against a background of slower sales.

With sales growth falling in central and eastern Europe as the markets mature, there are three opportunities to exploit:

- **Sales outside the main cities.** Before 2004 many companies took the view that reaching out to the small towns and rural areas simply was not worth the effort. Procter & Gamble was one of the first to go against the trend and to invest locally, compete with domestic brands, do local research and offer new propositions to consumers with smaller incomes. EU membership has also made a big difference for some countries in the region. By the beginning of 2005, the incomes of rural families had risen by 30%, and by mid-2005 the year-on-year increase was 65% in Poland, Hungary and the Czech Republic. This was attributable partly to direct EU payments but more to booming exports of food products to European markets, especially the UK, Germany and Scandinavia. A huge new market had opened up for products such as meat and milk at high prices, and the removal of customs barriers meant that goods arrived quickly because trucks were no longer stuck at the border for days at a time.

  Now that rural consumers in the region are better off than they were, more western companies are following Procter & Gamble and reassessing their investment and business models. Not all are convinced even now that a market composed of smaller towns and rural areas merits big investment, but most agree that it is worth taking a second look at any growth opportunities in tightening markets. Intel, an IT company, has reported that sales of personal computers in rural areas of Poland have soared, albeit from a low base. And a US food company says that it will probably put more effort into these rural regions.

◢ **Sales per head.** Several companies report that their sales per head in central and eastern Europe are barely 50% of those in countries such as France. The logic then is that with convergence, good GDP growth and rising western investment, sales per head should increase steadily.

◢ **More credit.** Consumer credit is rising across the region by around 50% a year, forcing banks in some countries to raise interest rates to stop things getting out of hand. The increase in credit available to companies and individuals has important consequences for business. In 2003, IBM complained that it could not make enough business-to-business sales in the Czech Republic because local companies could not borrow from the local banks. Now they can, and being better financed can act as better partners, suppliers and competitors. Increased access to credit means that consumers are taking out loans to buy cars, white goods and houses – which may mean that they start cutting back on other spending.

Some of those involved in the region may be asking themselves, "Is this as good as it gets?" But as well as the three opportunities outlined above, the things that companies should be looking at, if they are not already, are as follows:

◢ Where to base their shared services, R&D and competence centres. Many will spread them around, but Budapest, Prague and Warsaw are attracting most attention.

◢ Whether to use local or global brands – or what mix to use in the region.

◢ Price and trade harmonisation. Some prices will rise in the coming years, but some western companies have been charging premium prices for branded products and pharmaceuticals. As price transparency increases, consumers will look for where they can buy western products more cheaply.

◢ More systematised IT systems, which are more closely integrated with and linked to those in west European operations.

◢ More pan-European supply chains and distribution.

◢ Consolidation – especially in retail, beer, paper and energy.

South-eastern Europe

Healthy sales and profit margins are being reported by a growing number of companies in south-eastern Europe. Sales in Croatia are bolstered by tourism receipts, a large grey economy and a stable inflation and currency outlook. Serbia, although small in absolute terms, has grown noticeably for several years, and most people expect it to be a sizeable and important regional market in the next few years if political risk can be controlled. The recently created free-trade zone for south-eastern Europe should boost sales, and the prospect of EU accession will sustain corporate interest. But these markets will become more competitive in the next few years, as is beginning to happen in Romania. Political risk remains high.

Western companies' corporate structure

Many western companies established small structures in central and eastern Europe that looked after small clusters of markets in order to give them critical mass and to reduce back-office costs. One big US food company and a European beer producer have set up a "Central Europe" unit which includes Germany, Austria and Switzerland along with Hungary, the Czech Republic and Slovakia. This more pan-European approach is likely to spread, though it seems sensible in the short term at least for some central and east European markets to remain separate from the major European markets because of the need to be closer to customers and clients, to be more flexible in distribution and not to introduce big, expensive, clunky western managerial systems.

The Middle East and North Africa

The Middle East and North Africa (MENA) region comprises:

- Algeria
- Bahrain
- Djibouti
- Egypt
- Iran
- Iraq
- Israel
- Jordan
- Kuwait
- Lebanon
- Libya
- Morocco
- Oman
- Qatar
- Saudi Arabia
- Syria
- Tunisia
- Turkey[a]
- United Arab Emirates (UAE)
- West Bank and Gaza
- Yemen

a But western companies tend to include it in their central Europe operations.

Winners and losers

Turkey was a boom market in 2003–06 and is likely to remain so. After

Table 16.5 **Middle East and North Africa: GDP, 2004–10**
(real annual % change)

	2004	2005	2006	2007	2008	2009	2010
Algeria	5.2	5.3	3.0	4.8	5.6	5.7	5.7
Bahrain	6.4	7.8	7.8	6.7	6.0	5.6	4.7
Egypt	4.1	4.5	6.8	6.9	6.6	5.7	5.3
Iran	5.1	4.4	4.3	4.6	4.0	3.7	3.5
Iraq	46.5	1.5	1.9	2.5	2.8	n/a	n/a
Israel	4.8	5.6	5.1	5.2	4.5	4.2	4.0
Jordan	7.7	7.7	6.2	5.6	5.2	4.2	4.0
Kuwait	10.5	10.0	12.6	5.0	5.9	4.8	5.2
Lebanon	4.3	0.1	−6.4	2.1	2.7	n/a	n/a
Libya	5.0	5.8	6.1	5.4	5.2	5.1	5.0
Morocco	4.2	1.7	7.3	3.9	4.9	5.6	5.3
Oman	5.4	5.8	6.6	5.0	5.1	n/a	n/a
Qatar	20.8	6.1	7.1	8.3	9.5	11.1	8.0
Saudi Arabia	5.3	6.5	4.2	3.9	5.0	4.6	4.5
Sudan	5.2	8.3	9.6	12.8	5.8	n/a	n/a
Syria	4.9	4.6	3.5	2.8	3.4	n/a	n/a
Tunisia	5.8	4.2	4.9	5.4	5.7	5.8	5.5
Turkey	8.9	7.4	6.1	5.0	5.5	5.3	5.0
UAE	9.7	8.2	8.9	7.3	6.5	6.1	5.3
Yemen	2.7	3.4	2.6	3.6	3.1	n/a	n/a

many disappointing years, Saudi Arabia started to boom in 2005. Since 2004 Egypt has begun to show promise. Dubai and other parts of the UAE are enjoying huge growth.

Israel, Lebanon, Jordan and Syria are likely to continue to underperform.

Risks versus opportunities
The Middle East is a region of great risk and, in parts, considerable opportunity. The oil booms of the 1970s ended badly for business and the economy. As oil revenue dwindled, debt and unemployment grew,

infrastructure crumbled and tensions increased. In Saudi Arabia, GDP per head reached US levels in 1981 but had sunk to less than a quarter by 2001. Periodically higher oil revenues reduced the urgency to introduce structural reforms, but the oil boom that started in 2005, driving the price of oil to over $75 per barrel in mid-2006, is different. The oil price is driven by demand and so should stay high for the foreseeable future. Oil revenues are being invested in the region as Arab investors see greater risks in US markets and greater opportunities at home; the oil windfall is largely being used to invest in infrastructure, diversification and reserves. Governments are pushing on with economic reforms in order to build a job-creating private sector to cope with a growing population.

Dubai's emergence as a regional headquarters for international business is increasing competition and making business more hands-on. Retail trade structures are being modernised and industrial trade is becoming more structured. Local companies are expanding regionally and moving beyond trading into manufacturing and services. The opening of Middle Eastern markets is cemented by World Trade Organisation (WTO) regulations and the negotiation of US free-trade deals with countries such as Jordan.

Only a dramatic downturn in oil prices would jeopardise the medium-term economic outlook. Any corrections in real-estate bubbles and stockmarkets should not affect underlying growth. In the longer term, the economic outlook will depend on the success of diversification strategies and the emergence of a dynamic private sector. Over the next five years or so, the principal risks are not economic but political, as tensions with the West (and within the region) have increased since the Iraq war and most regimes are trying to control change, not adapt to it.

Business growth is being driven in much of the region by massive public spending on transport and infrastructure, and the opening up of power, water, telecommunications and transport sectors to foreign investors. Consumption is being boosted by increased public-sector wages and private-sector activity. Oil revenues are behind much of this.

Tourism has become an important diversification strategy for some countries but has been hurt by political troubles in others. The WTO is exerting pressure on Saudi Arabia and the Gulf states to open up to exports and investment. The real-estate sector is booming with over $300 billion in construction projects announced. This is being driven by Arab investment in property and the opening of property markets to foreign and local ownership. A new focus on gas-based manufacturing – aluminium, petrochemicals and fertilisers – has the potential to create competitive niches.

Western companies are paying more attention to the region as the Middle East booms. The markets are still extremely dependent on distributors – more so than in most regions. A good or bad distributor and his inside-track contacts can make or break your business, so companies are generally moving away from exclusive distributor relations.

It is difficult to find good staff in the region. In Saudi Arabia, most western expatriates have left and international companies have started hiring people from India, Syria and Lebanon. In Dubai there are many expatriates, but wages are rising rapidly. Another human resource problem is that most women are kept out of the workforce. Hiring talented local women requires close attention to legislation and social mores, so few western companies do this. There is strong pressure to hire locals (and obligatory quotas for local staff are common), but many companies hire locals and also hire expatriates to do the actual work. The region suffers from too much red tape and from corruption.

Profits have been good in the region but margins are starting to decline, most markedly in fast-moving consumer goods. The reason is higher fixed costs, more active marketing and stronger competition. In other words, the Middle East is becoming more like the West.

Companies are increasingly focusing on how to make branding and marketing more locally relevant. There is no such thing as a typical Middle Eastern consumer – the markets are made up of locals, expatriates and tourists.

Security, ease of expatriate living and the relative ease of doing business make Dubai the obvious location for regional headquarters. New companies continue to be attracted to the emirate, but rents, wages and the cost of living are rising massively. Qatar and Bahrain are cheaper alternatives but lack the critical mass. Istanbul is a possibility for those who do not see Turkey as part of their European operations.

Saudi Arabia
The Saudi market was performing well below potential in the 1990s and until about 2005, with the exception of energy companies. Since then business has been growing strongly, boosted by government spending and an increase in disposable income. Riyadh and Jeddah are the fastest growing cities in the Middle East and will double in population by 2015.

Reform of the financial sector and diversification into metals, petrochemicals and fertilisers are moving ahead. The United States signed a bilateral trade agreement with Saudi Arabia, clearing the way for WTO membership. Despite a crackdown on al-Qaeda cells in Saudi Arabia, security remains a concern. All those involved in business in Saudi Arabia realise that it is a high-risk market.

United Arab Emirates

GDP growth in the United Arab Emirates (UAE) is being driven by the development of non-oil industry and services. The population is expanding rapidly and is already around 5m, with over 75% expatriates. The UAE federal government is implementing a new company law, making foreign ownership easier and changing the restrictive agency law. Spurred by Dubai's success, Abu Dhabi has woken up to the potential and is focusing on developing energy-intensive manufacturing as well as tourism.

Dubai's development continues with attempts to move into financial services, outsourcing and manufacturing. Construction is booming but the transport infrastructure is inadequate, costs are rising and labour is getting harder to find. Some companies also report that getting the necessary licences and permissions has become much more difficult – which may simply be because of the volume of paperwork the authorities are having to process.

Egypt

After a decade of poor performance, a shift in policy direction and the implementation of economic reforms, things began to pick up in 2004, with many firms reporting healthy growth. Industry performed best, reflecting a tooling up in manufacturing and a catch-up in the investment that had been lacking. The quality of engineers is high and it is likely that Egypt will follow the booming Gulf markets in building up its industrial base and investing in much more sophisticated equipment.

Consumer goods companies are generally the most optimistic about the market potential of such a large population, providing individual purchasing power increases. Total personal disposable income rose from $45 billion in 2004 to $58 billion in 2006, and private consumption per head from $770 in 2004 to $950 in 2006. FDI leapt from virtually nothing in 2003 to $3.5 billion in 2005–06 and should be sustainable at something like that figure as more companies are privatised.

The political outlook is less rosy. In power for more than a quarter of a century, President Mubarak, who will be 80 in 2008, has provided Egypt with stability. But the management of his succession will be of crucial importance, especially given the rise of the Muslim Brotherhood, which has 20% of seats in Parliament which is half of those they contested in the 2005 election. Terrorism is a further threat to stability and to the contribution made to the economy by tourism.

A number of critical and long-standing problems for business have been resolved, including foreign-exchange shortages. The government has succeeded in pushing through cuts in income tax and custom duties, and it has promoted privatisation and consolidated the banking sector. Public-sector wages are to be boosted and private consumption and investment have been helped by the tax cuts. High real interest rates should keep GDP growth stable at around 5% for a few years.

Israel

It is not that long since Israel was a thriving market and an engine for growth for several neighbouring markets, but it has been mostly downhill for the region since 2001 and its political problems are likely to hold it back in future. It is a tough market in which to generate good profits and is notorious for being distributor dependent: if you do not have a good local wholesaler or partner, doing business is extremely difficult.

Iran

Iran is the fourth largest oil producer and the largest supplier to China. The country has tremendous potential for western companies attracted by young, wealthy and sophisticated Iranian consumers, but it is threatened by political risk. Demand for western products is strong and far from being satisfied. More than half of the western companies involved enjoy high sales growth, but they are worried about the extent to which politics will damage business. Politics have so far impinged little on most business operations and many well-known western firms, including Unilever and Tetra Pak, have a presence in Iran. The automotive sector is growing strongly and Peugeot, Renault, Volkswagen, DaimlerChrysler have all invested in the market. As Renault's managing director in Iran says:

> It's a huge market that was closed to foreign companies for 30 years. The pioneers get the biggest part of the cake, so I think it's better to hurry than to wait.

Getting pricing strategies right for the poor urban and rural markets is difficult as genuine market research is rare. Local partners are essential for good relations with government but are difficult to control. European companies have an advantage over American companies, which are hampered by the Iran–Libya Sanctions Act of the US congress. Nevertheless, US branded goods are much in evidence in Iran because companies can circumvent the sanctions by not using US staff and by keeping US product content below 5%.

The business outlook for 2007–10 is generally good, although corruption is likely to be just as bad as it has been. The government's antagonism to western influence is reflected in its clampdown on market researchers, fast-food restaurants and western-style advertisements, and the prime minister's backers in parliament and among the Revolutionary Guards have been antagonistic to liberalisation and foreign business. But it is more a matter of making life more difficult for business than destroying it.

The country is cash rich on oil revenues and the government is spending freely. The next few years are likely to see an increase in government-controlled subsidies and pricing policies, higher tariff rates to protect local industry, little effort to implement WTO reforms in private and foreign ownership, and insistence on Iranian majority ownership and control in all FDI deals.

During 2006 the US administration exerted more pressure on western banks to stop financing deals with Iran and this policy started to hurt investment. However, companies will continue to seek legal ways into the market. As long as the United States and Israel hold back from military action, good levels of business will persist, especially for European companies.

Turkey
Since the arrival of a new government in 2002 much has changed for the better in Turkey. Macroeconomic discipline has been introduced and the government has stuck to maintaining a primary budget surplus, which excludes interest payments on debt. Interest rates came down from 100% in 2002 to 12% in 2005 before bouncing back up to 22% in 2006. The lira stabilised and became overvalued before falling in 2006. There has been a dramatic clean-up in the banking sector, to the extent that western banks are lining up to buy into Turkish ones.

After 13 years of chronic mismanagement under ten coalition governments, the 2002 elections resulted in a two-party parliament for the first time in 50 years and a single-party government for the first time in 15 years. The Justice and Development Party (AKP), which has Islamist origins, is generally described in the western media as a "moderate, centre-right party".

Turkey was a boom market in 2003–06. If it can manage its debt repayment and related fiscal issues successfully, it should remain a boom market for several years to come. And if it were accepted for EU membership, an upswing would have much more chance of being sustainable than it did in the past. EU funds prior to entry would boost investment in transport, infrastructure, retailing, banking, telecoms and electricity distribution.

Political stability should strengthen if the AKP is re-elected in 2007 with a sizeable majority in parliament. Political parties and the military will have to resolve the issue of electing the president but this ought to be settled in 2007–08. Cyprus remains a thorn in EU–Turkish relations. Negotiations over EU membership will drag on and Turkey will not join the EU until 2015 at the earliest, if it ever does.

But the process of reform which continues in the effort to join is worthwhile for the Turkish economy. Turkey has a good chance of digging itself out of its debt hole without another major crisis. The risk of a financial crash in the next few years is as low as 20%, although more conservative western analysts would put it a bit higher. Things have certainly changed since 2002, when the chances of a financial collapse were over 90%.

Turkey is rated by many companies as the best growth market in the Middle East and North Africa region and also the central and eastern Europe region (excluding Russia).

With regard to the economy, the current-account deficit is the biggest concern, but high oil prices rather than consumer goods imports are a large part of the reason for it. The economic reforms that have been entrenched and the fundamentals of the economy should help Turkey through any storm that arises, and the United States and the EU would ride to its rescue if necessary. Turkey currently offers high rewards at an acceptable level of risk, although price pressure is intensifying, which makes it more important to build scale.

Turkish consumers are becoming more affluent, sophisticated and open to western products, and as the birth rate slows, average household size is falling. Greater consumer credit has boosted the market for consumer goods overall and especially for housing, household appliances and cars. Marketing costs are rising, another regional trend, and TV advertising costs have risen hugely in the early 2000s. The retail sector is consolidating and putting more cost pressure on manufacturers. Imports run into bureaucratic protectionism and lack of respect for intellectual property is a problem.

Advice from investors in Turkey is not to sacrifice market share for price and that it is best not to create too big a cost structure until you know the business is there at the right price. FMCG has proved a good sector to be in but is getting tougher.

The healthcare and IT sectors have been experiencing heady growth. Wages remain low and good, hardworking staff not too difficult to find. In the words of one western manager, Turkish staff are "excellent at imitating and adapting quickly, but are less strong on innovation".

Africa (excluding North Africa)

Sub-Saharan Africa is largely a human tragedy and a commercial mess. It is the weakest emerging market region in terms of attracting business, and it has slipped backwards while the rest of the world has moved on. In the 1990s real GDP per head in the continent actually fell and, on average, is lower than it was in the 1960s. There have been no improvements in these indicators to 2006. Africa's share of world GDP is now 1%, a decrease of around 30% over the past 50 years; its share of world exports has decreased by over 60% over the same period. In 1980 Africa accounted for 28% of global foreign investment; 20 years later the figure was only 7%.

Too much African infrastructure is designed to ship out exports and not enough is built for internal trade and markets. Many economies are dependent on volatile commodity prices. Intra-regional trade, although rising, still accounts for only 10% of African exports. IMF programmes have done little for Africa: either the funds were misdirected in the first place or they have been squandered or stolen by local officials. Debt is a huge burden, and many African countries still spend more of their annual budgets on interest payments than on education or health.

Africa needs a concerted combination of aid, trade and implementation of the debt relief agreements already signed. This might encourage reform and support programmes such as the New Economic Partnership for Africa's Development (NEPAD), which promises good governance and a better business environment. But Africa's economic and political track record does not inspire confidence, let alone hope. Development of the oil industry in Nigeria, and especially in western Africa, will mean that revenues of some $200 billion will flow into African government treasuries in the next ten years. But how much of the money will be put to good use, and how much will be wasted on prestige projects or diverted into private bank accounts?

Africa is also blighted by AIDS. UN reports estimate that in 2002 sub-Saharan Africa accounted for 71% of the more than 40m adults and children living with AIDS around the world, and that average sub-Saharan life expectancy was 47 years in 2002, 15 years lower than it would have been without AIDS. Human development in the region will be harmed more in the coming years as more children become orphans and do not attend school. On the economic front, countries will suffer from more labour and skill shortages, especially as men in the age range 20–45 fall victim to AIDS. Medical costs, both public and private, will increase; a few companies are beginning to provide specific medical and insurance coverage but this is unlikely to become prevalent.

GDP will grow more slowly and poverty levels will rise, which will have long-term effects over the next decade and beyond. It is estimated that in 2012 the South African economy will be 20% smaller than it would have been without AIDS. In a survey of South African managers, 60% thought the epidemic was a "serious threat" at the national level but only 20% thought it would seriously harm their business. This may prove to be an optimistic assessment. Outsiders are taking a gloomier view. Investors are now asking for premium rates of return of 18–20% in South Africa and 25–30% in the rest of sub-Saharan Africa on account of the higher risk associated with AIDS, according to the Economist Intelligence Unit and Business Map.

It is therefore not surprising that the African continent is overall a poor market. The exceptions are energy and mining companies, which do well in several countries. Sales for western consumer goods and pharmaceuticals companies will, on average, grow slowly if at all over the next few years. However, the big IT companies are reporting reasonable business, especially in South Africa but also in West Africa and parts of North Africa. Some mobile telecoms and food and beverages companies are also doing well.

Consumer goods companies have been reporting good growth in some parts of the continent, especially when they enter new markets in francophone West Africa. Western commercial interest in eastern Africa picked up in 2002–03, but this was not sustained in 2005–06 as the markets did not meet expectations. However, companies will continue to monitor Kenya, Uganda and Tanzania in the coming years for any improvements in this potentially interesting subregion. Even Nigeria (one of the world's most corrupt places to do business, according to Transparency International) has proved to be a profitable market for companies that have been able to build onshore operations to circumvent tariff barriers. However, some of the shine has come off this market too, with investors becoming disillusioned with the sustainability of reforms, and the outlook is uncertain. Higher raw material prices boosted GDP in 2005–06 and China has been taking increasing interest in Africa, investing in energy and infrastructure and getting involved in countries that most western companies would not go near, such as Sudan and Zimbabwe.

For most manufacturing and consumer goods companies, the continent boils down to a triangle of three key markets: Egypt, Morocco and South Africa. Except for energy and raw materials companies, the rest of the continent is a small and disappointing market with extreme levels of risk. There is little reason to expect significant improvement in the next few years.

South Africa

Business has boomed since 2004 and this has generated much western interest in South Africa. Most companies now rate the country's mid-term growth potential as very good. There are many reasons for this. GDP growth is over 5%, driven largely by consumer spending, which has been encouraged by a stronger rand and low interest rates. High prices for gold, platinum and other commodities have brought in substantial profits. FDI is increasing, especially in banking, real estate, business services and IT, and the automotive, manufacturing and mining sectors. Investment is coming from China, Russia and India as well as the West, with FDI reaching $7 billion in 2005. A sustainable figure for the years to 2010 would be in the range of $5 billion–$8 billion a year.

Some of the worries people had about South Africa have evaporated, although crime remains a serious problem.

Challenges that the country needs to address include:

◪ making the currency less volatile;
◪ improving work skills – the shortage of skills is a major constraint on growth;
◪ improving the infrastructure, such as telecoms, which will help reduce business costs;
◪ tackling AIDS – 20% of the population is infected and the government's policy response is ineffective;
◪ reducing crime and improving security – these two issues constrain investment despite some improvement and the beginning of regeneration in inner city areas.

Over the next few years government policy is to invest heavily in physical and social infrastructure in order to lessen income inequality, which is second only to Brazil, and to achieve sustainable GDP growth of 6% by 2010.

Some $730m is to be spent on upgrading infrastructure (including $400m for the 2010 World Cup), which will lead to a construction boom, heavy investment in the electrical power sector and a capital goods boom. Consumer spending is likely to slow as inflation rises and house prices become sluggish. Competition from Asian and Chinese companies, in particular, is increasing strongly in sales to the consumer goods sector and in tenders for infrastructure projects. For western business South Africa remains a good market, especially for business-to-business and business-to-government, but companies will have to focus on price if they want to move deeper into the market and to compete with local and Asian competition.

India

While western companies wonder whether the shine is going off China, they are taking a fresh look at India, which has prospered markedly in a number of sectors. The economy is doing well with GDP growth seemingly stable at around 7%. But India needs to grow its GDP at around 8% a year if it is to reduce poverty levels and ensure strong investment – investment in India is only 24% of GDP compared with 50% in China.

A buzz continues in the consumer and industrial sectors, with the liberalised automotive sector – of which Tata Motors has a 15% share of the domestic market – now producing more than 1m cars a year. Most other sectors are doing well too, including textiles, cement, steel, consumer durables, tourism, real estate and transport. Growth in manufacturing is healthy, though much stems from drawing down on spare capacity and not enough from new projects. The growth and expansion of the IT and outsourcing business in India are well known. Its well-educated, English-speaking workforce gives the country a competitive advantage, but western companies report high staff turnover and many question the quality of service they receive. But this is a feature of outsourcing in general and not a problem specific to India. Expectations often start too high, and some 30–40% of the companies that outsource question whether this was the correct decision.

Inflation is running at a manageable level and the government has wisely tried to temper any inflationary pick-up by cutting import duties and excise duties rather than raising interest rates. The economy has been helped by low interest rates but if inflation does not respond to tariff cuts, rates are likely to rise. Following through on its election promises, the government is spending on infrastructure, agriculture and basic health services. But spending growth is curbed by a high federal budget deficit of 4–5%, even though this is half the level it used to run at.

Table 16.6 **India: key economic indicators, 2005–10**

	2005	2006	2007	2008	2009	2010
Real GDP growth (%)	8.5	9.2	8.4	8.0	7.5	7.5
Consumer price inflation (av; %)	5.6	6.9	6.0	5.1	4.4	4.4
Budget balance (% of GDP)	−4.1	−4.0	−3.5	−3.6	−3.9	−3.5
Current-account balance (% of GDP)	−0.9	−2.3	−4.1	−3.5	−2.8	−2.0
Lending rate (av; %)	10.8	11.3	11.8	10.8	10.5	10.2
Exchange rate Rs:$ (av)	44.1	45.5	46.5	47	47.5	48
Exchange rate Rs:¥100 (av)	40.1	39.8	46.4	49.2	50.8	52.5

Source: Economist Intelligence Unit, 2006

The money markets have improved as a result of the easing of capital controls, the liberalisation of equity pricing and the creation of a regulatory authority, which has boosted portfolio investment.

Against this broadly positive picture, most of the caps on the levels of foreign ownership in key sectors have not been lifted, although the cap on telecoms was raised from 49% to 74%. This is one reason FDI was only $7.5 billion in 2005. Sectors which have not liberalised include retail, banking, defence and the media. Retail in particular is proving a tough nut to crack, and with communists in the coalition government, it is unlikely that the cap on foreign ownership levels will be raised much. Lack of reform in the energy sector will mean continued poor distribution of electricity.

Among the things that would help improve the business environment are keeping interest rates down; implementing the VAT system more broadly; encouraging state governments to reduce their budget deficits; opening up the non-liberalised sectors; land reform; urban renewal; amending laws on asset recovery from bankrupt companies; simplifying labour laws; and better protection of intellectual property.

Typically, India accounts for 1–2% of global sales of the average western multinational company. Rapid credit growth and consumer demand have helped sales and business confidence, and most multinationals operating

Table 16.7 **India: market outlook, 2006–10**

	2006	2007	2008	2009	2010
Population (m)	1,110.4	1,125.4	1,140.2	1,155.0	1,169.7
GDP ($bn at market exchange rates)	854.9	928.7	1,038.4	1,166.0	1,302.0
GDP ($bn at PPP)	4,234	4,681	5,176	5,693	6,252
GDP per head ($ at PPP)	3,813	4,160	4,540	4,929	5,345
Personal disposable income ($bn)	714	812	911	1,000	1,121
Median household income ($)	2,210	2,419	2,651	2,910	3,176
Household consumption per head ($)	470	500	550	590	640

Source: Economist Intelligence Unit, 2006

in India report solid sales, good profits, flat prices and cost-cutting efficiencies. In 2005, among over 100 western multinationals surveyed by the Economist Intelligence Unit, revenue growth was good: 15% of companies reported sales growth of 30–50%, 20% growth of 20–30% and 20% growth of 15–20%. The survey revealed that the two main concerns were cost structures and human resources, whereas in 2003–04 the major concern had been revenue growth. Companies were also questioning the government's commitment to reform.

Multinationals face many operational difficulties. Domestic Indian companies are tough competitors. They are often run by talented, well-educated, English-speaking senior executives, and they are helped by the usual advantages insiders have in emerging markets, including close relations with federal and local authorities. Other difficulties are weak awareness of western brands; large income differentials among consumers; the country's north–south divide, which makes national marketing and distribution campaigns difficult; high levels of corruption; and poor infrastructure and transport.

Areas in which the multinationals surveyed say India is better than China are listed in Table 16.8.

Table 16.8 **Proportion of companies reporting business problems in India and China (%)**

	China	India
Counterfeiting	70	30
Grey market	44	25
Data security	62	40
Repatriating profits	40	32
Transfer pricing	54	30

Source: Economist Intelligence Unit Survey of client companies, 2005

Latin America

The most important markets for business in Latin America are:

- Argentina
- Brazil
- Chile
- Colombia
- Mexico
- Peru
- Uruguay
- Venezuela

The Latin American market is a little larger in terms of GDP than China or central and eastern Europe, and its GDP is about three times that of India. The region's combined population, which is growing at 1.4% a year, was around 530m in 2006.

Many western companies have invested or do business in Latin America, but economic and political volatility over the years has meant they have committed fewer resources than in China or central and eastern Europe. However, things are looking up. Average annual growth in GDP of 5% during 2004–06 was the best sustainable run in five decades. The current account is in surplus and foreign-exchange reserves stood at $320 billion in 2006, more than those of both the European Union and the United States. The foreign debt burden went down from 45% of GDP in 2003 to 24% of GDP in 2006, and in Mexico and Brazil it was down to 15% and 19% respectively. This is lower than for most countries, including those in the developed world. The annual financial requirement (the amount needed to pay for deficits and past debts) has also gone down from $170 billion a year in 2000 to under $70 billion in 2006, the lowest level since 1992.

Investment from abroad is increasing. After four years of decline compared with 2001, foreign direct investment (FDI) in the region reached $70 billion in 2006, roughly similar to China but less than central and eastern Europe, where it exceeded $100 billion for the first time. Furthermore, Latin American multinationals are investing abroad, thus providing further stimulus to economic performance.

Political stability has increased, with democracy well established throughout the region, and on the whole politics have become more pragmatic. Fears that President Luiz Inacio Lula da Silva in Brazil would follow policies of the far left have proved unfounded as he embraced an approach similar to many European social democracies. Similarly, in Chile, the centre-left did not radically change the right-wing policies of the previous government but adjusted them. This is leading to increasing continuity in government policies, something that was previously lacking.

Economic stability has also increased. There were almost 30 economic crises in the region during the 1980s; in the 1990s there were ten; and since 2000 there have been just two, in Argentina and Uruguay.

Chile and Mexico have escaped the debt trap (paying large amounts to service past debts, which hinders more productive use of government revenues) and Brazil is on the way to achieving the same. These three markets account for about 80% of the region's GDP, over 90% of Latin American emerging multinationals (so-called *multilatinas*) and about 90% of Latin American market capitalisation.

This is encouraging news for companies seeking to enter or increase their activity in Latin America, and they would do best to take action sooner rather than later.

The downside and risks for the region are as follows:

- ⬛ It is still heavily exposed to the US economy, which is likely to slow down in 2007 and 2008.
- ⬛ It is dependent on exporting commodities. This is fine while prices are high, but a weakening of commodity prices would expose structural and competitiveness weaknesses.
- ⬛ It has attracted a fair share of portfolio investment, often of a speculative and high-yield-seeking nature. Consequently, there is a threat of sudden outflows of liquid capital, although the region is much better placed now to withstand an outflow of "hot money".

- It has a large grey economy estimated at 35–50% of economic activity (and about 40–45% in Brazil), compared with 25% in India and 15% in China. Such tax evasion limits governments' ability to spend on necessary infrastructure.
- Chile is the only country that has reduced its GDP per head gap with the United States since the mid-1980s; in all the others the gap has increased. But the trend is now gradually changing.
- It is not doing enough to help business. Research by the Economist Intelligence Unit indicates that in the period to 2012, the business environment rankings (which indicate how business-friendly countries are) of all larger Latin American countries will fall. Areas of concern are labour laws and other regulations, red tape and corruption.
- It is slow to improve its competitiveness and move up the value chain. The rise of real exchange rates, particularly in Brazil and Chile (thanks to booming commodities exports among other things), is making it harder for local manufacturers to compete.
- It suffers from poor infrastructure (see earlier point).

Overall, however, the pluses outweigh the minuses and the attractions of the region (or at least some countries in it) to western companies should increase over the next 5–10 years.

Brazil

Brazil has been one of the laggards among the BRIC (Brazil, Russia, India and China) countries in recent years, with corporate sales and profit growth largely slower than in the other three. The economy has been choked by exceptionally high real interest rates. Despite rapidly falling inflation and good macroeconomic indicators, the central bank kept nominal rates high to keep portfolio investors happy. They have started to come down but are still high (11% in real terms in the second half of 2006). The fact that real incomes and lending are rising should boost domestic demand among Brazil's 181m population, a prospect that western firms will find enticing. However, it should be borne in mind that some 30–40% of the population continue to live in poverty and the earnings of 50% account for little more than 10% of total incomes.

The macroeconomic stability that was missing for many decades is now entrenched. External debt as a percentage of GDP has dropped to under 20% and will fall to 10% of GDP by 2012–14. The current account is in surplus and will stay largely balanced in the foreseeable future (provided commodity prices stay on the strong side). Exports have more than doubled from under $60 billion in 2001 to $140 billion in 2006 and will exceed $200 billion by 2011 (again provided that commodity prices stay acceptably high). Public-sector debt, at 45% of GDP with a forecast drop to 35% by 2013, is better than in most west European countries. The need to go to the capital markets and cover budget deficits has been reduced. The government now runs consistent primary budget surpluses, a marked change from several years ago, and it is investing hugely in infrastructure.

If President Lula's first term was about stabilising the economy and setting the foundations for growth, his second term is about accelerating growth. This has pleased the business community and should succeed if the central bank relaxes its conservative stance and lets interest rates fall to where they should be considering the massive improvements in macroeconomic fundamentals.

Growth will gradually come closer to 4% a year and by around 2010, if interest rates do come down to 3–5%, it may hit 5% and continue at that level. Foreign investors are taking notice and expect strong performance. FDI is likely to continue at between $18 billion and $21 billion a year for the next 5–10 years, with Brazil possibly taking over the regional number one FDI spot from Mexico. The biggest bonus is that for the first time in ten years Brazil has no debt with the IMF or the Paris Club of creditors. Furthermore, tax collection has become more efficient, allowing greater government spending, and education standards have improved. Unlike Chile, Brazil has a well diversified export base, but this has recently been hurt by its strong exchange rate, a fact to be noted by foreign companies planning to export from Brazil. As for those selling in Brazil, they should be aware that the currency may weaken as speculators decide to move out. The local currency has strengthened not only through strong exports of commodities but also by attracting portfolio and speculative investment through high real interest rates. In turn capital investment has been cramped by the higher cost of capital.

Government officials now claim that by 2009, or at the latest 2010, Brazil should be able to achieve an investment grade credit status. This would allow the government and domestic companies easier and cheaper access to the international capital markets.

Despite improvements, day-to-day business in Brazil continues to be hampered by a complicated tax system, bureaucracy, red tape, corruption, skills shortages and infrastructure shortcomings (from electricity shortages to transport infrastructure).

Mexico

Foreign companies operating in Mexico can be more relaxed than in other Latin American economies because in the event of an economic crisis, its membership of the North American Free Trade Area (NAFTA) means that the United States will intervene to stabilise the situation.

In many ways, Mexico is increasingly seen by companies as a market that is more closely linked to the US economic cycle than the cycle in the rest of Latin America. In the short term this implies a slowdown because some 85% of Mexican exports go to the United States, where the economy is slowing down, but there has also been good trend of macroeconomic convergence, with inflation rates falling and risk premiums on debt falling to low levels.

Mexico is now seen by many international companies as a sounder and more predictable market than it was previously. The structure of its exports helps: it used to be heavily dependent on oil exports (over 60% of exports were oil-related), but the economy is now more diversified and oil accounts for 10–15% of exports depending on oil prices. From 2002 to 2006 FDI was the highest in Latin America at $16 billion–$22 billion a year, and it should continue to exceed $20 billion a year for the next 5–10 years. Foreign investment has largely gone into in the *maquila* free economic zones, with the fastest growth in the automotive industry. Mexico has developed an extensive network of free trade agreements, making it attractive for companies that seek a base for export manufacturing.

However, between 2002 and 2006, growth has exceeded 4% a year only twice and early in that period it was hovering around 1%, barely enough to keep up with population growth. As the US economy slows, it is likely that Mexico will on average grow at 3–4% from 2007 to 2012, driven primarily by corporate investment, exports and to some extent private consumption. But without the forecast US slowdown, Mexico would no doubt enjoy growth of well over 4% in 2007 and 2008. Business and consumer confidence are high following the inauguration of a centre-right president, Felipe Calderón, in 2006.

Macroeconomic stability is underpinned by exports, which in the ten years from 2002 are expected to grow from around $150 billion to $350 billion, one of the fastest export growth rates in the world. Imports are expected to grow similarly, highlighting opportunities for companies operating or planning to operate in Mexico. The current-account deficit is small and manageable. The budget deficit is small and accumulated government debt is remarkably low at 23% of GDP (compared with the international benchmark of 60% of GDP). External debt is safely below 20% of GDP.

The risks for Mexico remain the potential inability of the new president to push through further structural reforms on such matters as tax and labour laws. That he does not control Congress will to some extent inhibit government effectiveness, which will not help improve Mexico's competitiveness. The peso has not strengthened much against the US dollar and so it is less vulnerable to outflows of hot money than the Brazilian real. Market nervousness can, of course, weaken the value of the peso, but the inflow of more than $12 billion a year in workers' remittances and strong FDI trends will ensure than any weakness is temporary.

Low tax collection (only 15% of GDP) has held back government investment in education and health (both of which are concerns for long-term competitiveness), and the country remains poor. Wealth is concentrated in a small proportion of the population, and Mexico has a long way to go to move up the human development index.

Other markets

Chile. In the external competitiveness and human development indexes Chile leads the region. It has signed probably more free trade agreements than any other country in the world, and it is the only Latin American country that has actually reduced its GDP per head gap with the United States in the past 20 years. Growth has been strong in recent years, combined with macroeconomic stability. The country's pragmatic economic policy serves as a model for other countries in the region, notably Brazil. However, Chile remains uncomfortably dependent on commodity exports: almost half its exports come from mining. The need to diversify is the main challenge for the government.

Argentina. In the early 20th century, the term "rich as Argentina" was almost as common as today's "rich as Switzerland". Some 50–60 years ago, Argentina accounted for about 50% of Latin American GDP; today it accounts for only about 8%. Now back on its feet after the crisis and deep recession between 1999 and 2002, the country has reduced its external debt to 50% of GDP compared with 150% during the crisis. Accumulated government public debt has also decreased, and the country has repaid its last IMF debt. The strong economic rebound has been a result of interventionist government policies and high commodity prices, but growth will slow to a more sustainable rate of 4%. The inflation rate remained stubbornly around 12% during 2002–06. In the 1990s Argentina attracted

FDI of more than $20 billion a year, but it now struggles to get $6 billion a year.

Venezuela. Like Argentina and Peru, Venezuela has been struggling to increase its GDP per head. Peru is now managing to do this but Venezuela's growth trajectory remains uncertain. More than 80% of the country's exports are oil related and the percentage is rising rather than falling. Although the country has about 60 years' worth of known oil reserves, there is a need to diversify. This is unlikely to be achieved under the increasingly left-wing policies of President Hugo Chavez which are aimed at reducing the country's huge inequalities.

Venezuela has been growing poorer since the late 1970s and has experienced some ten recessions in the past three decades. Wealth, as in Argentina and several other countries in the region, has accumulated in the hands of just a few people, many of whom have moved it abroad. Estimates indicate that Argentines have moved well over $100 billion out of the country and Venezuelans between $40 billion and $50 billion.

Colombia. Both economic performance and security, which was a problem during the left-wing guerrilla insurgency, have improved. Interest rates and taxes have come down and fiscal policy has been tightened. The outlook for Colombia is solid if it manages to avoid the resurgence of guerrilla warfare.

Uruguay. The government of President Tabaré Vazquez, the first leftist government in Uruguay for about 200 years, is proving to be moderate, similar to Brazil and Chile, which should lead to better economic performance in the next few years.

17 Russia and other CIS markets

Russia will be our biggest market in Europe in ten years.

Peter Brabeck, CEO of Nestlé, speaking in November 2002

We invested a couple of million in Russia a few years ago. It was the best business decision of my life.

Regional manager, American pharmaceuticals company

For the last two years, Russia has posted the best sales growth in the world.

Regional vice-president of one of the world's largest IT companies

China and Russia are our key growth markets in the world for the next five years.

Regional manager of one of the world's largest soft drinks companies

One of the major themes of this book is that many western multi-nationals are ignorant of the opportunities in emerging markets and how to develop their business in them. The Russian market is a prime example of western prejudice and ignorance.

The experience of hundreds of western companies operating in this market would indicate that media portrayal of Russia as a place where you will get cheated or even killed by the Russian mafia if you attempt to do business there is simplistic and wrong – and becoming more wrong. How successful a business can be in the Russian market is one of the best-kept secrets in the business world, although no one would deny that the market is difficult, painful and problematic.

Where in the world?

For global multinationals searching for sustainable growth, the answer is often China, Russia and India, in that order. Russia is getting more attention, and no wonder, as companies report sales growth of 30–45%. But until mid-2002 it was difficult to get the attention and commitment of senior management to do something in Russia or to develop existing operations there. However, an increasing number of companies are now getting involved in or are at least willing to look at Russia.

The reason Russia has been ignored in the boardrooms of major multi-nationals probably has a lot to do with the history and politics of the

20th century. Many board members grew up in a culture where, since 1945, Russia and the rest of the Soviet Union were the number one enemy and bogeyman. This still colours their thinking, as is clear from what the manager for Europe of one of the best-known corporate names in the world said:

> We do some good but below potential business in Russia. But when I brought this on to the agenda our CEO screamed at me that "we will not do business with those damned communists".

Some US companies no longer think this way, but many still do.

What's good about doing business in Russia?
Growth in western sales is among the best in the world
Sales figures of 30–40% are strong by any criteria but few businesses anywhere can grow organically at that pace, and many have been trying to gauge what the "sustainability figure" is. The consensus among companies in all sectors is that they are aiming for about 20% annual growth over the next five years. This is not a small target, and 20% is not set in concrete. The point is the relativity. Companies that were achieving growth of 40–50% in 2001–04 feel that a sustainable figure during the period 2007–10 is around 20%, about half of what they were achieving in earlier years.

During 2005–06 market leaders, especially in the fast-moving consumer goods (FMCG) sector, saw their sales levels fall as international and domestic competitors took more market share and often undercut market leaders on price. One of the largest American FMCG companies saw top-line sales fall from 40% in 2003 to about 15% in 2006. But because this is 15% growth on a much larger volume than three years earlier no one is complaining. As one Russia country manager for a large Swiss food multinational says:

> Our sales and those of our main competitors have trended downwards from about 28% per annum to around 22% in the last two years but this is no big deal and it does not surprise us.

The figures in Table 17.1 refer to average organic sales growth based on private surveys carried out by the authors of some 100 western companies. Some companies will have reported significantly higher results after large new investments or significant jumps in headcount; there will also be wide variations.

Table 17.1 **Western sales growth in selected commercial sectors, 2004–10 (%)**

	2004	2005	2006	2007	2008	2009	2010
Pharmaceuticals	23	30	33	28	25	20	15
OTC pharmaceuticals	25	33	35	30	25	22	16
Chemicals & industrials	28	32	28	23	20	18	15
Fast-moving consumer goods 30	30	35	25	23	18	18	13
Food & beverages	26	22	18	15	15	14	13
Information technology	35	35	33	30	25	25	25

Source: Daniel Thorniley

As one IT company noted in mid-2006:

Depending on whether we win one or two large tenders in 2006–07, our sales can rise 150% and we are quietly hopeful.

Pharmaceuticals sales have fallen more quickly than sales in other sectors for industry-specific reasons: certification, registration and VAT.

The market remains strong. Eventually a slowdown will occur, so expectations need to be managed downwards. More than 80% of companies operating in Russia report sales growth in double digits, but profits are coming under pressure as a result of salary increases and higher utility and rental costs. In 2005 many companies were enjoying growth in profits of over 20% and some were enjoying profit growth of over 50%. This is why the majority of western companies doing business in Russia have plans to expand their operations there. Some companies are rationalising their office structure by, for example, combining branch offices or putting more staff in offices outside Moscow to cut costs.

For McDonald's, which employs 18,000 people in 37 cities, Russia was among the top ten most profitable markets in the world between 1997 and 2005 and sales growth is running at 25% a year. As for many companies, Moscow and St Petersburg are where most of its business is, with 90% of sales and profits coming from these two cities.

Russia is already the 12th largest consumer goods market in the world and it is growing at over 15% a year. Russians are aware of quality and product content. Cadbury Schweppes, for example, gets more sophisticated questions on its hotline from Russians than from anywhere else in the world. It also thinks that Russia is the most brand aware market in world. Market leaders feel that they must customise their product portfolios, and several companies have products that are sold only in Russia.

Several Russian retailers have annual sales of between $1 billion and $3 billion. Retail sales are growing at over 15% a year and should continue to grow at over 10% a year. Consumer credit is increasing by 50% a year and will continue to grow by at least 25%. Russia is now the fifth largest beer market in the world and the market is consolidating and maturing. Other markets are certain to follow suit.

Consumer goods sales will do well as incomes rise: GDP per head went over $10,000 for the first time in 2005 and is likely to be $15,000 by 2010. Personal disposable income rose by 25% year on year in 2005 to $410 billion and household consumption was $350 billion, but disposable income may have been 25% higher if the grey economy is taken into account. Total consumer expenditure was $335 billion in 2005 and is expected to rise to $500 billion by 2008, driven by rising incomes and soaring credit. Mobile phone penetration has doubled each year since 2002, with 509 subscribers per 1,000 people in 2005. Low levels of ownership of consumer durables mean market openings.

Russian retail sales are booming, rising by 25% year on year in 2005 to $240 billion, and are likely to continue to grow annually by 20% in value terms and 10% in volume terms. By 2009 the Russian retail market should overtake those of Spain, Brazil and Mexico. Retailers rank it as the market with the best potential in the world for expansion. Almost 1m square metres of retail construction is under way in the Moscow region; by the end of 2005 there were 100 square metres of retail space per person (still behind the European average of 159 square metres). In 2005 the household cleaning products market was worth $3.3 billion and is likely to rise to $4.4 billion by 2009; cosmetics and toiletries sales were expected to increase from $9 billion in 2005 to $13.5 billion by 2009. Local brands are getting a stronger foothold in the market.

Most western executives believe they can build a sustainable business

Russia appears to be set for a fairly long period of normality. Business grew well from 1990 to the first dip in 1993 and then surged for several years before the rouble crash of 1998. The bounce-back was reasonably quick for most companies, and one manager of a western health company summed up the situation in 2002, saying: "The real work starts now." He meant that in the 1990s there were surges, volatility and the 1998 crash. The trend thereafter would be for some steady slog, steady growth models and managing corporate expectations – most of the normal issues of day-to-day business anywhere in the developed world. The Russian business environment may be becoming more normal, but there will be highs and lows and surprises on the way.

Although international companies often put current profits before investing for future and profits, no one seems to be cutting back on investment in Russia.

For many western companies the Russian market is highly profitable

Average profit margins in 2005–06 ranged from 15% to 20%. Some companies had focused on growth in market share rather than profit margin, but many have been achieving high profit margins. Large consumer goods companies often report profit levels three times higher than in western Europe and 50–80% higher than in central Europe. For many consumer goods, food and beverages, packaging, chemicals and machinery companies, Russia is their most profitable market. According to a manager of a big international consumer goods company:

> We aim for and achieve profit margins of 4–8% in the West,
> 12–15% in central and eastern Europe and 17–21% in Russia.

Tetra Pak, a packaging company, notes that Russia is its second most profitable market in the world after Brazil. One US consumer goods company reports astonishing figures for Russia: it is the company's second largest profit market in Europe in absolute profit terms (Spain is the largest), bringing in some $110m of profit in 2006, compared with $30m from Poland and $20m from Germany.

Why has the market been profitable? Several companies have found that they can charge premium prices for products in Russia, whereas this is no longer the case in larger central European markets such as Poland, Hungary and the Czech Republic. Pricing pressure is increasing in Russia, but many Russian customers – both individuals and businesses – are willing to pay premium prices for quality products. They are not stupid and will rarely be taken in by glib marketing: if a product can differentiate itself on quality, there is a better chance in this market that the customer will pay more. This has been a trend since soon after the collapse of the rouble in 1998 and was underlined in a telling way by the regional manager of a western food company:

The Russians really do look for quality – obviously those who have discretionary purchasing power. They want quality and will pay for it. In the food sector especially, they won't buy what the average German consumer will eat.

This may have implications as the retail sector takes off in Russia. Going for the discount market may not – at least initially – be the key to success for retailers as they engage in price wars. Nevertheless, market forces will surely drive prices downwards eventually, if with a little more resistance than in other markets. In the short to medium term, western consumer goods, food and beverages companies in Russia may tell western retailers that "you don't have to impose your global strategies and price structures here because it's a different and more discerning market". And they may be right.

Moscow is cool
The managing director of one of the world's largest consumer goods companies said: "Moscow is a cool place." She was not referring to the climate but to the atmosphere of excitement and of things happening. In the past a posting to Russia was not always regarded as a career-enhancing move or an enjoyable prospect, but this has now changed. The manager mentioned above says she is "bombarded with requests from colleagues to come and work for me in Russia". Many western expatriates whose term in Moscow is nearing an end do not want to leave, and now that business is booming and is easier to conduct many others are keen to join them – and as salaries for Russian staff are rising, some companies are considering increasing the number of expatriate workers.

Growth prospects in the regions
The Russian Federation is broken down into 89 administrative units or regions. In 2006 most western consumer goods and food and beverage companies were doing business in 8–11 regions. The main ones for business are Moscow city, Moscow region, St Petersburg and the Leningrad region (curiously, when the city changed its name, the surrounding region did not). Only a handful of western companies do business in more than 20–30 regions, including Coca-Cola, PepsiCo and Dandy/Stimorol, a Danish chewing gum company bought by Cadbury Schweppes in 2002.

As competition tightens in Moscow and St Petersburg and their surrounding regions, more western companies are looking at the relatively untouched markets of the outer regions. There are a number of "usual suspects" of second-rank regions, including Yekaterinburg, Nizhnii Novgorod, Samara, Rostov, Novisibirsk and Novgorod. One of Europe's largest food companies reported that in 2006 Moscow was only the third largest sales region in the country as a result of sales growth outside the capital. The second-rank regions offer good scope for organic business growth, but as many as 40 or 50 other regions offer relatively little to western firms as their populations are too small and/or too poor, or they are geographically too remote. However, overall, the regions offer business opportunities that do not exist to the same extent in central Europe. A good comparison is China, where western companies are expanding out of Beijing and the coastal zones.

Managers can use the regions like a concertina in their budgeting process, expanding or contracting at their own discretion the number of regions into which they plan to expand business in order to meet budget targets set by headquarters. A manager in Moscow may consider expanding into five new regions in the next budget year, but if a tough budget is set, the expansion can be ratcheted up to seven or eight new regions. However, if a less stretching growth target is set, the manager may choose to go for only two or three new regions.

Competition in Russia is not yet fierce

Competition is not as intense as it is in some of the central and eastern European markets. It is reasonable to say that in terms of competition, Russia is 3–4 years behind Poland and 1–3 years behind Hungary and the Czech Republic. However, it is catching up quickly. The type of competition is also different from the more established central and eastern European markets, as a manager of a consumer goods company noted:

> We bump into each other in the market but we are not yet at the stage of savaging each other for 1% of market share, not even in Moscow. The market is big enough and the regions have a lot of scope for geographical growth. But the cake will stop expanding in size and then market share will become the driver.

How long will the window of opportunity for other competitors to enter the market stay open? For those not in the market, this comment from the managing director of a major western company will be food for thought: "We think anyone who wants to be a player must be in during 2007–08." A Danish executive noted the change in the competitive environment:

*In the mid-1990s we were making a lot of money in Russia for
not doing very much. Now we're making a lot of money in
Russia, but we are working damned hard for it.*

The retail sector is improving

The form of competition for consumer goods companies will change
radically as western retailers flood into the Russian market. Western
retailers will also introduce their global business models, which will
squeeze the margins of consumer goods companies. This trend is already
apparent in central and eastern Europe.

Moscow has a population of at least 8m with an income per head of
almost $6,000 (almost five times higher than St Petersburg). Muscovites
spend 45% of their income on food and alcohol, 20% on other non-food
consumer products, 16% on shoes and clothing, 5% on electronics, 3% on
public transport and just 4% on housing and 1% on education. The proportion of retail spending is significantly higher than in other European cities.
Currently, just one-third of retail spending is in shops and supermarkets;
outdoor markets and kiosks account for the remaining two-thirds.

Western consumer goods companies have benefited from a lack of
consolidation in the retail sector which has enabled them to display their
products in prime positions within stores without paying a lot to do
so. Some companies think that the retail sector will soon become more
difficult for them; others think that any tightening up will take a few
years. Russian retail companies are also expanding rapidly and starting to
achieve sales of $1 billion or more. Prime locations are being snapped up,
so if western retailers want to enter the market, they may have to consider
acquisitions.

Human resources is the biggest problem for business in Russia

The Soviet educational system trained students to high levels, especially
in subjects such as maths, sciences and engineering. It was rigorous
and strict, and taught students to work hard and learn hard. Western
companies have been able to draw on this pool of talent for some 15
years. Salary levels were also modest until about 2003–04, when more
companies started to report that their Russian staff were asking for bigger
pay increases.

One of the biggest operational issues for Russian country mangers will
be getting the right staff at the right price and keeping them. As an industrial company stated quite bluntly in 2006: "The only thing stopping us
growing even more is the lack of people." A major IT company said that it

would be increasing its headcount by 50% in 2005, and other companies have said they would be raising staff levels by more than 10%.

Salary levels continue to creep up. In 2003–05, most companies kept pay increases in line with inflation (10–15%), but with good staff now in shorter supply, wage levels in many companies are increasing by more than inflation. Most managers agree that to attract and keep good people in key positions you simply have to pay what you have to pay.

Salary inflation is driven in part by Russian companies. One major western bank says:

> We are losing staff to Russian banks or firms which simply tell
> our staff they will double or treble their salaries. That's game
> over for us.

As a result, a number of western companies have either increased the number of expatriate staff or are seriously considering doing so. One health company reported it had recruited 20 Russians studying in the United States who were willing to go back to Russia if the package was "right". This was not the same package as that for expatriate staff, but it included a 20% bonus and recognised that they were regarded as "privileged and on a fast-track" within the company.

Until 2005 hardly any western companies noted a fall in the high educational standards of the people they hired. During 2005 some western executives remarked that some of the people they were hiring were of lower educational standards than before, but this may simply be a result of the surge in demand for labour.

Staff turnover remains low (7–12% on average a year) for most companies, but there is an increasing trend for the more talented Russians to want to change jobs every two or three years. However, few want to leave Moscow, at least for another location in Russia.

Corruption
Meetings the authors had with executives in Moscow during 2005–06 revealed that companies with a local presence do not find that corruption sabotages their business. Several people were firmly of the view that there was less corruption and nearly all argued that it is at manageable levels. Corruption in Russia is no worse than in India or China.

Distribution
Although some firms have thought about doing their own distribution,

few have taken the plunge. As an executive from the services sector says: "I don't think any company has changed its distribution in the last year." He went on to note that some may have modified their activity but no one has gone it alone. However, western companies are being more forceful with their distributors and insisting that they are more compliant with western laws on corrupt practices. They do not want their reputation damaged by their distributors' behaviour.

Increased rigour in the enforcement of competition law may influence how western companies draw up contracts with distributors they are using on an exclusive basis.

Russia as an export base?

One or two FMCG companies are looking at Russia as an export base for central and eastern Europe and therefore the EU. Average export tariffs for Russian goods entering Poland have fallen from 15% to 4–5% since Poland joined the EU in May 2004. However, few companies are looking at the option yet. Ensuring that manufactured products are of high enough quality for export is still a challenge. One US industrial company points out that the appreciation in the value of the rouble and the rising costs of inputs have made the export business significantly less attractive.

Political risk is manageable

There is political stability and there are fairly clear markers for business. The badly handled Yukos affair may have provided a good excuse for conservative western companies to stay out of Russia for a while longer, but it should be seen as a one-off which did not affect western business interests.

In addition to complying with normal due diligence rules, companies need to pay attention to those who have business interests that it might not be wise to compete with. If doing business in the regions, bear in mind the power of regional governors and local council committees to make or break your business.

President Putin's managed democracy has given the people the stability they crave, and under him the middle class has grown and poverty has been reduced. He has reined back the power of the oligarchs and has built up restructured state and semi-state interests. When he leaves office, he will have supporters in most of the important political positions but also in most important economic positions as well: Gazprom, Rosneft, Lukoil, TNK-BP, Surgutneftegas and Rusal (a metals conglomerate) among others in automotives, armaments and other raw materials and metals. There is some risk in who will follow him, but he is preparing the ground for a centre rightist like himself, probably Sergei Ivanov or Dmitri Medvedyev, both first deputy prime ministers.

Internationally, Russia has changed in recent years and it sees itself again as an important geopolitical force, not least because of its energy resources but also because of the problems of the United States in the Middle East. At the forefront of Russia's concerns is its relations with the Islamic world and any impending "clash of civilisations", given that Russia is home to 15m Muslims.

The economic outlook

In 2006 all the main economic indicators looked good and will remain so as long as the oil price stays over $40 per barrel. Russia had almost $100 billion in the oil stabilisation fund and central reserves of $150 billion. Its budget surplus was over 4% and the ratio of domestic government debt to GDP was as low as 18%. These are impressive figures.

More good news is that gross fixed investment picked up well in 2005 with growth of 11% and it should stay above 10% a year until 2010. GDP growth in 2005 was just over 6% and should remain over 5% in 2007 and 2008. Medium-term pressures on growth are capacity constraints, poor demographics and low labour mobility.

Russia makes money on oil at $14 per barrel, good money at $17 and "happy days" at $23. With oil at over $60 per barrel in 2006 and the price looking set to remain high, government spending ought to pick up. This in turn should ensure continued fixed investment growth of 10% a year and thus western companies selling into the industrial sector will do well. Domestic demand and consumer spending should also stay strong at over 10% up to 2010. As inflation drops below 10%, real wages should grow at over 10% a year for the next few years.

The country is cash rich but will the money be spent wisely? The big debate is what the money in the oil stabilisation fund should be spent on. The finance minister wants to pay back debt and save the money for pension commitments. Other ministers want to spend the money on infrastructure and current consumption. Whatever happens, it is likely that spending on large projects will increase. Spending on health and education is also likely to increase, as it needs to.

Probably the most difficult challenge for the government is how to bring down inflation and keep it low.

Table 17.2 **Russia: key economic indicators, 2005–10 (%)**

	2005	2006	2007	2008	2009	2010
Real GDP growth (%)	6.4	6.7	5.8	5.5	5.0	4.8
Consumer price inflation (av; %)	12.7	9.0	8.0	7.5	7.5	7.2
Budget balance (% of GDP)	7.5	7.5	5.4	4.9	4.5	3.9
Current-account balance (% of GDP)	10.9	10.8	9.5	7.0	5.0	5.0
Central bank refinancing rate (end-period; %)	12.0	11.0	10.5	10.0	9.0	8.0
Exchange rate Rb:$ (av)	28.3	26.3	26.3	26.5	27.2	27.4
Exchange rate Rb: € (av)	35.2	35.5	35.8	36.6	37.2	37.3

Source: Economist Intelligence Unit, 2006

WTO *membership set to happen*

The government's stated aim is to join the World Trade Organisation (WTO) as soon as possible. Negotiations are under way but membership is not likely before the end of 2007. Overall, WTO membership should be beneficial to western investors, but changes made to achieve it may disrupt current business strategies or at least make them more complicated or expensive.

Receivables: not too many bad debts

Any notion that it is difficult to get paid in Russia is wrong. Most companies report extremely low levels of bad debt in the Russian market at 0.2%–0.4% of sales volume. Western companies extended their payment terms during 2002–06 and now usually offer terms of 90, 120 or 180 days to Russian distributors with whom they have built up trust. Obviously companies must manage their receivables (payments due to them) carefully, but Russia is a good trading environment. It should remain so as the market continues to enjoy liquidity and customers will generally have the money to meet their obligations. One large American engineering company says: "We have been doing business in Russia for 20 years and never lost a dollar in payments."

Tax: huge improvements have been made

Some 95% of western managers, together with big law and accountancy firms agree, that there have been huge improvements in taxation in Russia in the past few years. The introduction of a much lower rate of personal tax (13%, compared with a range rising to 35%) did not dent tax receipts. Corporate tax has come down to 24% from 35%. A radical overhaul of the tax penalty system has been implemented and tax inspectors can no longer harass western companies and get away with it. In the courts, the burden of proof in tax cases is in favour of the western company. The main change in the tax environment, however, is that firms can now deduct all necessary and evident business expenses, including advertising, training, recruitment, legal, consulting and auditing.

Intellectual property: mixed at best

The laws on intellectual property look good on paper, but implementation leaves something to be desired. Microsoft has had some successes as have brand names such as Reebok, but infringements in the pharmaceuticals sector have been getting worse. The Russian civil and criminal authorities are now working together better, which will help improve matters. Most importantly, Russia's desire to join the WTO provides an incentive to get on top of intellectual property issues.

The legal environment

Russia is not the "Wild East". It is a paper-driven society. If you have the right papers, you will win in court; if you do not, regardless of the spirit of the law, you will not. Western law firms report that they are winning 90% of their cases in Russia compared with 50% in the West. Western companies of any size can win, and the cost is lower than in the West. An average commercial case takes 5–7 months.

Another positive trend is that, in general, laws are now not just Yeltsin-era decrees but are federal in nature and enacted by the Duma, so they have more chance of being properly implemented. But some western industrial companies complain that there can be a lack of consistency, especially outside the big cities. As one American manager complained: "They simply haven't heard what the new laws are."

In the past, companies generally set up a representative office in Russia.

Now they are increasingly forming legal entities and subsidiaries. This is encouraging the "Russification of business and law", with structures and litigation referring more to Russian law and courts. Western companies are becoming increasingly comfortable with this. Indeed, for arbitration, western law firms advise their clients to choose Moscow as a location rather than Stockholm or Geneva as it simplifies the process and there is just as much chance of a positive result. Attaching assets after a successful arbitration can be as difficult as it is anywhere else. Often, though, the threat of a court case frightens companies into settling.

When a western company loses a case in a remote region, it can often appeal in a regional centre and win, and as the case gets closer to Moscow, its chances of winning increase.

Nothing is perfect, however, and lawyers advise caution when taking organisations with powerful Russian vested interests to court. It may not be so simple to get a favourable ruling in the Moscow courts against an organisation that has the support of, say, the mayor of Moscow.

You can trust your Russian business partner – most of the time

"Our Russian distributors are more trustworthy than our German ones," says the regional manager of a large American IT company. The Russian commercial environment is built on personal relationships, trust and part-nerships, and commercial judgments are often based on instinct. This is not always easy to incorporate into a company's business processes. Time, effort and thoughtfulness are needed to build relationships with distributors or joint-venture partners to get good returns. This can take a lot of energy, but if western companies and investors want to build solid commercial relations, this is part of the deal.

Following the rouble crash in August 1998, it was commonly assumed that Russian companies fleeced their western partners. Some Russian distributors pretended to go bust and did not pay their bills, but just as many did go bust and could not pay their bills. What is less well known is that many Russian partners went the extra mile to pay their western suppliers in the months following the crisis. Dozens of western pharma-ceuticals, consumer goods and manufacturing companies reported that their distributors were paying them via bank accounts in Liechtenstein, Vienna and London.

Managers at a German automotive company found themselves with a $21m exposure to a new Russian business partner when the rouble crashed. They thought their careers were over as they went to their ultra-conservative German board to tell them of the loss. But then the Russian company deposited the $21m in the German company's bank account in Moscow.

Of course western companies do get ripped off in Russia, just as they do anywhere in the world. One consumer goods company operating in St Petersburg says that it has lost a couple of shipments each worth $100,000 in recent years. But it also says that this is not something that happens only in Russia.

One manager supports the general view that partners and distributors in Russia are trustworthy but elaborated as follows:

> They are generally very honest partners and individual relationships work well. But it is when you get beyond personal contacts that you find there is more graft and corruption within institutions. It is nothing outrageous for an emerging market but institutional graft does exist.

Western lawyers speaking in 2006 seem to share this view: "There is bribery in Russia but really nothing above the norm of emerging markets."

Personal safety

Moscow and other large Russian cities are as safe as most cities in Europe. Of course it has "no-go areas", and sensible caution is required. Muggings and even carjackings do take place, but again nothing more than in London or Amsterdam. Often the biggest danger to personal safety is the potholes in the street.

What's not so good about doing business in Russia?

A lot is going well in Russia, but few executives are naively optimistic. The drawbacks of the economy and business environment include the following:

- Domestic investment is volatile.
- There is still dependence on oil and commodity prices and diversification into non-energy manufactures is still slow.
- Corporate governance standards are still too low.
- Foreign direct investment is picking up but remains low.
- The banking sector is immature, inefficient and lacks probity. It will take time to get it into a shape considered acceptable by western standards. More western banks entered the market in

2005–07, with Raiffeisen International leading the way with its $500m acquisition of Impex bank. With credit in its infancy, many western banks think the Russian retail banking sector has huge potential. Russian banks provide only around 12% of the financing resources required by Russian enterprises, which obtain the remainder of their financing predominantly from reinvested profits, from capital being repatriated and from investments by western partners.

- It can take an inordinate amount of managerial time and energy to do business in Russia because regional executives often have to put so much effort into challenging and overcoming the prejudices of senior managers at headquarters. With better commercial results being reported from Russia, more companies are investigating the market. In 2002 more than 80% of western regional managers complained that their global headquarters did not understand the market and did not really want to build the business there. This figure had fallen to about 45% by 2007. But it is still remarkable that nearly half of all companies, mainly those from the United States and UK, remain sceptical about or wary of Russia.
- Minority shareholder rights remain inadequate.
- Corruption remains a concern.
- The customs regime continues to present operational difficulties, though it has improved since 2004. More companies are doing their own customs clearance and taking on more of their own distribution within the country or at least considering this option. Further improvements are likely in the next few years.
- Capital flight is still a problem.
- Some sectors, such as food, beverages, consumer goods, consumer durables and IT, have been better for western companies than others, such as agriculture and construction.

Why is foreign direct investment so weak?

Before 2003 annual foreign direct investment (FDI) in Russia was running at under $3 billion. Slowly more and more companies began to see Russia as an investment location, and in 2003 FDI rose to $8 billion. Since then it has exceeded $20 billion a year, and will probably reach $30 billion in 2008. Local mergers and acquisitions boomed in 2005–07 and this will continue as consolidation takes hold. The sectors attracting more foreign and domestic investment include oil, gas, metallurgy, mining, packaging, beer, food and consumer goods. Despite well-publicised tussles in the energy sector in 2006, western investors will not stop investing in Russia – it is too big an opportunity and too big a part of their plans.

FDI levels should be higher than they are now, given the size of the Russian economy. Paul Melling, a senior partner at Baker & McKenzie and one of the most experienced western lawyers working in Moscow, gives several reasons for the low levels of investment:

- Western companies have strong memories of the 1998 crash when some were taken to the cleaners by Russian partners or heard stories of such events. Some Russian companies left bankrupt shells. Corporate governance has improved among the larger Russian companies but there is still a long way to go.
- The Russians themselves have a love-hate relationship with all things western and this applies to western business and western investors. They want the benefits of FDI but are unwilling to do what is necessary to attract it.
- Only a handful of Russian regions make outside investors welcome, including Moscow, Moscow region, St Petersburg, Novgorod and Nizhnii Novgorod. The other 84 regions are either indifferent or do not have the experience to work professionally with outsiders. However, since 2006 there have been improvements.
- There are virtually no tax incentives. Russia must understand that it has to compete with other countries to attract inward investment.
- The government should employ a good PR agency. The message about Russia is simply not getting across. All the good news is swamped in the negative portrayal of the country, which is largely unfair and inaccurate.
- The authorities would be well advised to revamp Sheremetyevo, the main Moscow airport. All the prejudices of senior managers (and tourists) are reinforced when they see the sleaze and gloom pervading the airport complex. This is mitigated by the bright lights and consumerism on Tverskaya Ulitsa, the main thoroughfare in downtown Moscow. (Thankfully, the authorities have taken the hint and in 2006, at least superficially, the airport started to look better.)

There seems to be an "emotional barrier" in convincing headquarters of the benefits of a Russian investment strategy. One executive underlined the risks:

You want to avoid looking like an idiot or a manic risk-taker.
Those who want to sabotage your plans will always find a case
and be able to question your financial assumptions.

The debate on Russia often takes place against a background of office power play among managers who want to invest in other regions of the world or not at all. Russia takes up a huge amount of managerial time and energy because the internal corporate debate is so demanding.

Other CIS markets

As stated in Chapter 15, as a general benchmark for the majority of companies (excluding those in energy or commodities), the "85-10-5" rule applies to doing business in the Commonwealth of Independent States (CIS – the former Soviet Union). This means that in most business sectors 85% of a company's business is carried out in Russia, 10% in Ukraine and 5% in the other republics.

Belarus

Belarus, where Alexander Lukashenko continues to run one of the last Soviet-style economies in the world, remains another isolated island for western business. Suppressed inflation of the Soviet kind is the only thing preventing a total economic collapse with severe social and economic consequences. There is no likelihood of any real currency or economic union with Russia until the regime changes.

Caucasus

Overall, there are few business opportunities in the Caucasus, a large region between the Black Sea and the Caspian Sea that includes Armenia, Azerbaijan and Georgia. The market is poor and the risks are high. Companies that do business in the region invariably do so opportunistically via distributors and insist on pre-payment.

Central Asian republics

The same applies to the Central Asian republics, where corruption is as rampant as in the Caucasus. Many of them are becoming family-run fiefdoms. In the 1990s, some general manufacturing companies tried to set up manufacturing operations in the region, as did some food companies, but all ended in failure. Large services companies that tried to enter the market were blocked by corruption, and opposition came from within the Kazakhstan leadership. Banks and health companies that set up operations or representative offices have been generally disappointed, and currency conversion is a major headache in the region. However, the business environment in Kazakhstan improved marginally in 2005–06 because of the windfall from oil revenues, and there are many reports that the banking system there functions efficiently. This is still not attracting much investment on the ground as the operational environment is still treacherous. But it may get better and Kazakhstan is likely to remain the number three market in the CIS after Russia and Ukraine.

Some western companies have reported sales growth of up to 50% but from fairly small bases. Again, most business is conducted at low risk with pre-payment the norm. Overall, the outlook is bleak for western companies that wish to conduct regular business in Central Asia on regular terms.

Ukraine

Political volatility during a two-year election campaign in 2005–06 damaged some western business interests, but overall they survived well. As one experienced western businessman in Kiev said: "Business is in much better shape than politics in Ukraine." Much of the good news could be coming from the large grey economy.

But opinions are mixed: European and Asian companies appear more upbeat than American ones, and managers on the ground in Kiev are gloomier than regional managers outside the country. Perhaps the locals are managing expectations downwards.

Consumer goods companies are experiencing sales growth of 10–20% and industrial companies are reporting sales growth of 10–15% with occasional big contracts. But the operating environment – high taxes and customs duties, unpredictable changes in legislation, lack of transparency and entrenched corruption – make Ukraine a tough market.

Since early 2005 many private Ukrainian companies have been looking at raising cash through an initial public offering (IPO), and some oligarchs are seeking to sell assets to raise cash to put away or to restructure and modernise their businesses. FMCG and over-the-counter drugs companies continue to do well; industrial companies are less upbeat. Business-to-business is progressing well in telecoms, glass, real estate and construction. Results are mixed within subsectors of consumer goods: one confectionery company reported terrible results in 2006 to the extent that it embarked on a review of its whole strategy, but a big detergents firm reports steady to good business.

The food, tobacco, beverages market was worth $35 billion in 2005 and

Table 17.3 **Ukraine: key economic indicators, 2006–10**

	2006	*2007*	*2008*	*2009*	*2010*
Real GDP growth (%)	7.0	5.8	5.7	6.2	5.8
Private consumption (%)	16.8	8.9	8.0	8.6	7.5
Fixed investment (%)	11.4	8.0	11.0	9.0	9.0
Inflation (end period; %)	12.0	9.0	7.0	6.0	5.8
Change in real wages (%)	18.4	6.3	6.1	5.3	5.0
Current-account balance (% of GDP)	−1.6	−4.8	−6.0	−5.1	−3.4
Budget balance (% of GDP)	−0.7	−2.5	−2.3	−2.5	−2.5
Exchange rate HRN: € (end period)	6.45	6.66	6.50	6.30	6.35

Source: Economist Intelligence Unit, 2007

should rise to $50 billion in 2010. The proportion of consumer spending on these items is high at 45% but is likely to fall to 35% in 2010, as consumers spend proportionately more on health, transport and communications, such as mobile phones and computer link-ups. It is estimated that housing and fuel costs will rise from $3.8 billion in 2005 to $6.2 billion in 2010.

In 2005 foreign direct investment shot up to $8 billion, but most of this was the result of the privatisation of Krivorizhstal steel mill and Aval Bank. Even so, FDI is likely to settle at around $3 billion a year over the next few years, compared with $1 billion before 2005. Russian investors have been aggressive in filling Ukraine's foreign investment void. When western companies get round to investing more in Ukraine, they may well find themselves dealing with men from Moscow.

Corruption remains a problem, and many western companies think it became worse during the political volatility of 2005-06 as officials tried to line their pockets before leaving office. An example of the level of corruption is the shortage of quality hotels in Kiev, which may have been encouraged by current hotel owners who want to keep new entrants out. It appears that more than 100 sign-offs are needed to set up a new hotel which opens up more than 100 opportunities for palms to be greased. On the plus side, law firms are noting more success in litigation and dispute resolution, but nothing like their success rate in Russia.

The government which took office in 2006 faced a number of crucial challenges, which are to increase GDP, control inflation, manage relations in general with Russia, keep local investors on side, instil confidence in western investors, and spell out its plans for privatisation and renationalisation.

Large business groups have become more influential in parliament (the Rada) since the 2006 election, but Ukraine's political and economic future remains uncertain. As Russia goes from strength to strength, Ukraine continues to underperform.

More companies are managing Ukraine separately from their Russian operations. This is because it does not look good to run Ukraine from Russia and in any case the Russia manager has enough to do. There is also a tax reason, as there are benefits to treating the two markets separately.

Ukraine is underperforming in every sense – politically, economically and commercially. As the Russian market matures and tightens in the next few years, western companies would love a reforming, booming Ukrainian economy to be waiting to take up the commercial slack. However, it is more likely that it will continue with stop-go improvements, probably more stop than go.

18 China

China is the world's fourth largest economy, accounting for 25% of world growth in 2006. It attracted foreign direct investment (FDI) of $86 billion in 2006, far more than any other country. It has the largest currency reserves in the world ($1,700 billion in 2006), exceeding those of Japan ($880 billion). It accounts for 25% of the US trade deficit, but runs only a modest surplus with Europe. Some 50% of its exports are generated by companies that have received foreign direct investment. It is set to be the world's largest exporter in 2008, with $1 trillion worth of exports. In 2004, it ran a trade surplus of $20 billion despite huge commodity imports. Imports have been rising at 40% a year. In 2005, it consumed 25% of the world's steel and zinc and 40% of its cement, as well as accounting for 30% of the growth in global oil consumption. China overtook Japan in 2006 as the world's second largest importer of oil after the United States. By 2010, the Chinese-language internet will be larger than its English-language counterpart.

Everyone wants to be in China

Seemingly all big companies want to be in China, either for the domestic market or as a supply base for exporting to the West. But some in other emerging markets feel their companies have focused too much on China. They may have a point. According to an executive from an American IT company:

> We have definitely put too much into China relatively. There are production delays and problems getting the right staff, and when the product is ready for shipment, it sits for five weeks on the Shanghai docks waiting in line with millions of other containers.

Making profits from business in China was difficult in the 1990s, and companies still find it hard because it has become much more competitive.

China has been a magnet for foreign direct investment and will continue to be so, although it is highly likely that western multinationals will diversify their investments more in the coming years. In 2002–04 annual foreign direct investment averaged $50 billion, but it leapt up to

$86 billion in 2006, an annual level that is likely to be sustained until 2010. Some of this is Hong Kong money going in and out of the country for tax reasons, but the trend is strong. Business is booming. Sales growth in many sectors is 20–25% and some companies are finally starting to report profits. The major cities have been "done" by western players, who now have to move to the more rural areas and adapt their pricing. Competition is picking up. Bureaucracy is still a burden and western companies need to get local players and the local authorities on board.

During the 1990s, generating profit in China was tough and the average annual return on equity was a mere 3%. Since WTO entry the Chinese market has rocketed and it is now getting big by all corporate criteria. Western companies have seen their sales soar and profits pick up. For example, in 2003 Philips's sales in China were $2.5 billion and exports were $5 billion, giving a total sales figure of $7.5 billion. By 2007 Philips expects China sales of $12 billion, which will represent 30% of its global revenue. It already has 20 joint ventures in China and its audio parts sales increased by 100% in 2003.

But China is not yet a profit rich market for the majority of investors, even though some are making more profits than officially booked as a result of transfer pricing. Some firms are investing in growing their business in the interests of long-term profits, while others are finding the going tough. Trends in earnings reported by US companies in China reflect this. In 1997 reported earnings were zero; in 1999 they had risen to $755m; by 2003 they had tripled to $2.4 billion. However, one-third of reported profits from mainland affiliates were accounted for by just five US companies; when affiliates' profits booked through Hong Kong and Singapore are included, with royalties and licensing fees, the 2003 total increases to $8 billion. In comparison, in the same year US companies made profits of $7 billion in Australia, a market with only 20m people, and $9 billion in Taiwan and South Korea combined. So even in the boom year 2003, most US companies were only reporting profit margins similar to their global average.

Telecoms companies did well in the late 1990s, but they have faced massive domestic competition in recent years and margins are down. The automotive market has been booming, but it started to take a hit in spring 2004. US fast-food companies (KFC and McDonald's) report good profits. Western companies in the foods and beverage sectors face the least competition and are less vulnerable on issues such as intellectual property protection. Overall, few western companies have "cracked" the domestic market and many are garnering the best results by using China as a sourcing base for exports to western markets.

Many western companies have struggled in China and average annual return on investment in the 1990s was a low 3%. But some have done better – for example, Siemens reported sales of $4 billion in 2003 with a profit margin of over 10%.

Within China, many western firms are choosing to operate as holding companies and putting more emphasis on buying part or all of state-owned and domestic private-sector companies. More companies will adopt "standard" emerging-market strategies, such as:

◪ adapting corporate structures to the local market;
◪ moving into new regional (poorer) markets, in this case inland;
◪ facing up to more competition, local and international;
◪ getting the best local and international management and being willing to pay for it.

Cracking the domestic market

Many companies and investors went into China with high expectations and have been disappointed with the Chinese market. But most big western companies want or have to be in China and will increasingly adapt their business models there.

Most companies use China as an export base and this is unlikely to change in the short term. However, they are increasingly looking at the domestic market, although few western companies have cracked it. One reason is that consumer spending is low – $650 per head in 2005. Even though this figure is growing, it will take China ten years to reach just 4% of the level it is in the UK. Those who want to get into the domestic market face fierce competition from local companies which often have good connections with government officials and are subject to a much less burdensome tax regime. But there is potential. There are 12m households regarded as "affluent" with annual incomes greater than $7,500; by 2015 there will be 60m such households. Today 30m people can afford to buy luxury goods (2% of the population); sales of chocolates will have tripled between 1998 and 2008. If it grows by 10% a year, private consumption will hit $1 trillion by 2009; and by 2018, on current trends, China will be the largest consumer market in the world.

Companies that have done well in local markets are now reaching beyond the main cities to smaller towns and rural areas. This brings challenges: how to source cheaper inputs in order to bring prices down and how to distribute and market products to a largely poor population. In rethinking their domestic market strategies, companies are undertaking more local market research and trying to determine at what rate rural incomes will rise.

In order to achieve this "rural strategy" and to expand existing business, companies are consolidating existing facilities and expanding through mergers with local companies. More companies will take the M&A route in order to break into the domestic market.

As companies go more local, they will realise that municipal governments are becoming more independent from the centre. There is thus a growing need to work more closely with local authorities. But at the same time they should be aware that central government is in places seeking to limit local industrial capacity. Companies need to identify the regions that are more amenable to FDI, and to do this they will need to hire government relations managers in the regions.

Competition

Western companies operating in China are reassessing their corporate structures, centralising some functions and outsourcing others. They are trying to come to grips with government policy on the WTO while the government is still openly or covertly supporting state-owned enterprises. They are also looking at Chinese domestic companies and assessing them as potential competitors or takeover targets. Competing with Chinese companies can be difficult because their cost structures are low and they often have inside contacts with federal or local government.

Western firms are also developing their procurement strategies, considering the sustainability of premium price strategy, acquiring the necessary licences for trading (import/export or selling) and organising distribution. Another issue facing western multinationals is how to consolidate production facilities. In central and eastern Europe companies are switching manufacturing plants from one market to another; the same is happening in China among the regions.

Staff and wages

An increasing number of western firms involved in China are reporting that Chinese staff are not good at taking the initiative or, curiously, at logistics. A major issue is competence in the English language and a lack of soft business skills. Their education has tended to be rigid and theoretical, and staff need a lot of training in team building.

Companies also report problems in recruiting the right staff at the right price. Average wages have been increasing at more than ten times the rate of inflation but are still well below wage rates in Hong Kong.

Corporate focus on Asia

In a poll carried out in 2006, multinationals were asked what proportion of their corporate focus (time and investment) would be dedicated to certain Asian markets in 2006 compared with 2002. The main results are shown in Table 18.1.

Table 18.1 **Corporate focus on selected Asian markets (%)**

	2002	*2006*
China	22	33
Hong Kong	17	10
Japan	12	10
South Korea	8	8
Singapore	12	7
India	35	6

Source: Economist Corporate Network, Asia

Members of the Association of South-east Asian Nations (ASEAN) are exporting less to the United States and more to China. These smaller markets will have to focus on their specialisations and relative advantages in their relations with China. This will mean moving up the production value chain, following Singapore, South Korea and Taiwan, or going for niche markets in energy and foodstuffs. If ASEAN loses some manufacturing to China, it will need to increase supplies and services to its massive regional neighbour. China is a large net exporter of light labour-intensive manufactures and a large net importer of machinery, equipment and primary materials. It will also seek to invest its large capital surplus abroad and this will benefit the region. This is not a zero-sum game.

Western companies will want to enjoy the benefits of the massive Chinese market while not being overly dependent on it for their regional strategy. Most companies will want to retain operations in both China and the rest of ASEAN and build operational synergies. Philips, for example, has moved manufacturing from Singapore to China and senior management to Hong Kong to be closer to the Chinese market. But the company retains a strong R&D presence in Singapore.

Economic outlook

The general economic outlook for China is good: annual GDP growth was just under 10% in 2003-06. Any slowdown is likely to be marginal, and annual GDP growth should stay close to 10-11% in 2007-10. It would be no bad thing if growth slowed to around 8% to counter the threat of the economy overheating. China's economy is the fastest growing in the world, at almost three times the global average. Despite this, inflation is still low and should stay so, at least in the short term.

Investment in 2005-06 grew at 15% after a surge to over 20% in 2003-04. But to generate $1 of GDP growth, China invests $5, one of the worst ratios in the world. Private consumption is increasing at about 10% a year because real wages are rising at the same rate. China has the highest savings ratio in the world (40% of GDP and 25% of household incomes). There are two reasons for this: repressed savings (people had nothing to spend the money on), which is good news for western consumer goods companies; and people's need to cushion themselves against further deterioration in the provision of state social security. In other words, they may not plan to spend a good part of this.

Structural reforms need to replace the pump priming the government has relied on. Whether the authorities will be able to engineer a soft landing for the economy is the crucial unknown. The government will introduce further austerity measures if and when it sees any of the following: a rebound in inflation; infrastructure bottlenecks; falling bank deposits as people turn to speculation. There were signs in 2005 that the balance of economic growth was improving with rising demand from Chinese consumers plugging the (potential) slowdown in investment.

Buying the world

The world is changing and we are seeing the first stages of China's rise as an economic competitor. The United States is not accustomed to this and does not like it, as the refusal to allow the proposed acquisition of Unocal, an American oil and gas exploration and production company, by the China National Offshore Oil Corporation (CNOOC) to go ahead showed. But American business leaders want to make acquisitions in China and worry that they are vulnerable to accusations that the United States does not support a global, level playing field.

China, like the United States, is trying to secure oil sources and is seeking to invest in the United States (it has mostly failed so far), Canada and Kazakhstan in order to do so. It has also invested and even tried to take a lead in Africa, where it has been willing to work with questionable regimes; for example, China is the biggest foreign investor in Zimbabwe. Its investments on the continent include $8 billion in Sudan, with a 41% stake in the national oil consortium and the construction of a 900-mile pipeline; a deal to purchase 30,000 barrels of crude from Nigeria, with investments in railways and rural telephony systems; oil pipeline construction in Libya; and the purchase of 25% of Angola's oil in exchange for credits for road, railway construction and electricity generation.

The Chinese currency debate

From January 1994 to July 2005 the People's Bank of China (PBC), the central bank, fixed the value of the currency in a "managed float" that allowed it to fluctuate in a narrow range around Rmb8.28:$1. On July 21st 2005, however, the Chinese authorities revalued the currency by 2.1%, maintaining the managed float system around a new target of Rmb8.11:$1. They also scrapped the renminbi's peg to the dollar and instead linked its value to a basket of currencies. Since this decision was made, the renminbi has slowly but steadily appreciated against the dollar. In May 2006 the renminbi went for the first time below the threshold of Rmb8:$1. The outlook in 2007–10 is for slow, steady appreciation.

The exchange rate peg was maintained to keep the value of the currency low relative to the US dollar, thereby allowing Chinese exporters to sell more easily into America. The United States is urging China to revalue the renminbi upwards by 20–40%, claiming that its cheap currency gives the country an unfair advantage in trading with the United States. However, although China has a trade surplus with the United States and the EU, it has trade deficits with its Asian partners and overall its trade is often close to being balanced. In recent years China has dramatically increased its market share in sales to the United States in certain sectors. However, this market share has not been "stolen" from American companies, but rather from South Korean or Taiwanese companies. A revaluation would have a minimal impact on the US trade deficit; for example, a 10% revaluation would improve the US trade deficit by a mere 1%. When Japan followed the same advice from the United States in the 1980s, the economy underwent a brief boom before collapsing into a 15-year recession.

There are two important reasons why China should not revalue:

◪ It would damage the Chinese banking sector. Revaluing dollar-denominated debt upwards could seriously hurt the fragile Chinese banking sector as its debt exposure would increase. A Chinese banking collapse is in no one's interest. Chinese consumption would fall, western sales to China would collapse, hurting corporate earnings, Chinese and Asian central banks would be forced to repatriate capital and the dollar would tumble, plunging the United States into recession and dragging Europe and Japan with it.

◪ It would reward currency speculators who have taken positions on the renminbi being revalued, which if it happened would simply put the currency under more upward pressure.

With the renminbi pegged to the US dollar, China's central bank is tied to US monetary policy and there are two scenarios, both of which involve the threat of importing US-driven inflation, that might encourage China to revalue the renminbi. One is if US monetary policy becomes too loose and interest rates too low for China; the other is if the dollar were to fall to 1.50/1.60 to the euro.

Hot stocks

Chinese investors have taken to the stockmarkets in a big way which has created a bubble that the authorities have sought to control by, for example, raising stamp duty overnight in May 2007. Eventually the bubble will pop or at least let out some air. The likelihood of a full-blown meltdown is small – say, 10% – and the government will do everything in its power to prevent a major financial collapse before the prestige-enhancing Olympics. So far, the knock-on effect of the downturns in the Chinese markets has been remarkably mild in global markets as investors take on more risk. Given maintained high growth levels in China, the fundamentals ought to stay good until 2010 with inevitable falls in stock prices and corrections. Investors will have to manage this.

APPENDIX

Comparative tables

Table A1 **Central and eastern Europe: market size, 2006**

	GDP (US$bn)	Imports (US$bn)	Population (m)
Bulgaria	32	22	7.6
Croatia	43	21	4.6
Czech Republic	142	93	10.2
Estonia	16	12	1.3
Hungary	112	73	10.0
Kazakhstan	77	24	15.4
Latvia	20	11	2.3
Lithuania	30	11	3.4
Poland	340	122	38.0
Romania	122	47	21.6
Russia	979	163	142.0
Serbia	31	13	7.4
Slovakia	55	45	5.5
Slovenia	37	23	2.0
Turkey	393	132	74.0
Ukraine	103	44	46.6

Table A2 **Western Europe: market size, 2006**

	GDP (US$bn)	Imports (US$bn)	Population (m)
Austria	322	135	8.3
Belgium	412	318	10.4
Denmark	275	88	5.4
Finland	211	73	5.3
France	2,235	520	61.0
Germany	2,897	920	82.6
Greece	308	65	11.0
Ireland	221	84	4.2
Italy	1,854	427	58.1
Netherlands	663	343	16.4
Norway	335	63	4.6
Portugal	195	64	10.5
Spain	1,225	317	45.0
Sweden	385	132	9.1
Switzerland	378	150	7.5
UK	2,373	603	60.3

Table A3 **North America: market size, 2006**

	GDP (US$bn)	Imports (US$bn)	Population (m)
Canada	1,267	360	33.0
US	13,250	1,860	300.0

Table A4 **Latin America: market size, 2006**

	GDP (US$bn)	Imports (US$bn)	Population (m)
Argentina	214	33	39.0
Brazil	1,070	92	187.0
Chile	146	36	4.6
Colombia	136	25	46.0
Ecuador	40	11	13.4
Mexico	840	256	107.0
Peru	93	15	28.0
Venezuela	182	32	27.0

Table A5 **Asia: market size, 2006**

	GDP (US$bn)	Imports (US$bn)	Population (m)
Australia	754	127	20.6
China	2,690	790	1,314.0
Hong Kong	190	333	7.0
India	910	185	1,100.0
Indonesia	364	71	245.0
Japan	4,366	533	128.0
Malaysia	149	126	26.0
New Zealand	104	25	4.2
Pakistan	129	26	160.0
Philippines	117	53	90.0
Singapore	117	245	4.4
South Korea	888	303	49.0
Taiwan	356	200	23.0
Thailand	206	113	66.0

Table A6 **Middle East and North Africa: market size, 2006**

	GDP (US$bn)	Imports (US$bn)	Population (m)
Algeria	112	21	33.0
Bahrain	15	8	0.7
Egypt	108	33	75.0
Iran	202	46	70.0
Israel	140	47	7.1
Jordan	14	10	6.0
Kuwait	98	15	3.2
Libya	47	12	6.0
Morocco	62	21	32.0
Qatar	52	12	0.9
Saudi Arabia	347	64	25.0
Tunisia	30	14	10.2
United Arab Emirates	163	86	5.0

Table A7 **Sub-Saharan Africa: market size, 2006**

	GDP (US$bn)	Imports (US$bn)	Population (m)
Nigeria	117	28	144.0
South Africa	255	69	42.0

Table A8 **Foreign direct investment in emerging markets, 2001–06 ($bn)**

	2001	2002	2003	2004	2005	2006
Central & eastern Europe	30	36	36	66	74	106
Developing Asia	101	84	88	141	177	160
of which China	44	49	47	55	79	86
Latin America & Caribbean	131	52	48	68	75	70
Middle East	7	8	12	16	33	35
North Africa	6	4	6	9	16	17
Sub-saharan Africa	13	9	13	12	18	16
Total	288	194	202	316	399	410

Note: Numbers for regional FDI have been rounded. Total is actual total.

Source for all tables: The Economist Intelligence Unit

INDEX

A

accounts payable 95
accounts receivable 95 *see also*
   receivables management
acquisitions 84–105
Adidas 13
advertising
   local 67–70
   price benchmarks 73
   social responsibility 121
Africa
   business outlook 182–4
   GDP/imports/FDI 182–3, 227–8
   product package size 69
   see also Middle East and North
      Africa; South Africa
AIDS 182–4
Aldi 157
analysts 24
Angola 44–5
Argentina 129, 193–4
Armenia 212
arrogance 8–9, 70
Asia
   definitions 2
   economic crisis 127, 130–2
   GDP and imports 226
   management groupings 65–6
   product package size 69
   see also Central Asian
      republics; Japan
Association of South-East Asian
   Nations (ASEAN) 220
audits
   environmental 97

external 30–7
financial 93–7
internal 37–9
legal 98
Austria 132–3, 157
autocrats 47
Azerbaijan 113, 164–5, 212

B

Bacardi-Martini 127
back office, local presence 12–13,
   67
Bahrain 177
Baker & McKenzie 211
Baltic states 163
banking sector
   Central and Eastern Europe 167
   China 222
   Egypt 179
   Russia 209–10
   Turkey 180
   see also risks, banking
Belarus 47, 212
benchmarking 19–20, 42
Bhagwati, Jagdish 137
black economy, exclusion from
   GDP figures 53
BMW 55
board membership 8–9
Booz Allen Hamilton 22
Brabeck, Peter 5, 10–11, 195
brand loyalty 2, 69
brands
   and distributors 72
   external audit questions 37